THE OMNISCIENT NARRATOR WOULD LIKE YOU TO KNOW THAT JORI AND ZAK HAD A CONVERSATION ABOUT NAMING THE BOOK THAT WENT SOMETHING LIKE THIS:

JORI: We need to give it a name.

ZAK: What do you mean a name?

JORI: Well, call it something, something other than *Book* or *The Book*.

ZAK: Why?

JORI: Because it's part of our life's work.

ZAK: All work is part of someone's life's work. For most people, life is the work.

JORI: OK, OK. Just give it a name because it sounds stupid and pedantic if you have to explain that to each person who asks you the title of the book and, even more, it comes off pretentious if you don't name it.

ZAK: Why is that pretentious?

JORI: Seriously? Don't bore or bait me. Just... you know what I mean. I don't really need to tell you more. You get it.

ZAK (*laughing*): I do, I do. A name will give it an easily referenced place in the world... something I've been avoiding my whole life, and in that regard I consider myself an abject failure.

JORI (*laughing*): Yes, let it fit in. The necessary evil, better for people to see it, find it, buy it than not... although the yurt is still an option. (Zak's eyes light up, daydreaming of the center of nowhere.) Let it fit into the list of projects we take on, are taking on. Have it be part of what we do, but not the whole.

ZAK: Right, right. It's not a summation but documentation: irrelevant to the time it's released, relevant only to the time it's produced.

JORI: Well, let's not sell it that way. But yes. This is a project just like the garden and we've incorporated the production into what it is we do.

ZAK: That train leads us to the notion that had we not worked on this book since Fish & Game's inception, it would be a different restaurant. Maybe that's the reason why our sign is upside down.

Well, anyhow, I've been calling it *Project 258*. I mean, not that I've made a list of everything we're working on, but it's one project on a long list of many... endless... It's one important project on our list of projects.

JORI: So it's a working title?

ZAK: Now we're back to this?

JORI: Ha! Isn't that what you want, or where you want to be? In a place that can't be categorized? Like Gil Scott, who you're always quoting, finding his records in the bin marked "miscellaneous."

ZAK: No, no. I mean, yes, you're right about my life goal, plan, eventual evaporation; we work, cells divide, die off, what have you. But the book. Talking about the book. I think this is the name: *Project 258*. Simple. Listen, each day has its own tasks, they are the subsets of a larger agenda... some tasks further the larger agenda, some are just about survival and an immediate means to an immediate end... this is, for lack of a better or worse number, task or project 258. Part of the larger agenda.

JORI: (*smiling*) "Project" is definitely better, softer. But it consists of so many smaller projects that have to reach completion so it isn't really just one project.

ZAK: Now you're baiting me.

JORI: Yeah, OK, but maybe it would be cool if on the back or inside the cover somewhere we can acknowledge all the other project numbers that contributed to the book's completion.

ZAK: Sure, yeah, why not? I leave it to you to number those...

JORI: So, we're calling the book *Project 258*, right?

ZAK: Right... I mean, unless there's a number more fitting...

JORI: Just part of your endless road of indecisiveness. I think *Project 258* is great. It's perfect.

FISH

&

GAME

PROJECT 258

Making Dinner at Fish & Game

by

Zakary Pelaccio

Peter Barrett

Photos and illustrations by PETER BARRETT With essays, comments, and recipes by JORI JAYNE EMDE, STEVE HERNANDEZ, and KEVIN POMPLUN

CONTENTS

Dramatis Personae

PETER BARRETT	*Omniscient Narrator*
ZAKARY PELACCIO (opposite, near left)	*Partner, Co-chef*
JORI JAYNE EMDE (opposite, far right)	*Co-chef*
KEVIN POMPLUN (opposite, near right)	*Co-chef*
PATRICK MILLING SMITH (opposite, far left)	*Partner*
STEVE HERNANDEZ	*Sous Chef*
KAT DUNN **MADISON MILLION**	*Bartenders*
MIKE RICE	*Natural Wine Apostle*
ZACH KALAS	*Cook-turned-farmer/gardener*
WALTER GROHS	*Baker*
WAYLON	*Zak and Jori's dog*
BLUE HERON BARN, OLD CHATHAM	*Zak and Jori's place*
FISH & GAME FARM, CLAVERACK	*Patrick's place*

How to Read This Book

FROM BEGINNING TO END, LIKE A NOVEL. Let it soak in. Then go back and find the recipe or technique that excites you the most and that fits best with your current mindset and available ingredients. Make it. Eat it (or wait however long until it's ready; in the meantime, make something else).

Did something hitherto unseen snap into focus? Did you feel good? That enthusiasm, and its origin in the existing culinary rhythms of your life, constitutes your way forward. The desire, the curiosity, and the inspired eye you bring to the day's ingredients will set the tone for your explorations.

The book follows the trajectory of a year, organized by seasons, with ingredient and producer profiles spread throughout to shed some light on the talents working upstream from your meal. Each season features a cocktail, except for winter, which includes several because you'll need them. And one full seven-course tasting menu rounds out each quarter.

EXIT

Cooking is a thinking man's game!

—KEVIN

WELCOME.

TO BEGIN: SOME WORDS OF ADVICE FOR *ALL* PEOPLE

"...it seems to me that the moralist is the most useless and contemptible of creatures. He is useless in that he would expend his energies upon making judgments rather than upon gaining knowledge, for the reason that judgment is easy and knowledge is difficult. He is contemptible in that his judgments reflect a vision of himself which in his ignorance and pride he would impose upon the world. I implore you, do not become a moralist; you will destroy your art and your mind."

—A letter from Gaius Cilnius Maecenas to Titus Livius as imagined by John Williams

OH, AND...

"If you are doing business with a religious son-of-a-bitch,
Get it in writing.
His word isn't worth shit.
Not with the good lord telling him how to fuck
You on the deal."

—William S. Burroughs

NOW PLEASE, SETTLE IN AND HAVE SOME WINE...

LAT: 42.252701
LON: -73.7918679

Fish & Game's mission statement can best be summed up in two sentences, one interrogative and one declarative: "What does this place taste like?" And, "Let's not waste food."

FINE RESTAURANTS SPECIALIZING IN THE EXHAUSTIVE EXPLORATION OF STRICTLY LOCAL PRODUCTS ARE NO LONGER A NOVELTY; this most welcome phenomenon has become the new normal, and we should all celebrate that development. The granular specificity of their recipes often means, however, that while they're very beautiful, many of these restaurants' books are about as useful as pornography; they're not applicable to your actual life in any direct way unless you live in the same part of the world. When a cuisine is so exacting and requires such unique ingredients, it's impossible for anyone living outside that region to duplicate the food.

Though there are recipes in this book, our main goal is to elucidate the processes—both intellectual and culinary—behind the food at Fish & Game. All these methods and techniques will apply to the food that grows where you live. More importantly, the approach—engaging intimately with nature both wild and domestic, building relationships with farmers, nurturing a wide variety of fermenting condiments—is one that applies to anyone, anywhere, who yearns to cook and eat better food.

In large part, the key to cooking this way is to invert the conventional contemporary relationship between cook and ingredient. In the standard model, we say "I feel like Mexican tonight" and go buy avocados, jalapeños, cilantro, tortillas, and beans. It's the same mindset as choosing a restaurant: our desire for particular flavors or a specific dish governs where we spend our money. Recipe-centered books presuppose a standardization of ingredients (an egg, an onion, a lamb chop) but, more insidiously, they assume that your cooking process begins with you choosing what you'll make for dinner. When handmade food is an integral part of your lifestyle, however, the forest, farm, and pantry tell you what's for dinner; the food chooses you and you can rejoice in your anointment as the vehicle through which the raw materials become cooked.

Part of the fun is that those building blocks will not be limited to what's perfectly mature; young sprouts or baby roots will need thinning, and other plants will have flowered or gone to seed. The Japanese Kaiseki tradition features, in addition to a given course's main ingredient, garnishes a little before and after their seasons, celebrating a fleeting moment by saluting the days that precede and follow it, stretching time so that one meal on one day can encapsulate a larger swath of experience, flatteringly illuminated from both the past and future. This kind of food is only available to cooks attuned to the daily progress of plants and who have those plants available at different stages of growth.

Foragers' practiced eyes develop the ability to notice choice fungi where a novice would see nothing but moldering leaves. Attentive browsing in the garden reveals far more food than would be apparent during a cursory glance; a dedication to wasting as little as possible means a modest garden can yield a great deal of food as well as help to sharpen concentration in the kitchen. Lacking a garden, the benevolent dictatorship of a weekly CSA delivery also demands efficient consumption: promptly dispatch an armload of rutabagas or marinate in yuppie self-loathing when they finally go bad in the back of your crisper drawer. (Sometimes there's a fine line between inspiration and guilt.)

The pantry—the cache of preserved fruits, vegetables, and condiments arrayed against the privations of long, hard winters—provides a wide spectrum of captured flavors, all modified by the means of their preservation, that can inform and enhance meals in the leaner months. If you live somewhere without winter, be advised that fermentation and preservation are still noble methods of transforming food into delicious and nutritious treats that will enhance your meals.

ALSO, WINTER BUILDS CHARACTER, DAMMIT.

This is a book for people who already know how to cook. But more importantly, it's an attempt to codify an improvisational aesthetic. Like jazz, the theory can be taught but the execution is up to you. Cooking should be thought of as a practice, like law, or medicine, or yoga. That practice—the daily engagement with ingredients, whether grown or foraged by you or others—builds a fluency that allows for spontaneous flights of fancy anchored in an understanding of how the foods interact and behave under different cooking conditions and at different times of the year.

But there aren't any shortcuts to this understanding. Zak, Jori, and Kevin, while masterfully advanced in their respective culinary practices, are nonetheless fairly new to this holistic, deeply place-based cuisine. As a result, they're all climbing the steepest slope of the learning curve together, open to experimenting in all sorts of directions, making mistakes, and steadily expanding the scope of their operation as they continue to serve splendid menus to their customers.

Changing the restaurant's menu most weeks—it works out to over forty unique menus a year—presents a challenge, but it also reflects the reality of the region, climate, and farming, all informed by the passage of time. If you sincerely want an answer to the question "what does this place taste like?" in a climate with four seasons then your menu must constantly shift to reflect the nature of what's available. It's also an excellent way to keep from getting bored in the kitchen and ensuring that your family or customers never become tired of your food.

Most great cooks work intuitively, so delineating that process can be a challenge. Building that instinctive response to ingredients can be the work of many years. Rewarding years, though. Tasty years. The goal is to motivate you, to help you listen to the food you grow or buy, and urge you to meet the people you buy from so the product speaks to you with their voices. We all respond to stories.

A NOTE ON THE RECIPES

You will likely notice that many of the recipes vacillate erratically between metric and English measurements. Don't be alarmed; this is perfectly normal. While it might be easier to convert entirely to one or the other, or to offer both every time like many books do, this is how this group of cooks talk, record, and communicate with each other; all of their notebooks and the official restaurant recipe archives use this mixture of measurements. If you have a digital scale, a set of measuring cups and spoons, and an immersion circulator that can switch between Fahrenheit and Celsius, you'll be fine. Think of mastering the blend as equivalent to being bilingual.

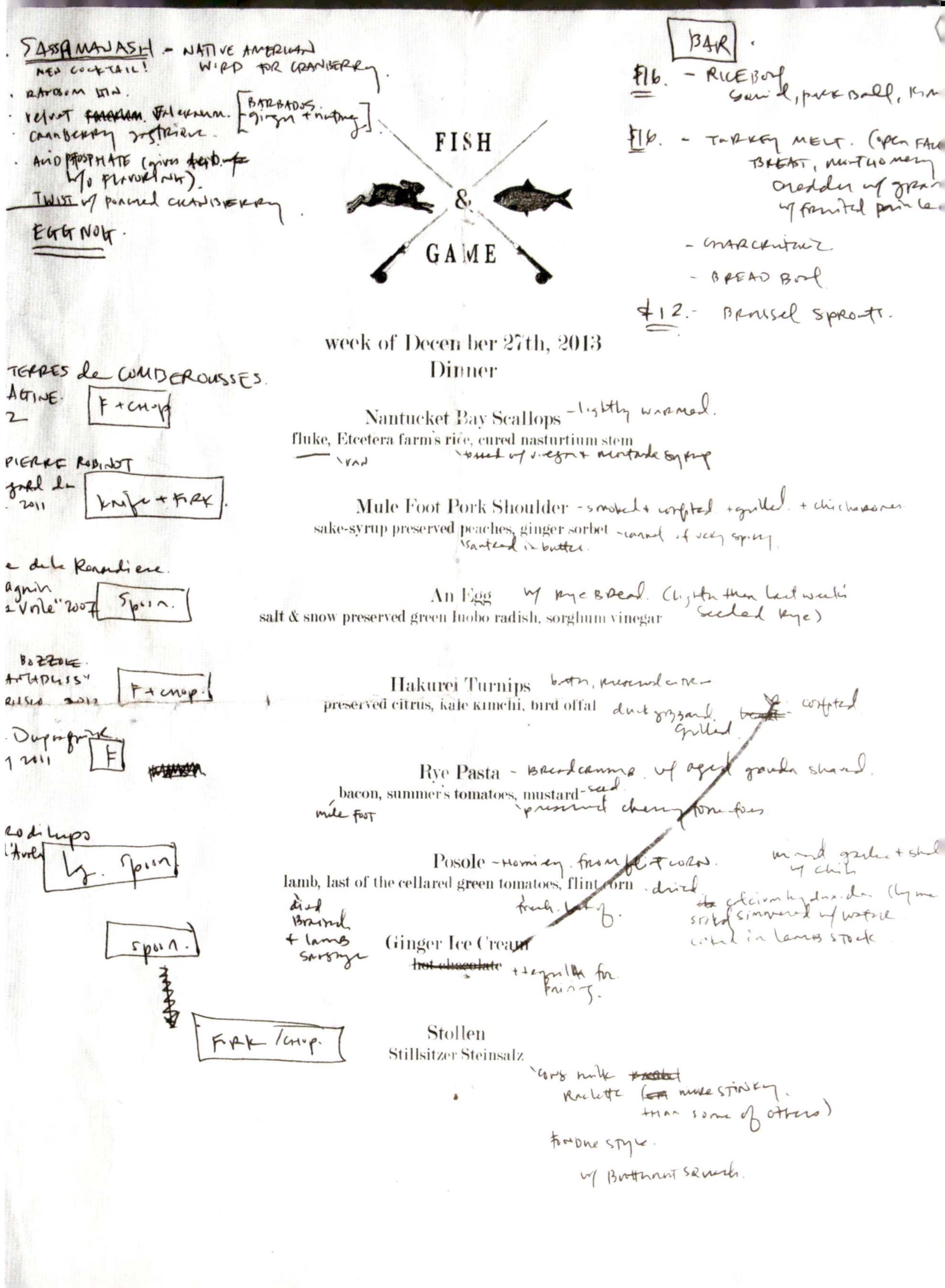

FISH & GAME

week of December 27th, 2013
Dinner

Nantucket Bay Scallops
fluke, Etcetera farm's rice, cured nasturtium stem

Mule Foot Pork Shoulder
sake-syrup preserved peaches, ginger sorbet

An Egg
salt & snow preserved green luobo radish, sorghum vinegar

Hakurei Turnips
preserved citrus, kale kimchi, bird offal

Rye Pasta
bacon, summer's tomatoes, mustard

Posole
lamb, last of the cellared green tomatoes, flint corn

Ginger Ice Cream
~~hot chocolate~~

Stollen
Stillsitzer Steinsalz

BAR

SASSAMANASH – NATIVE AMERICAN WORD FOR CRANBERRY

EGG NOG

$16. – RICE BOWL

$16. – TURKEY MELT

– CHARCUTERIE

– BREAD BOWL

$12. – BRUSSEL SPROUTS

THE DYNAMIC IN THE KITCHEN AND THE RELATIONSHIP BETWEEN THE PRINCIPAL PLAYERS IS CLOSER TO A BAND THAN ANYTHING ELSE: hierarchical, yet collaborative, with constant reworking and refinement of old and new material alike. Each of the three chefs has a distinct role; though they frequently overlap, they focus their energies on different disciplines to get the most work done. As with music, being able to switch seamlessly between improvisation and repetition is a prerequisite for inclusion. It also reflects another essential musical parallel: like a concert, each meal will be different, a unique and memorable experience that vanishes into the past after it's over. Unlike music, the taste and texture of food cannot be recorded for posterity. Like music, however, the final product gets served to an appreciative audience in real time.

Zak's describes himself in his Instagram profile as "the spiritual leader of a very small church." He steers the ship and creates the menu every week. His approach generally consists of writing up the framework for each week's menu, articulating 80–90 percent of the details of each dish, usually pursuant to a conversation with Kevin and then followed by another. He assumes that Kevin understands the unarticulated remainder; sometimes that understanding meshes with his conception, and sometimes it's different. When it differs, it can be either better or worse than his original idea. If it's better, it stays; this is the principal means by which other members of the team influence the menu. If it's worse, Zak explains what he wants. Fish & Game is not a democracy.

He tries to get outside every day, to walk in the woods, foraging in season, and just breathing the air and thinking in winter. Each week's menu arises initially during these sojourns; the weather and smells trigger desires, impulses, and cravings for particular flavors. On his way in to the restaurant, more often than not he stops by a farm or two to pick something up or swings by Patrick's to check in on the garden or animals. These direct experiences, refracted through his knowledge of what's coming in that week, inform the choices he makes for each menu.

Some weeks are ambitious and involve a lot of technical cooking. Others are simpler, more down-home and humble. Zak describes this expansion and contraction using exercise as a metaphor: "Sometimes you want to hike up a mountain and sweat your ass off, and sometimes you just want to take a nice walk." That fluctuation—a gentle, pendular oscillation between soigné elegance and casual comfort—provides a natural rhythm, the heartbeat of the improvisational process. It also underscores the ways in which the food one eats at Fish & Game strives to be the food one would eat as a guest at Zak and Jori's house—what's on hand, what they're craving, what the weather or occasion demands—just on a grander scale.

Kevin is a Taurus. He likes walks on the beach, puppies, and yelling. He dislikes people, paying for things, and sobriety. Kevin is the principal moderating force between Zak's abstract free-association and the reality of running a business. He manages the kitchen, keeping the cooks on course and making sure

6

cooks quit because
Kevin yelled at them

We don't keep getting angry, we just replace you.

—JORI

each week's menu has all the components it needs in plenty of time. He orders the seafood, haggles over per-pound produce prices, and cooks his ass off during prep and service alike.

Kevin's thorough understanding of inventory—what's in the freezer, what needs to be used up, what should be run as a bar snack—modifies Zak's initial vision, making it more efficient and cost-effective. They've worked together long enough, and their styles are similar enough, that they speak in a sort of shorthand: "braise it out," "ginger it up," and the like. "Johnson" or "Johnny" also frequently stands in for any elusive noun: "Have you seen the Johnson?" "I think whatsis Johnson had it up in the Johnson" are sentences that have been uttered—and understood—in the kitchen.

When necessary, though, language gets very specific. Discussing some ember-roasted leeks meant to be enfolded in sliced pork and dipped in broth, shabu shabu–style, for example, Zak made sure to specify that post roasting the leek segments (about three inches long) should be sliced thinly enough that their inherently stringy nature wouldn't cause them to all be pulled out on the first bite, interfering with easy eating.

Jori's path meandered the most in the first year. She began in the kitchen, working on the line and expediting in turn. After a staff change, she took over front of house duties. She hated it. Though she's warm, charming, and often gregarious, Jori's talents find their most eloquent manifestation far from the madding crowd. She is happiest, and most productive, when ensconced in house or garden (with Waylon, her trusty familiar, by her side) like a witch—a good witch, but still a little scary—stirring her cauldron in solitude. In this context she can best express her nature: a savvy, nurturing supertaster with extraordinary culinary gifts.

Jori has a growing collection of vintage cookbooks, most with housewifey themes. From these, she gleans both direct technique and inspiration for all manner of concoctions and preserves. As she deepens her understanding of plants through countless hours in the garden and kitchen alike, she works towards a synthesis of time-honored preservation techniques and contemporary refinement in all her products. She leaves daikon in soy sauce outside all winter to freeze and thaw, concentrating its flavor, and uses a rotary evaporator to distill herbs for bitters.

Once the first year bloomed into full summer, she repaired to their "barn in the woods" and began preserving the harvest full time. After that tapered off in the fall, she returned to doing prep on service days and working at home the rest of the time on her Lady Jayne's Alchemy line of tinctures, potions, and condiments. Come the following February, she began starting seeds over at Patrick's, which transitioned into an additional position as gardener, assisted by Zach Kalas. She works closely with Zak, discussing each week's menu during the planning phase (usually their nominal days off on Mondays and Tuesdays) and often coming in to eat at the bar so she can give him feedback. A year later, by which point a wide range of her boozy concoctions had come online, the bar program transformed into an utterly handmade and profoundly original line of beverages.

67

average hours Kevin, Zak and Jori work together during a week

Monk's Comment on a Conversation

ZAK

In the bath pretending to rest
Having dined on rabbit, killed by the dog
And grilled over old, rotted barn wood
I stop sipping and reading and I listen

Monk bangs at the keys, playing a fight
Or grooving at a speed I've yet to get
Unsure and entranced I feel him
Pleading and I can't tell if he wants to spend
More time with the unyielding immediacy
Spin it backwards, stop it or die

I put down my chartreuse and rye
And drop Gilbert's *Everywhere and Forever*
I don't know if what I told him when I told him
To go for it, to not hold anything back
I don't know how can I do that now, too

This trio keeps everything moving through a flexible combination of division of labor and frequent collaboration. Because Zak and Jori live together, and they see Kevin almost every day, the conversations and shared experiences continue constantly. Other staff frequently come up to Blue Heron Farm for work and play alike: garlic planting, wine tastings, the one-year anniversary pool party. The result is a tightly knit, adaptive group that thoroughly understands the repertoire and consistently performs at a high level (except at the pool party, which was not a high-functioning function).

Music plays constantly in the kitchen; it energizes the air. The chefs use their phones to choose tunes for working; during prep it can be almost anything. The music played during service comes from a curated mix of about twelve thousand songs from Zak and Jori's collection. It's played a little louder than it might be at similarly fine establishments, though without overwhelming conversations. The songs span a wide range of genres, drawn from different periods of their lives, and are meant to provide a festive atmosphere while inspiring nostalgia and creating interesting transitions. Music can fill a space without diminishing enjoyment of food or companions: a transparent overlay that enhances an experience.

In the kitchen, besides the perpetual music, there's also a busy counterpoint accompanying the soundtrack: the syncopated clatter of pans on the flat top, squid on the grill sizzling like the rivets in Elvin Jones' ride cymbal, and the constant low roar of the vent hood, all punctuated by intermittent calls of "Fire two menu!" and "Pick up!" from Kevin (Zak says "Pick up, please!" when he's expediting).

Zak usually adds whole albums to the playlist, which occasionally results in an inappropriate song booming out during service. Someone is usually quick to jump on their phone and skip to the next track. At Zak and Jori's house, though, vinyl provides the score. Many of their records are old, obscure, and out of print; unlike with their cooking, the deepest cuts stay at home.

Foundations

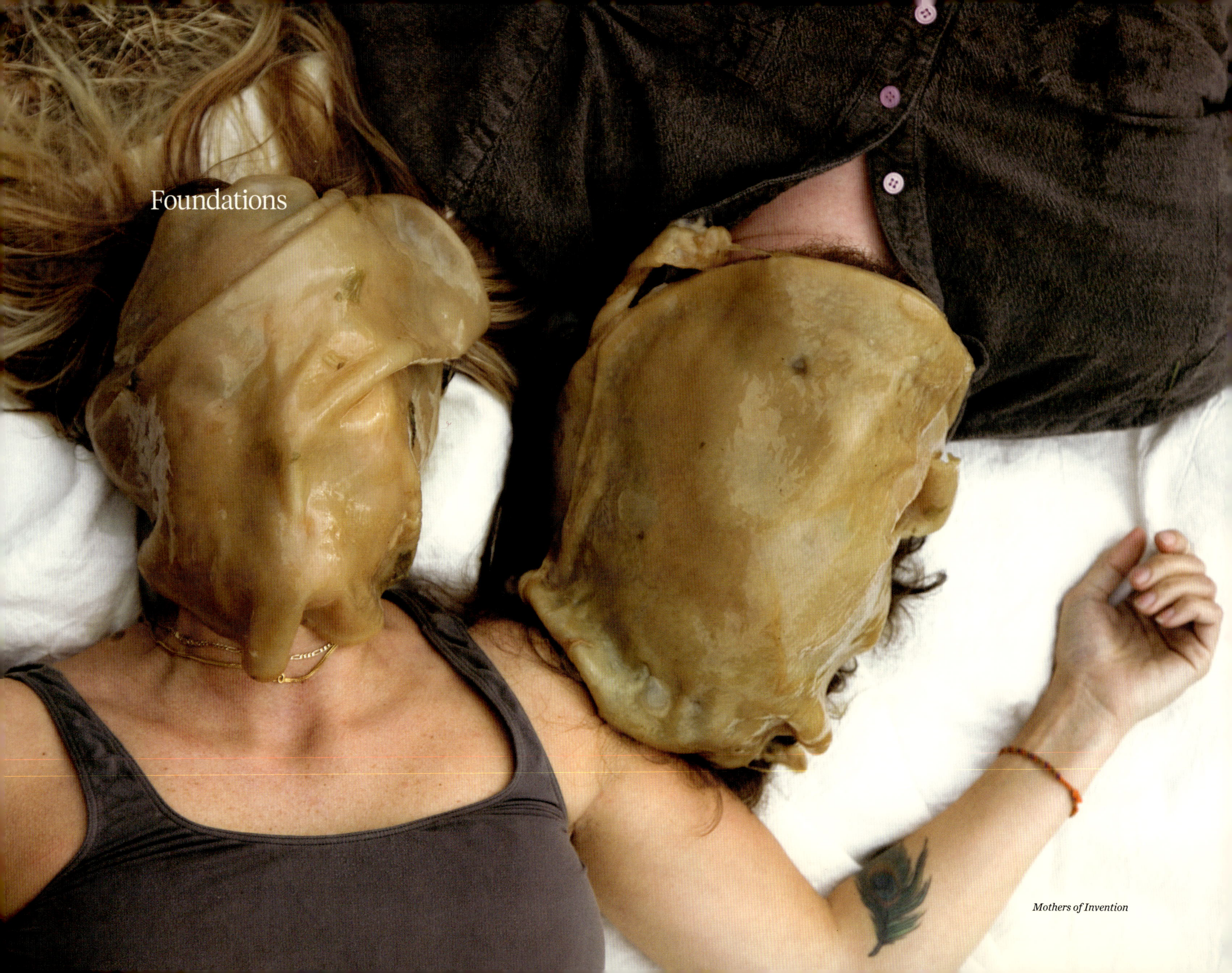

Mothers of Invention

"HOUSE-MADE," A PRECIOUS EXPRESSION, BORDERING ON PRETENTIOUS, adorns many menus today. It's important, of course, to draw attention to the handmade products featured on a menu, but there's a point at which it becomes cumbersome. The solution is to make everything in house, obviating the need for the term. Creating the building blocks from scratch also enables the creation of food with unique character and depth.

Along with local maple syrup and homemade vinegars, fish sauce makes up one third of Fish & Game's Holy Trinity of seasonings. Those axes—salty umami, acidity, and sweetness—happen to be the three-legged stool upon which Southeast Asian cuisine rests, but in this case they're all homemade products, fundaments of a foreign flavor profile translated into northeastern terroir.

Fish sauce allows food to stay nimble while still packing a strong punch of flavor, and vinegar's acidity sharpens the focus. Like salt, fish sauce works as an amplifier for flavor. It also makes the mouth water. Because Jori produces so many kinds of vinegar, the kitchen has a broad palette of tastes, extracted and honed by bacterial fermentation, to complement or contrast with the ingredients in a given dish. Sugar rounds flavor, fattens mouthfeel, and lengthens the finish. It moderates spice and acidity, allowing more intense flavors to harmonize, even if there's no detectable sweetness.

The Pliable Algorithm

ZAK

Fish + Salt + Water + Container + Time + Temperature = Fish Sauce

IF I WERE A RELIGIOUS—AS DISTINCT FROM SPIRITUAL—MAN, with a penchant for symbolic iconography, or simply fetishistic, I would have a shrine of amber-hued fish sauce and coffee-colored dark maple syrup, which I'd genuflect in front of while anointing myself with holy vinegar, regularly leaving offerings of brilliantly colored fresh chilies.

In the wet markets of Southeast Asia I learned to see in all directions at all times and keep moving through the frenzied action that's always edging toward chaos. This was the first time I felt the joyous and exhausting rush of all aspects of life happening, at once in one spot. The thumping of pestles methodically crushing their mortars' content released intoxicating aromas into the air. Bags of sauces: red, green, orange, and amber, tied tightly with rubber bands, sat stacked beside grilled fish, fried pork, and skewers of meats (some identifiable and many not) all highly seasoned with an orchestrated pungency that indelibly imprinted itself upon my brain. I awoke to flavor. I learned to smell and taste all over again; I learned there is no substitute for the trinity of fish sauce, sugar, and lime juice.

Fish sauce is one of the triumvirs of our base seasoning at Fish & Game, and it's probably the most important. (Though maple syrup and vinegar are both forces to be reckoned with.) Fish sauce contributes far more than salt's flavor-enhancing properties; it imparts depth, roundness and sometimes even a little sweetness.

My passion for fermented, liquified fish began when I first arrived in Thailand, in 1996, where I discovered the profound pleasures of high-quality *nam pla* and *nam pla raa*. As I moved along and settled, for a time, in Malaysia, I became enamored with *belacan*, *terasi*, and *cincalok*, different forms of fermented shrimp paste and sauce. And then I discovered the preeminent *budu*: a bold, unfiltered fermented fish sauce produced along the Malaysian Peninsula's eastern coast.

The sauces and pastes, forward and pungent as they are, do not season a dish unaccompanied, and for good reason; a mouthful of straight *budu* would assault your palate in the most unpleasant way. Working with Thai and peninsular Malay cuisines taught me how to temper the pungency of fish ferments, most often using palm sugar and lime juice. These three elements balance a dish, enabling one to elegantly push it in different directions, making it as assertive as it needs to be. Also, a chili product of some sort must always be close at hand. Though the chili is a revered fruit, it does not share the omnipresence of the sweet-sour-umami triangle.

These electric flavors turned me on in my early twenties, and I have yet to find any other cuisines that brazenly walk that high wire of sweet, hot funk with the same dynamism. In planning our project in the Hudson Valley, Jori and I knew we would have to create an equivalent triumvirate to govern our cuisine. We'd riff on what Southeast Asia had taught us, creating our own versions. Back in 2006, when our move upstate was only the stuff of late-night dreams, Jori created her "fermentation station" in in our New York apartment and began developing recipes. Carboys of fish sauce, jars of vinegars, and pots of kimchis bubbled alongside experimental wines and our sofa. We had more than a few complaints from neighboring tenants, but she was on a mission and the threat of eviction did not deter her.

At Blue Heron Barn we have now determined that delicious fish sauce can be produced in the Hudson Valley. We ferment whole fish, cut up fish, and fish guts: some in barrels, some in glass jars, and others in crocks. We play with salt percentages, types of northeastern fish, water volumes (and water types), and time in barrel or other vessels. The results so far have almost always been usable. Some have been phenomenal. This season we're considering heat sources other than the sun.

The recipe is simple:

FISH + SALT + WATER + CONTAINER +
TIME + TEMPERATURE = FISH SAUCE.

Is that clear?

It'll have to be clear enough for now as the experimentation continues and there's no end in sight.

Vinegar has replaced lime juice, and our own maple syrup proves to be a fine substitute for palm sugar. I'm writing this in April and the sugaring season has just come to a close. This was our best yield to date, taking in over six gallons of syrup at approximately 67° brix. We're drinking the fresh sap, which usually has a sugar content of 2–3%, and serving it to diners as an opening salvo during the few short weeks it stays fresh. It's lightly sweet, cold, and refreshing. There are few things as beautiful as drinking water straight out of a tree.

The spectrum of Jori's vinegars currently in our pantry is massive: white wine, green tomato, peach, rhubarb, carrot top, cherry and bread, rosé, grape skin, red tomato, cherry, red wine, and herb... and that's just off the top of my head.

Her vinegar production really shifted into high gear when we visited our friend Bob Machin up at his farm in Vermont six years ago. Bob has an old cider press and sells his fresh cider and cider vinegar in local co-ops. He fills his old oak wood *foudres* with fresh cider every fall and leaves them alone in the mill, where beautiful strains of bacteria make some of the most indescribably delicious cider vinegar anywhere. He presented Jori with a gift: a big chunk of his mother. With that mother, Jori has been mighty prolific. Over the ensuing years her brood has grown and generations of new mothers from all types of vinegars now live in our barn, which we hope will one day possess a bacterial beauty equal to Bob's mill.

These three condiments (the magic number) form the cornerstone of our cuisine; they find their way into everything we cook from the beginning process to the final seasoning at the pass. Each station has them sitting in glass jars, ready to be spooned into sauce, onto meats and fish, or tossed with vegetables again and again and again. The combination comprises our lifeblood, for which there is no recipe.

Fish Sauce

FISH SAUCE PROVIDES FOUNDATIONAL FUNK, the irresistibly insistent and addictive bass line that amplifies flavors and throws their details into sharp relief. The crew makes several kinds, using the most local fish they can get: trout and shad from the region and herring from the North Atlantic. Also, because the pull of tradition can sometimes overpower devotion to local products, one summer saw the creation of a cuvée: a mixture of anchovy, mackerel, and sardine from the Mediterranean. Jori also made a barrel of squid sauce the following winter. Some of the sauces ferment and age in charred oak barrels from Tuthilltown distillery; the oak adds further complexity to an already compelling product. After about a year, the resulting liquid is sweet, salty, pungent, and packed with umami. It makes everything that it touches taste better.

The Romans made fish sauce and called it *garum* or *liquamen*. It almost vanished after the Roman Empire collapsed, but fish sauce is still made in Italy: *colatura di alici* remains an artisanal and culinary tradition (albeit an obscure one) in Campania, the region around Naples. Like a coelacanth, it remained largely invisible for millennia before being rediscovered in recent years. There are numerous Scandinavian and Inuit traditions for burying and fermenting fish, many of which make Fish & Game's barrel-aged versions seem like fine wine in comparison. Swedish *suströmming*, for example, is herring fermented inside sealed cans, the tops and bottoms of which bulge out from the pressure of gases released by microbes digesting the fish.

20	+	367	=	2
pounds of fish		days fermenting in an oak barrel		gallons of fish sauce

Fresh fish are essential, either whole or cut into chunks; the digestive tracts contain enzymes that are instrumental in breaking the fish down and accelerating the effects of fermentation. Oily species are traditional, but the trout experiment yielded a milder yet still compelling flavor. Modern versions use somewhere around 25 percent salt by weight, but *garum* was usually made with significantly less. A lower percentage of salt allows fermentation to have more influence on the result, since salt impedes microbial growth. More microbial activity seems to develop a richer, more umami-laden flavor. For safety reasons, though, it's essential to have at least ten percent salt. Oak barrels are not required; glass or ceramic work fine, though glass containers should be kept out of direct sun to protect the contents from UV radiation.

The time to maturity varies largely due to temperature; anywhere from six months to a year is a good bet. More time will tend to improve the result. The first experiments at Zak and Jori's place sat out in an uninsulated barn that ranges from well below freezing in winter to jungle hot in summer, so your garage or basement will probably work fine. (Keep in mind that fish is fermented from the Arctic Circle to the tropics.)

Opening the barrels can be intense. The trout batch reeked like baby diarrhea when the top came off, but beneath the surface scum lurked a limpid liquid that tasted noticeably sweet. There's a fine line between fermentation and rot, but underneath, protected from air, lies a magical elixir.

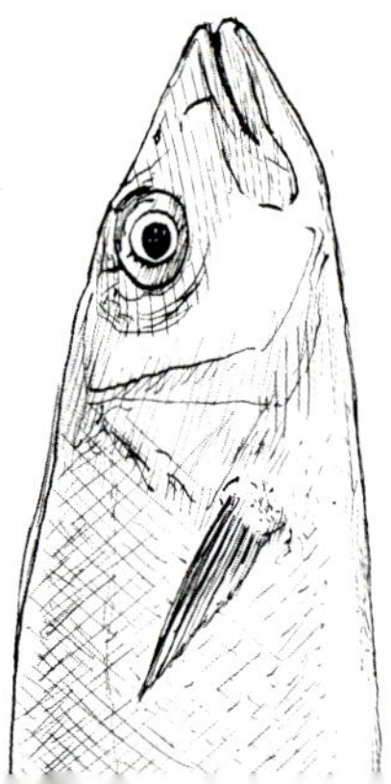

AFTER A YEAR, strain the liquid through cheesecloth and bottle it. If you're feeling extra adventurous, strain it through a colander or medium mesh strainer to remove the bones and fins, then strain it again through a fine filter. The paste remaining in the filter after you squeeze or press the liquid out of it is also a great condiment, albeit an intense one. The Romans called it *allec*; those too poor to afford *garum* used it. Waste not, want not.

There is no subtlety in necessity. Stick your nose in a barrel full of fish, each one consuming itself from the inside out. Enzymes in the gut slowly eating away the flesh. Processes such as these provide the nutrients & healthy bacteria for us to go on being. —ZAK

Vinegar

JORI CONTRIBUTES MANY, MANY INGREDIENTS TO THE RESTAURANT, BUT THE UNUSUAL ASPECT OF THE RELATIONSHIP IS THAT THE KITCHEN SENDS HER FOOD AS WELL: past-prime fruit, vegetables, peels, and trimmings. She spins them into gold. Vinegar comprises a central and ongoing component of this process and is essential to the kitchen's proper seasoning repertoire. With the one-time exception of some cider vinegar from friends in Vermont—from whom Jori got the mother to start her acetic endeavors years ago—Fish & Game has never bought vinegar.

The kitchen uses a lot—about sixty gallons a year—so Jori fills crocks and carboys with wine and various flavorful agents on a regular basis. They ferment all over the place, under tables and in corners, openings covered in several layers of cheesecloth to keep the fruit flies out. The wine comes from the restaurant's too-long open bottles, donated samples, and cases of dodgy old stock in distributors' warehouses that the restaurant buys in bulk for pennies on the dollar.

There is a risk with buying cheap wine, since many companies use copious chemicals to preserve their products. An entire batch of vinegars once failed when some boxed Finger Lakes white turned out to be so heavily treated that fermentation never took place. That mass failure set Jori back significantly; it took her a year to catch up with the demand from the kitchen. (The Vermont vinegar filled the gap.) Since vinegar takes between six and twelve months to fully ferment, and gets even better after two or three years, it's a product that requires planning and patience to ensure a steady supply. It took two years before her inventory had recovered to the point where she was finally able to set some aside for longer aging into reserves.

TOMATO
VINEGAR
9/21/13

NEW MOTHER
OLD MOTHER
OLDER MOTHER
LOVAGE

VINEGAR IS ONE OF THE EASIEST OF ALL HOME FERMENTATION PROJECTS: the gateway drug. Left to its own devices (and exposed to air) fruit juice will turn to vinegar in a two-stage process. First, wild yeasts present on the fruit or botanical being fermented metabolize the sugars into ethanol, also known as alcohol. Second, acetic acid bacteria take over and oxidize the alcohol into vinegar. This is a simplification, but it's all you really need to know to make extraordinary vinegars at home out of almost anything that grows in your area. Vinegar mother is a diminutive ecosystem of bacteria and yeast living on a cellulose raft built by the microbes' own metabolic processes.

Growing mother is easy; it forms as a natural result of fermentation. Cider grows it best and fastest; leave some unpasteurized organic cider at room temperature (and out of direct sunlight) for a few months and a pale disc of mother will appear on the surface, thickening as time passes. It's also possible to buy raw cider vinegar "with the mother" at health food stores. Adding mother to new batches of other kinds, especially wine-based examples, will jump-start the process and increase the success rate. Apart from red wine, which can sometimes grow a contagiously purple mother, the flavors and color of the vinegar the mother grew in shouldn't contribute too much to whatever sort they're deployed in next. Variations, however, are natural and every potion behaves a little differently. Make sure all jars of vinegar at every stage are covered with several layers of cheesecloth to keep fruit flies out.

Check your vinegar jars regularly. Think of them as your microbe farms and don't neglect them. It's also important, once the mother gets nice and thick on top, to gently twist the jars back and forth until the mother sinks. This opens up more surface area to oxygen, which vinegar needs to thrive and complete its long fermentation. Jori also blows air into her jars, using a length of tubing, to aerate them and accelerate fermentation.

Apart from apple cider, which is a local, organic product that makes for a complex and balanced result, Jori prefers white wine as the base liquid for most of her flavored vinegars: it's more neutral than cider, and clear. Red wine, with its overpowering flavor and color, is fermented as is into straight red wine vinegar, but most of the others are made with whites. Sometimes there are very old, very oxidized wines among the warehouse bottles; those tend to get used separately since they often have a compellingly sherry-like quality.

When it's homemade, vinegar offers a vivid example of the qualitative difference between artisanal and industrial products. They're quite literally different foods. Good vinegar can and should be drunk in shrubs, fire cider, or as a health tonic.

While pickles and charcuterie like cool basement temperatures, vinegar prefers warmer climates. If you're comfortable, it will be. The ambient temperature will make a big difference to the rate of fermentation: warmer means faster. Nonreactive containers (glass, ceramic, or stainless steel) are essential. Other factors being equal, a wide-mouth vessel will ferment faster due to the larger area exposed to air. A pH meter is useful, especially if you plan on using your vinegars to can foods; a specific acidity is required to ensure safe preservation.*

**Commercial distilled white vinegar is standardized at about pH 2.4. If you want to can foods, there are books devoted to the subject. Buy and read them. And remember, the lower the pH, the more acidic something is.*

CARROT

(see p. 68)

CARROT TOP

The oft-forgotten and neglected leafy carrot tops in white wine.

CORN COB

Cut the dekerneled cobs into thirds and pack into a jar with wine and herbs.

CELERY LEAF

As flavorful and full of natural salinity as the stalks.

CHILIES

Macerate 11 oz fresh chilies per gallon of white wine vinegar for 5 days, then strain. Save the chilies for something else. Add 2 cups of lemongrass shrub per gallon of chili-infused vinegar. The result, besides conveying sharp heat, also possesses a complex depth and richness enhanced by the sugar.

LEMONGRASS SHRUB:

4 cups cane sugar
¼ cup fine sea salt
3 cups white wine vinegar
2 cups water
3 thai/bird chilies
30g fresh garden lemongrass

Puree everything, bring the mixture to a boil, then let it cool to room temperature. Strain through a fine-mesh filter.

Chilies also become a fermented mash in a barrel with apple cider (see p. 248).

HERB

Jori makes this with white wine and an assortment of tired, wilting herbs from the restaurant, plus all the woody garden herbs cut at the end of the season: mostly summer savory, rosemary, thyme, and sage, plus whatever else might be around. It's one of the most versatile liquids in the kitchen: bright, sharp, and richly complex. Herb vinegar, fermented with the herbs, not just macerated after fermentation, is as flattering to food as the herbs are in their raw state, but it penetrates the flavor in a way that a sprinkled garnish could only fantasize about. Herbs fresh from the garden are also covered in yeast and bacteria, so they can jump-start sluggish fermentation. Jori usually doesn't bother to add mother to herb vinegars as they produce their own very quickly.

PEA SHELL

Shell the peas, put the shells in wine. Herbs make a nice addition.

PEACH

White wine and peach peels. (The pits macerated in booze for a liqueur, the flesh cooked down into peach butter, and the fibers left from food-milling the flesh went in the vinegar as well.)

RHUBARB

White wine and peels, butt ends, and scraps from making rhubarb kimchi.

SUMAC

Strip the fuzzy fruit off the woody stems and ferment with wine or apple cider.

TOMATO

Cores and seeds from fresh tomatoes before they're processed for winter canning or ketchup and the like.

VERJUS

Milling unripe grapes for verjus (a beautifully sour liquid with many uses, especially behind the bar as a citrus substitute) makes a lot of waste: skins, seeds, and pulp. Ferment all of it with white wine for some hot grape-on-grape action. Jori made hers with verbena and borage as well.

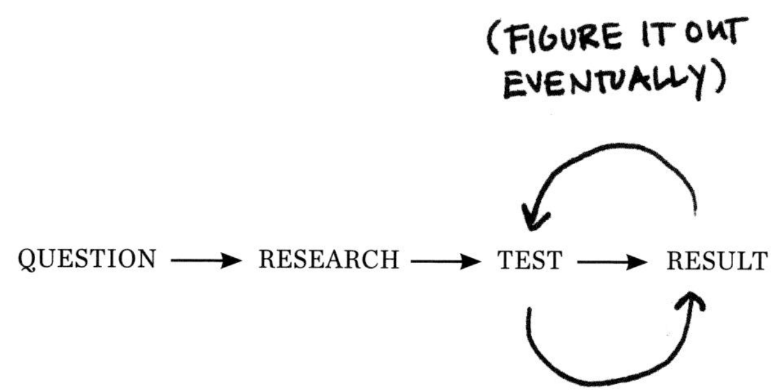

Maple Syrup

STARTING IN MID-FEBRUARY, THE SUN CLIMBS SIGNIFICANTLY HIGHER IN THE SKY EVERY DAY THAN IT DOES DURING WINTER, about the width of a hand held at arm's length each week. This acceleration of change quickly becomes apparent, even on frigid days, as we feel the heat on our upturned faces when we walk outside. Snow disappears more quickly on sunny surfaces. It's a quiet little miracle, but pretty profound after so much cold and dark.

When daytime temperatures climb above freezing but the nights drop back below, another miracle takes place inside the region's many sugar maples: sap begins to flow as the trees slowly wake from their long winter dormancy. Lacking the showy splendor of their autumnal display—sugar maples are scarlet peacocks of fall foliage—this marvelous transformation is no less beautiful for being invisible. It's the first waypoint in a new year's nascent growing season, a potent reminder that spring's leading edge lies buried deep in winter, just as the sap lies sequestered underground.

50 + 9 = 1

gallons of sap + hours boiling outdoors = gallon of syrup

Maple syrup holds pride of place among the region's most magical ingredients. It's the stuff of fairy tales; you drill holes in a tree and sugar flows out. The process, though it demands patience, is extremely simple. Drill, taps, tubes, containers—prosaic technology extracts ethereal nectar. A mature tree can easily spare ten gallons of water-clear sap per day. Drunk straight, the faintly sweet elixir provides an energizing tonic for the chilly outdoor work of lugging buckets. It's always worth putting a few jars of sap in the fridge to enjoy later; given enough freezer space there's no better summer quencher than cold sap. It's also lovely in cocktails and makes a hell of a braising liquid for pork.

Fifty gallons of sap, boiled down over a propane burner or wood fire, yield a gallon of thick, dark syrup. Wide, shallow evaporating pans and wood fires are traditional, and wood smoke adds a certain something to the result, but it's not rocket science. The first eighty percent is easy; a rolling boil sends billows of sweet steam into the air, and there's not much more to do than feed the fire and skim foam off the surface from time to time. As it thickens, though, your attention should sharpen since it can stick and burn if left alone for too long. At 66° brix, the syrup is sugary enough to be shelf stable when canned. Go past that point and you get into candy territory pretty quickly, which is not a bad place to be if that's how you live your life.

Maple syrup is superbly useful in the kitchen. Added in moderation, it sweetens marvelously without imparting too much of its taste which, though distinct, is nowhere near as assertive as honey. (And trees make easier pets than bees.) Occasionally, maple gets featured as a prominent flavor. The pre-dessert on the next page, which ran for three consecutive weeks one spring, featured stinky sheep cheese from Consider Bardwell Farm in Vermont melted between halves of little spelt brioches, doused tableside with a sauce of maple syrup and melted cultured butter. A tangle of kohlrabi sauerkraut and grated fresh apple added crunch, acidity, and a veneer of civility to what was otherwise a late-night stoner snack for the ages.

Fish & Game Farm sits on Patrick Milling Smith's property a few miles outside Hudson. Patrick's place has a large sugarbush, so as the tapping infrastructure gets scaled up over the next couple of years Fish & Game should attain maple independence. Combined with the honey from the hives down the hill, this means just about all the sweetness will be home grown. (Sugar is still called for in some instances, like ice cream and certain baked goods.) Besides its potent sweetening properties, maple syrup's sticky, viscous glory also derives directly from its status as the very definition of terroir: the concentrated essence of an ongoing collaboration between tree and soil.

The wondrous, cuisine-defining character of terroir lies in the inherent compatibility that tends to attend indigenous products. In Southeast Asia, palm sap is cooked down to make palm sugar, which acts as a moderating counterweight to the many strong flavors of the region. Chief among these, it makes seamless liaisons with fermented seafood by polishing that acrid stink to an appealing shine. Besides flattering the funk of shrimp paste, that supplemental hit of sugar also balances the acidity of citrus, blunts the sting of chilies, and elevates the finished dish into a rarified space of perfect culinary harmony. These same principles undergird the food at Fish & Game. Even if you can't taste it, maple syrup has enhanced your meal. You would notice its absence.

Fire

AMONG MANY TRANSFORMATIVE CULINARY PROCESSES, FIRE REMAINS THE MOST DIRECT, THE MOST PRIMAL. Zak, Kevin, and Jori love cooking with fire. It requires a visceral intimacy with the food, a deep feeling that comes with time, with burns, and a strength born out of passion to cook. Fire demands your attention. Taming the flames is not just about adjusting a burner; it's physical. Cooking with fire means managing the fire itself: feeding it, registering the hot spots, moving embers, adding wood at the right time. It's demanding work and it can't be ignored. It's dirty, too. The effort, however, pays off handsomely; the resulting food can achieve profound flavors and textures not attainable by any other means. And in a heavily forested region like the Hudson Valley, hardwood is an integral expression of terroir.

Fish & Game's wood-fired oven, built from brick salvaged when the exterior wall was demolished to add the kitchen, sits in the corner closest to the bar. It roasts fish and oysters with hollandaise and finishes any dish that requires an infernal broiling. Walter bakes all the bread in it. The grill to the right of the oven has two levels, and though the lower one is adjustable by means of a large wheel and pulley system on the side, it generally stays at counter height. By keeping the fire in one corner of the firebox, the cooks are able to create a gradient of heat and move the food around accordingly. Up top, there's a high grill, fixed at about three feet above the lower one. This shelf hosts loins and other cuts that want a low, slow smoking, usually after they spend some time lower down getting licked by flames.

Besides the oven and grill, the dining room fireplace also sees service as a cooking tool. That fireplace was also built from salvaged brick; it looks like it grew there. In addition to the light and heat it radiates, and the homey smell with which it perfumes the place, it provides some of the heartiest fare on the menu via a custom-made rotisserie and an old school swinging arm with a hook for hanging an iron pot or *raclette*.

The rotisserie sits on the left side of the hearth. Inactive, it's an unobtrusive black box decorated with brass. Fitted with spits and turned on, however, it revolves whole birds, shoulders, or joints in front of the fire, steadily darkening them to a seductively brunneous patina. A steel trough sits below the meat, more often than not populated with peeled potatoes that greedily catch the fat and slowly crisp outside while softening within. Dishes as diverse as hot chocolate and venison stew have simmered in a big pot hanging from the hook, while the *raclette*, a flat iron circle, melts its namesake cheese as well as finishing halved or sliced fruit like apples or peaches for various dessert applications.

Spring

SPRING TAKES ITS SWEET TIME ARRIVING. Although winter weather fluctuates—very cold/not that cold, lots of snow/no snow—the land in the Hudson Valley remains largely unworkable, frozen, and unproductive.

Spring, when it comes, transforms the earth from barren to verdant in short order. Columbia County springs tend to look a lot like winter until mid-April, so when it finally begins to thaw, months of planning and longing for sun and fresh produce shift quickly to production; the restaurant's expansive plans, pent up for so long, burst forth in several directions. As the sun creeps higher in the sky and a slow-motion wave of green breaks over the landscape, the crew eagerly rides it forward, building, planting, and foraging.

Because the restaurant opened in May of 2013, that season was mostly taken up with final preparations. The following spring, though, saw Fish & Game Farm take shape. Over the course of the next eighteen months, it mushroomed into a small farm: chickens, bees, rabbits, goats, and cows all joined the party, each with their own space, shelter, and requisite fencing.

MAY MARKS THE BEGINNING OF SERIOUS FORAGING. Wild onions and ground ivy appear earlier, but the warm sun and regular rain bring forth a proliferation of ramps, marsh marigolds, angelica, garlic mustard, dandelions, yarrow, mint, and spruce tips, among many others. Zak and Jori's place and Zak's parents' adjoining property comprise a diverse mixture of terrains: meadow, forest, stream, and wetland. Most of the land slopes fairly steeply down to the stream that wends through the valley.

Zak spends each morning before service walking the fields and the woods, digging and snipping roots, stems, and leaves for the week's menu. This daily perambulation, largely on their land, allows him to connect with the granular details of the season: what's popping up, what's peaking, what's past prime. Besides the sheer pleasure of the endeavor—seasoned with occasional tedium in the form of pouring rain or poison ivy—his ongoing interaction with the wild land informs the menu by providing both rich sensory stimulation and extended quiet for thinking.

All of these wild delicacies, many with unusual and slightly feral flavors, appear on the menu as soon as they arrive: marsh marigold bud "capers," grilled ramps, wild onion broth for poaching halibut, angelica ice cream, pepperwort roots puréed into crème fraîche for anointing braised beef, and plenty of delicate leaves and flowers used as garnishes. The most elegant of these, spear-shaped trout lily leaves mottled like patinated bronze, gracefully adorn prestigious dishes like halibut and spit-roasted duck. Most precious of all, elusive morels begin to appear in April, marking the beginning of a long mushroom season.

JORI'S RAMP KIMCHI

ABOUT HALF A GALLON

3 LB RAMPS

1 CUP WATER

¼ CUP SEA SALT

1 LARGE HAND FRESH GINGER, JUICED

¼ CUP HIGH-QUALITY FISH SAUCE

(Mega Chef, Red Boat, homemade)

¼ CUP UNPASTEURIZED YOGURT

(optional)

75G KOREAN CHILI FLAKES

25G BLACK SESAME SEEDS, TOASTED

8G ANISE SEED

1

Toss ingredients together and allow them to macerate for 24 hours at room temperature.

2

Pack the mixture into a fermentation crock or another nonreactive vessel where the food can be kept submerged in the brine. Store container at basement temperature.

Fermentation takes 3–8 weeks depending on temperature and batch size.

WEEK ONE

SPROUTED PEAS

Sprouted peas from Blue Star Farm were among the first fresh greens that arrived in the kitchen, about a week before the first day of spring. The sprouts were an easy sell, given how eager everyone was to eat new growth. The peas themselves—halfway between dried and fresh, lacking the pert and verdant optimism of the sprouts—needed a little love to become palatable. After a quick (one-minute) blanch in boiling salted water to tenderize them a bit, the peas were reheated for service in a stock made from roasted crab shells. A few peas and some claw meat nestled in the bottom of the deep bell-shaped bowls from Caroline Wallner in Tivoli, followed by a ladle of stock and finished with a scattering of sprouts, made for a bright and complex introduction to the March menu.

WEEK TWO

The following week, which included the equinox, Walter's blond rye (his name for bread made with white spelt flour and rye berries) anchored a dish of smoked shoulder ham that used the sprouted peas in a creamy fondue. Between supplemental cheese courses and frequent use of the fireplace raclette, the kitchen often has cheese rinds on hand. Full of flavor but difficult to chew, they're ideal for infusing into cream. Four hours at 120°F in the combi oven results in cheesy cream and softened rinds; the mixture, briefly blended and then strained, has depth and complexity and almost zero waste. Kevin thickened it with a bit of cornstarch and added the peas. It came out in little copper pots for spooning tableside: ham and cheese on rye reimagined as a subtle salute to the vegetable kingdom's vernal stirrings.

This version of the blond rye was essentially his porridge bread (see p. 230) but with spelt flour in place of all-purpose and fermented rye berries for the grain. The addition of caraway and nigella seeds emphasized that deli-redolent rye vibe. These loaves were baked in little fluted molds and bisected horizontally for service, but could be shaped into rolls or loaves as needed.

WEEK THREE

This combination of peas and cheese carried over into the next menu. A pasta course of extra-thick pappardelle offered a substantial texture offset by a rich sauce made from buttermilk—the by-product of making actual butter, not cultured milk—the raclette-infused cream, and the cultured butter that begat the buttermilk. On pickup, the pasta got tossed with a little citrus mostarda and garnished with a few more slivers on top. As well as the bright citrus and funky sauce played together, this dish was as much about texture as taste; both the sprouted peas and pasta offered significant resistance to chewing, qualities both illuminated and lubricated by the silkiness of the sauce. By this time, the little pea sprout garnishes had been supplanted by actual pea shoots: bigger, darker, greener.

THE BASIC FISH & GAME PASTA RECIPE is eleven eggs for every kilo of flour, combined in the mixer and kneaded for five minutes or so with a tablespoon of olive oil and a few tosses of salt. A small amount of water can be added if the dough is too tight. Strictly speaking, egg pasta doesn't require a ton of kneading, but the more you work it the more supple it gets. The dough should be wrapped tightly and rest in the fridge for an hour before rolling and shaping.

Texture is one of the trademarks of the place. Some things need to be chewed. When you come to Fish & Game, remember to bring your teeth.

BLUE STAR FARM

Stuyvesant, New York

10.9 miles from Fish & Game

Sue Decker grew up on a small farm in Pennsylvania but left that life behind to work as a graphic designer and producer in New York City. She and her husband, Mark, were members of a CSA, and she served as a board member for Windflower Farm in Washington County, developing recipes to include in each week's delivery so customers could have some tips on how to use their boxes in interesting ways. That weekly contact with the farmer, hearing about what was coming up and catching vicarious glimpses of the life, ultimately led her to close her office and become one herself: "It's in my blood."

After a year working for Windflower Farm, she returned to Pennsylvania in 2005 to apprentice at and then manage another farm for three years before they bought some land in Columbia County. The publication of this book will mark her eigth season running Blue Star Farm in the little riverside town of Stuyvesant about fifteen minutes north of Hudson. The farm is Certified Naturally Grown, but practicing organic. USDA organic certification is an expensive and burdensome process; many of the region's best farmers don't bother with it. As with all the other farms Fish & Game buys from, their direct experience with her sound methods and estimable produce trumps any institutional imprimatur.

Decker met Zak and Jori when they approached her to grow some specialty crops, something she enjoys doing because "it's challenging, different, and exciting." Their first list included celtuce, lemon drop chilies, and orach, and it gets longer every year. She is now also growing a dozen types of chili, fava beans, kabocha squash, and numane melons (*oshiro uri*), a Japanese variety prized for pickling. She sells half her produce at local farmers' markets and the other half wholesale to restaurants and institutions like Kripalu and the Omega Institute.

Blue Star Farm employs four full-time workers in season, and it's a long season; they do markets from March through December, and wholesale continues year round. The field crops grow on leased land in nearby Kinderhook, but their own six-acre plot produces a significant volume as well, courtesy of the large greenhouses that sit next to the driveway behind the old farmhouse. Between root crops and baby greens and sprouts, there's always plenty of produce available in the greenhouses. It's worth remembering that Hudson sits at about the same latitude as Barcelona and Rome. Though the climate is dramatically harsher in winter, the amount of solar energy is identical. With a bit of shelter and expert ministrations, fresh food can be harvested even when the ground just a few feet away is rock hard.

CARROTS

Pedestrian yet sweet, iconic yet humble, carrots embody opposites. (And, appropriately, boast vividly complementary hues of orange and green.) Carrots number among our closest and most familiar vegetable friends and are always available to party, whatever the season. With a bit of planning and protection, they can be harvested all year long. Given modest shelter—an unheated greenhouse, or even plastic stretched over hoops covering a bed mulched with straw to keep the ground from freezing hard—and steady succession planting, carrots can be dug all year long, man. They also store admirably in a root cellar or walk-in, and there are lots of wonderful ways in which they can be preserved.

In this climate, carrots don't actually grow in the winter, but the summer's crop remains accessible throughout if the soil can be kept soft. An autumn planting will begin to mature by spring; as soon as the days begin to lengthen dramatically in mid-February, sheltered plants begin straining upward (and downward, in carrots' case) in earnest. Pulling them from the soil, bright spears against the dark dirt, evokes all sorts of precious gem metaphors. It's magic every time. Bright, both sugary and earthy, they still retain their untamed essence despite having been domesticated. In fact, their wild progenitors still thrive in the meadow surrounding the Fish & Game garden; pick a Queen Anne's lace flower, crush it between your fingers, and smell it: *Daucus carota*, carrot.

CARROTS WITH MAPLE AND LAMB PANCETTA

This carrot dish from the end of March was the first course of the year to consist almost entirely of vegetables. During spring's long, slow supplanting of winter, this plate marked a pivot point, a fulcrum on which the kitchen's perspective flipped from looking backward at the pantry to forward at the soil; the governing inspiration for each week's menu moved from the interior (the various preserved concoctions and carcasses filling the cellar, fridges, and freezers) to the exterior, to fresh food growing in the ground. Not fully outside yet, in this instance, but rather the vast and immaculate greenhouses at Blue Star Farm, from whence these carrots came. Planted in late September, the equinox found the carrots fat enough to pull.

The following week flowering claytonia (also known as miner's lettuce, and among the most cold-tolerant greens available) replaced the watercress as a garnish, along with slivers of Jori's brown butter pickled onions.

1

When your raw materials have sterling provenance, they don't need much polishing to shine. The carrots, still with greens (carrot greens, especially young ones, are delectably edible) got a quick sauté in butter lifted with a bit of maple syrup.

2

To complement the bright orange carrots, Kevin made a spinach-watercress purée (that also possibly contained some arugula) by blanching the leaves, then blending them smooth with olive oil and about .005 percent lecithin by weight to give it some body and keep it from weeping on the plate.

3

Once tender yet al dente, the carrots moved to a warmed plate for embellishment with a spoon of verdant purée, a watercress leaf, a few cubes of diced pickled watermelon radish, and a couple ribbons of Jori's pickled carrots from the fall.

4

To finish, a paper-thin curl of lamb pancetta, cured in salt and spices and hung for a month is placed on the plate. Chilled for easy cutting on the deli slicer, then layered between sheets of plastic wrap until service, the fat melted on the hot carrots so that the strip of belly flattered them like sheer silk draped over shapely legs. It also provided the requisite hit of cured, meaty umami: a salty, savory exclamation point to round out the flavor spectrum and enhance both the sweetness and earthiness of the carrots.

WHAT'S UP, DOC?

2 OZ SIEMBRA AZUL BLANCO TEQUILA

.5 OZ CORIANDER CORDIAL (see next page)

.75 OZ CARROT JUICE

.25 OZ LEMON JUICE

.25 OZ GRENADINE

2 DASHES ANGOSTURA BITTERS

2 DASHES LADY JAYNE'S ALCHEMY PINEAPPLE SAGE BITTERS

1

Combine all in a highball glass with crushed ice and swizzle. Garnish with a baby carrot (with greens on) or a sprig of cilantro.

Another fine use for carrots that are still firm enough to juice, this cocktail arrived on the bar menu shortly after the carrot dish graced the dining room.

Note: All cocktail recipes make one drink.

CORIANDER CORDIAL

8 TBSP CORIANDER SEEDS

12 GREEN CARDAMOM PODS, CRUSHED

4 STAR ANISE, CRUSHED

12 CLOVES, CRUSHED

4 LONG PEPPERCORNS, CRUSHED

2 CUPS CANE SUGAR

3 CUPS VODKA

1

Add everything to a saucepan and boil, igniting the alcohol. Once lit, turn off burner and allow flames to subside.

In a half gallon jar, combine:

1 BUNCH CHOPPED FRESH CILANTRO

HOT SPICES WITH LIQUID FROM STEP 1

2 CUPS VODKA

½ CUP GRAPPA OR MOONSHINE

2 CUPS WATER

2

Leave the lid a bit loose so evaporating alcohol can escape; tight lids create a risk of exploding, which is dangerous. Circulate for 2 hours at 170°F. Let cool, strain through a fine filter into a glass bottle, and store in a cupboard.

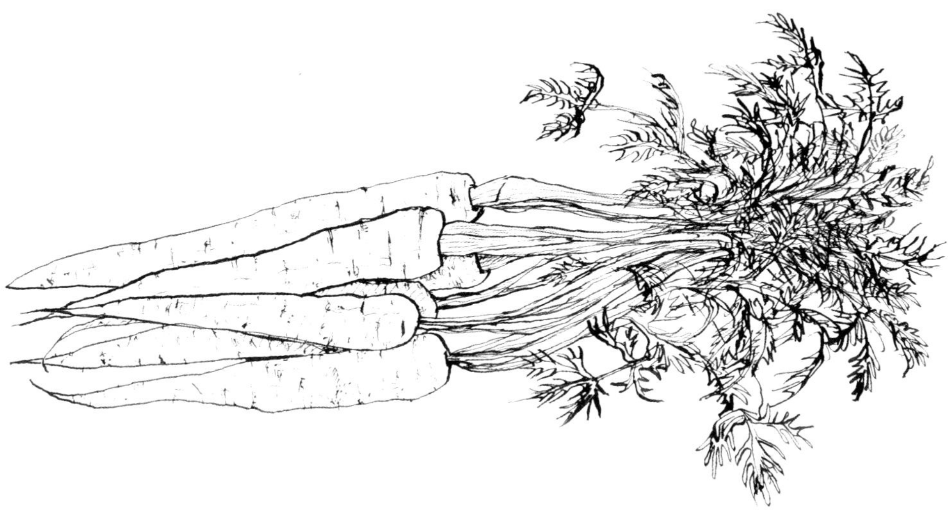

CARROT CAKE

ABOUT 20 SERVINGS

DRY MIX:

150G SPELT FLOUR

20G BAKING POWDER

¾ TSP BAKING SODA

¾ TSP CINNAMON

180G COLD BUTTER

1

Sift together all dry ingredients, then blend in butter with your fingers until the mixture is crumbly, much as you would make biscuit or pie dough.

Carrots can be dug all year, man.

WET MIX:

120G CHOPPED NUTS

340G SHREDDED CARROT

2.5 TSP SALT

162G BUTTERMILK

124G STARTER

74G POOLISH*

200G EGGS

300G MILK JAM**

2

Blend all wet ingredients together thoroughly in mixer bowl, then add in dry while the paddle churns.

3

Pour into molds and bake at 350°F for 12–15 minutes, turning once, until a cake tester comes out of the center clean.

4

Bake immediately after the batter is ready; waiting will cause all the leavening to activate and the result will not be as tender. Garnish with candied carrot slivers.

**A poolish is equal weights of water and flour fermented overnight with a pinch of yeast.*

***Jori found this recipe in Alain Ducasse's* Flavors of France; *milk is slowly reduced with some sugar. The result is a thick, sticky paste much like* dulce de leche. *Jori makes a lot of it.*

2 POUNDS ORGANIC CARROTS, PEELS AND SCRAPS, OR CARROTS THAT AREN'T BEAUTIFUL ENOUGH FOR THE MENU

2 QUARTS WHITE WINE
(Jori prefers Riesling because of the high sugar content, which promotes fermentation)

1 QUART WHITE VINEGAR WITH A PIECE OF THE MOTHER FROM A PREVIOUS BATCH OF CARROT VINEGAR
(see p. 37)

1 GALLON GLASS JAR

CHEESECLOTH

1

Young carrots don't require peeling, but the peelings and greens from bigger ones don't get thrown away. Instead, Jori puts them in white wine to ferment into vinegar. Another carrot vinegar, with a more pronounced carrot flavor and color, can be made using whole carrots that aren't pretty enough to eat.

2

Rinse the carrots (no need to peel them) and grate them on the large holes of a box grater or chop them finely. Add the grated carrots to the glass gallon jar. Add the wine and mother and ferment it according to the method on page 37.

AND ONCE THE GLUT ARRIVES, when there are too many to use fresh, the pickling begins. Jori makes these pickles without any added flavors so they can play well with whatever ingredients the kitchen might use in a given dish later on. If you want them as a stand-alone condiment, feel free to add whatever herbs or spices you like. If you're making pickles for the fridge, the pH matters less than if you plan on canning them for long-term storage. If you're going to process the jars in boiling water, dilute your vinegar with water until the mixture has a pH of 4.0 (commercial white vinegar that's five percent acid has a pH of around 2.4).

CARROT PICKLES

ONE QUART

1

Pack the carrots into a sterilized quart jar, alternating points up and points down to fit as many as possible.

2

In a saucepan bring 2 cups of water and between 1/4 and 1/2 cup of vinegar (depending on its strength) to a boil with a touch of sugar and salt to balance.

3

Boil to dissolve all solids. Taste the solution and adjust to your liking: if it's too acidic, add more water. If you want it more acidic, add more vinegar. Be advised that hot vinegar always tastes sharper than cool. Pour hot vinegar over carrots and seal jars.

CARROT MUSTARD

6 PINTS

2 CUPS MUSTARD SEEDS

4 CUPS MUSTARD POWDER OR FINELY GROUND SEEDS

1 TBSP FINE SEA SALT

1 CUP WHITE OR CIDER VINEGAR

2 CUPS WATER + ½ CUP WATER

1 CUP HONEY + 3 TSP HONEY

5 LARGE CARROTS

¼ CUP FISH SAUCE

2 BUNCHES ANISE HYSSOP LEAVES, CUT IN CHIFFONADE, STEMS RESERVED

1

Put the mustard seeds in a large heatproof bowl. In a large pot combine the vinegar, salt, 2 cups of water, 1 cup of honey, and the anise hyssop stems. Bring to a boil. Immediately strain the boiling liquid over the mustard seeds in the bowl. Let rest at room temperature until completely cool and the mustard seeds have soaked up most of the liquid.

2

While the mustard seeds cool, prepare your carrots. Add the chopped carrots with the fish sauce, 3 tablespoons honey, and the ½ cup water to a pot and simmer until the carrots are very soft and falling apart. When ready, add them to a high-powered blender and puree until smooth.

3

In another large bowl, add the mustard powder and lightly whisk the powder to break up any clumps. Slowly add the bloomed mustard seeds to the bowl of powder and stir constantly until a paste forms. Slowly blend in your carrot mixture. If the paste is very tight, add a bit more water.

4

Cover the mixture and allow to rest at room temp for two hours. Stir the mixture well and check the consistency. If it is tight, add more water and let it rest a while longer. If it is lovely and spreadable, jar it up and store it in the fridge.

Fish & Game Farm

THE FIRST WINTER FOUND JORI AND ZACH KALAS GERMINATING SEEDS IN PATRICK'S HEATED GARAGE. In February they built shelves, hung grow lights, and cloaked the racks in translucent covers for added warmth. The ground outside was still covered in snow, but within that garage glowed a Kubrickian assemblage of fluorescent light and organic material: a synthetic harbinger of spring's impending fertility.

That April, as soon as the weather improved enough to work outdoors, Kevin, Kalas, and Steve began building a chicken coop on an old trailer chassis bought from a farmer and towed from the roadside spot where it had languished unused for years to house the laying hens that had just arrived as a passel of sixty tiny, fluffy, multicolored chicks. As they knocked the coop together on the first truly warm day of the year, maple sap tapped from the sugarbush down the hill reduced over a nearby propane burner.

Inside the garage, the tented racks of seed starts flourished while the baby birds peeped, pecked, and scurried under heat lamps on the floor. The fast-growing chicks moved outside to a metal cage on the grass for a few days before getting introduced to the coop, which got towed out and parked in the field beyond the garden and ringed with a solar-powered electric fence.

By the time the hardier starts were ready for planting outdoors in mid-April, there was enough happening at the farm that Kalas could leave the kitchen and become the restaurant's dedicated farmer, working alongside Jori tending vegetables, chickens, and bees alike. In season he delivers eggs and sprouts to the restaurant, communicating the day's news to Kevin and Zak; in the winter he keeps the livestock fed, watered, and cared for.

By the time the restaurant celebrated its one-year anniversary at the end of May, much had been accomplished. But there's no doubt that more ground got covered, literally and figuratively, in the last three months of that first year than the rest of it combined.

The following June six beehives arrived. The goal was twelve gallons of honey, a year's supply. The restaurant also split the cost of a centrifugal extractor with the Steve Melnyk, Patrick's beekeeper neighbor, who supplied the hives. They sit on a gentle slope next to the orchard, across the drive from the rabbit hutches.

A year later found the cows and goats ready to be milked, the garden with another year's worth of compost enriching the soil, and the rabbits ready to breed. The first Fish & Game-raised goat appeared on the Easter menu, and the propane burner for boiling maple sap had been supplanted by a proper wood-fired evaporator built from an old oil barrel. The next crop of seeds sprouted, snug in their bright tents, waiting to go outside and feed on the warmth of the sun.

Jori had a dream that she spun a spider web for the peas, and the next morning she woke and made this trellis.

Sometimes the high road is taking the redneck approach.

—KEVIN

WE PLANT GARLIC IN OCTOBER
AND WAIT PATIENTLY UNTIL
JUNE/JULY TO START EATING IT...
WE START SEEDS IN FEBRUARY
FOR A PLANT WE WON'T HARVEST
UNTIL AUGUST. WE PLANT
PUNTARELLE AND ASPARAGUS
AND WAIT THREE YEARS TO
START HARVESTING THEM...

WE DO THESE THINGS BECAUSE OF THE BEAUTY AND THE REWARD OF HAVING THE CONNECTION, EVEN THOUGH IN THIS DAY AND AGE IT SEEMS LIKE THE WRONG WAY BECAUSE THESE THINGS TAKE SO LONG.

—JORI

MARCH 15
Start seeds indoors

Pile manure
to compost

5 days: germination begins

turn,

30 days: till the garden, form the beds, plant the peas & beans

turn,

60 days (frost-free date): begin transplanting hardy and tender plants

turn.

75 days: strawberries fruiting, peas and beans getting big

HUDSON VALLEY ORGANICS

Old Chatham, New York

17.2 miles from Fish & Game

110 days: harvesting peas and beans, first tomatoes, and cucumbers

125 days: first chilies

140 days: begin fall planting

180 days: clear the garden and lay winter cover crops

210 days: first frost

turn,

turn,

turn.

210 days: compost ready for use

GOOD SHIT

Shiny vegetables get plenty of attention because they're as pleasurable to look at as they are to eat. But ask any farmers what the real star of the farm is—the ingredient for the ingredients, the produce producer—and they will tell you, to a person, that it's the soil. Sun and rain matter immensely, obviously, but dirt is the medium in which plants grow and the medium is the message. Soil amendments are the sine qua non of organic gardening; without copious and easily available nutrients, plants struggle to grow in the heavy clays that this region is lousy with. While pastured animals fertilize their own feed, vegetables need compost to thrive. Modern technology be damned, decomposed herbivore shit remains the most powerful tool for transforming solid ground into fertile tilth.

Byron Clough and his son Cameron produce roughly seven thousand cubic yards of compost a year at Hudson Valley Organics, based in Old Chatham, just a few miles from Zak and Jori's place. Their compost is composed of a mixture of horse and cow manure from a handful of local farms that meet Byron's standards for sound stewardship of land and animals alike. His compost is not certified organic, but it is approved for organic farming. It's the best in the Hudson Valley; more than a few avid gardeners pay a significant delivery fee to have it brought across the river and beyond. Seven thousand yards would amount to about a thousand trips in their truck, but many of their customers come with their own vehicles to pick it up.

Byron started working in the commodity livestock feed business, but over time his journey led to raising dairy cattle and ultimately to his current vocation, where he is happily self-employed specializing exclusively in what comes out of animals rather than what goes into them. Compost is all they do. He and Cameron both attended the Maine Compost School, a week-long intensive course, that over the course of almost twenty years has provided nearly a thousand people with expertise in this most fundamental of agricultural processes.

Soft-spoken, with a philosophical demeanor, Byron brings the same care and attention to his form of fermentation that Jori does to her many endeavors. Which makes sense, since composting is microbe ranching in exactly the same way that cheesemaking or lacto-fermenting are: set up ideal initial conditions for the organisms you want and watch them thrive. There are some tricks to it—knowing exactly when to turn the pile and what to add if it gets too hot or too cool—but as with something like vinegar, when given half a chance compost makes itself. Things want to rot.

Making great compost requires understanding the four necessary components (carbon, nitrogen, water, and oxygen) and ensuring a proper ratio between them by attentively mixing the raw ingredients. Many species of bacteria and fungi act in concert to break down the matrix of organic material into humus, which provides nutrients, moisture retention, and naturally pesticidal properties to soil. It also encourages earthworms, which aerate the soil and further digest anything not fully broken down.

To monitor their diminutive mountains, the Cloughs use thermometers that look just like the ones you'd stick in a roast but with much longer probes. A couple of feet below the surface, an innocuous-looking heap of recently arrived manure—still dotted with horse pucks and shaggy with protruding hay—has a temperature of 140°F. This is about ideal; it promotes rapid decomposition, kills pathogens, and cooks any weed seeds that might be mixed in so they'll never germinate. When Cameron drives up their hulking yellow Komatsu and scoops a bucketful, clouds of steam erupt and envelop the loader as he dumps it back on top of the mound.

That heat is both real and metaphorical: some farmers heat their greenhouses through the winter by piling their fermenting compost against one wall, and the resulting substance represents the concentrated essence of the previous year's plant life converted into fuel for the new crops. Over time, with turning and decomposition, those lumps and stalks disappear, and the mixture darkens. The result is a crumbly umber, both fluffy and substantial. It has what plants crave. Once it's fully cooked, the Cloughs mix in wood chips for porosity. When the compost is deployed in the garden as top dressing, rain causes the smaller particles to settle down, and the mulch floats to the top and suppresses weeds. Compost can thus be a dual-use technology, making life easier for plant and farmer alike.

In the kitchen, the key to fermentation lies in arresting the process at the point of maximum flavor, where the vegetables and the microbes both contribute equally to the culinary experience. In the garden, the trick is to rot everything to the point where it no longer resembles what it used to be. That's when it can become something new.

Natural Wine

WHILE JUST ABOUT EVERY OTHER INGREDIENT COMES FROM CLOSE BY, FISH & GAME'S WINE PROGRAM FOCUSES LARGELY ON WINES FROM EUROPE, SPECIFICALLY NATURAL WINES. Why does a restaurant so avowedly local in its approach to cuisine boast a wine list full of bottles from thousands of miles away? The answer lies in the word "natural." While it's not a binding designation—every country has different classifications ranging from strict to nonexistent, it refers to a style of winemaking that took hold in France over the last couple of decades and quickly spread throughout Europe and beyond.

Natural wines' rapid growth in popularity arises from the same expectations that many people now bring to the provenance of their food: organically grown, unprocessed, produced in a way that builds the soil rather than depletes it, and at a scale that's sustainable. Some sommeliers, merchants, and critics are leading the charge, while others rush to meet the demand. The beginnings of a tectonic shift may be underway. In New York, Eminence Road winery in Sullivan County, which buys grapes from the Finger Lakes, makes serious natural wine, and Bellwether, a new operation in Trumansburg, is off to a promising start. In California, Tony Coturri has been letting his vinous freak flag fly since the mid-sixties, and more domestic producers follow suit with each passing month.

Wines made in this way can range from funky homebrews—sour, cloudy, urine-yellow whites, faintly fizzy rosés that smell like candied sweat,* reds redolent of the feet that stomped the grapes—to elegant expressions of some of the world's greatest terroirs. Plenty fall somewhere between these two extremes, but all worthy examples possess vitality, honesty, and magnificent sympatico with food. Most clock in under twelve percent alcohol, since wild yeasts die somewhere around that point. Oxidative flavors, like those in sherry or vin jaune, are not uncommon, and contribute to an enthusiastic compatibility with a variety of foods.

The genre can suffer from inconsistent quality control, to be sure. Importers with discerning taste should be your guides; what's written on the back of the bottle is as important as what's on the front. And even some well-made examples can require an adventurous palate, while others would fool the most ardent naysayer (and there are plenty, including the Hugh Hefner of wine, Robert Parker, whose influential love for obvious, cloying, artificially enhanced wines has deformed the industry for a generation).

Wines made in the international style—from heavily sprayed vineyards, with lab-bred yeasts, chemical additives, and sterile filtration—often tend toward opacity and high alcohol, crushing food, blunting tastebuds, and overwhelming regional character. Natural wines can feel closer to cider, or even beer sometimes, with a light touch that meshes beautifully with a meal. And with nothing added or subtracted, what one tastes reflects the essence of the terroir that nourished them. Almost all natural winemakers grow their own fruit; organic farmers first, their wines are built from the soil up.

**Sweat exists on a spectrum, of course, a continuum from pheromonally irresistible to rank and repulsive. On one end there's your lover after yoga class; on the other end there's Wayne Coyne's taint at Coachella. The best of these wines possess a seamless integration of animal, fruit, and mineral: sexy, quenching, and complex. They make us want to cook, and eat, and laugh, and fuck. That carnal element, that simultaneous arousing and slaking of desire, connects these wines to Bacchus himself, to the primal impetus of drinking and eating with others.*

Mr. Natural

ZAK'S NATURAL WINE EPIPHANY CAME IN PARIS, IN 2006: a bottle by the legendary Jean-Marc Brignot was "an electric purple I had never seen before; it was so vibrant and alive, the taste complex but still very light." He promptly ordered another Brignot, a white, which was "this orange, hay-colored wine, and equally delicious." Now, as Zak tries to build the best natural wine list in the country, he relies on importers who specialize in similarly revelatory and idiosyncratic expressions of fruit and soil. In the last five years, Zev Rovine has become one of the most important purveyors of natural wines in America. His roster is well represented on Fish & Game's extensive list.

Zev came to New York to be a musician, and while pursuing that career he worked as a waiter in a number of fine establishments, picking up wine knowledge all the while. After a year in San Francisco and a stint in Utah as a ski-bum-turned wine bar owner, he returned to New York to begin distributing and then importing the kind of wines he had fallen in love with during his travels: wines made with minimal intervention—a light touch both in the fields and in the winery—by producers earnestly and expertly collaborating with nature. It's hard to make good wine this way; everything must be kept super clean (tanks and hoses especially), but it attracts kindred spirits: creative people taking risks to stay true to their personalities and the land.

In 2009 he took a crash course in French and began visiting the country regularly, drinking in the Paris bars that focus on natural wines and driving far and wide to meet the producers, shipping a palette of wine back to New York after each trip. He was in the right place at the right time; these wines were just beginning to break into popular consciousness. A few places—Uva, Diner, Marlow & Sons, all in Brooklyn—were early supporters, and over time he landed Manhattan clients, among them Chambers Street Wines, Astor Wines & Spirits, and Gramercy Tavern. As with the winemakers, there's a self-limiting aspect to the business; only so much production is possible when something is made by hand, and thus the business grows at a measured pace.

Is it just a fad? Maybe, but there are many trends that would be far worse for producers and consumers alike. The increase in both supply and demand for these wines is a sure sign that more and more people want their drink to be grown and made as carefully and sustainably as their food, and that's hard to scoff at. Besides, the unusual colors (often cloudy) and flavor profiles (which can veer into pretty feral territory on occasion) plus the perennial possibility of a little unexpected carbonation mean that this is likely to remain a niche market for quite some time. That's not a problem; Zev sells out of everything he imports.

ZEV'S CONCISE REQUIREMENTS FOR INCLUSION IN THE NATURAL WINE CLUB:

1

Grapes must be grown organically. Biodynamic and Fukuoka methods are subsets of organic and equally valid. (Frank Cornelissen, who makes some astonishing wines on the side of Sicily's Mount Etna, is a big proponent of Fukuoka.)

2

No added yeast. Commercial yeast contributes a lot of flavor, so true fidelity to terroir requires only indigenous yeasts.

3

No sulfur prior to or during fermentation. Ten to twenty mg/l of sulfur before bottling is sometimes acceptable, but ideally there should be none.

4

No fining or filtration of any kind. Sterile filtration makes for great shelf stability, but it strips the life out of wine.

These are useful guidelines, but they mostly address what's left out, all the chemicals and techniques that may not be used. The rules miss the spirit, the artisanal handwork present in great wines. Besides their fascinating flavors, that diligent attention to every stage of production is what connects these wines to the cooking in the restaurant.

At the end of the day, though, what matters most in a wine is the taste and the pleasure it brings. These wines are uplifting, lip smacking, and have a peculiarly compelling quality that makes it hard to reach for something made conventionally once you've been bitten by the natural bug. It's a lot like having to put on trunks after getting used to swimming naked. In addition, unsulfured wines are far easier on the body: they feel better, are more uplifting, and, most importantly, given how easy they are to drink, tend not to cause hangovers.

JEAN-PIERRE ROBINOT

Chahaignes, France

3,512 miles from Fish & Game

Jean-Pierre Robinot is a godfather of natural wine and one of the principal forces behind its ascension over the last two decades. Robinot worked as a plumber in Paris for twenty years, but every weekend he and his wife Noëlla would travel throughout France, visiting winemakers in all the great regions. In 1989 his passion led him to open one of the city's seminal natural wine bars, L'Ange Vin ("Angel Wine"). He also co-founded *Le Rouge et Le Blanc*, a well-regarded and influential magazine about natural wine, and has written extensively on the subject over the years.

In 2001 he sold the wine bar and at fifty-two moved back to his birthplace in the Loire Valley, buying a house in Chahaignes plus vineyards, caves, and a building in Le Présidial, a cluster of medieval houses outside the village. He bought parcels of old vines and planted more in 2002, the year of his first vintage; now he has about seven hectares total. Robinot is a purist, an evangelist, and an *éminence grise*. He looks the part: lanky, bright-eyed, with long, disheveled gray hair and boundless energy. It comes as no surprise that he used to run marathons. A visit with him lasts all day: seeing the vineyards, tasting in the caves, then a leisurely meal revisiting the bottles opened underground. The conversation never stops.

Although their vineyards fall within the Jasnières and Côteaux du Loire appellations, since 2013 all their wines bear the label Vin de France, a generic designation that avoids hassles from authorities. Noella explains: "The people who regulate the appellations all treat chemically; they don't understand anything about what we do. So it's easier to be outside that system." The rambling, messy stone building now serves

as a winery; it's flanked by two natural hollows enlarged and excavated into a series of caves over five hundred years ago. The disorderly space—rolls of labels, cases of full and empty bottles, tools and implements scattered everywhere—belies Robinot's extraordinary focus and intimate knowledge of his wines.

Wrestling with a ring of enormous old keys, he opens the cave containing the sparkling wines. His *pétillants naturels* are all made according to the ancestral method: bottled with 16–20 grams of residual sugar, the wine ferments for between 12–24 months before disgorging and topping up with the same vintage. He grabs a bottle and heads outside, deftly opening it with a spurt of foam. Light, delightfully delicate but with a bit of chewy malolactic viscosity, this wine embodies easy drinking. The bubbles are very fine, and even though it's entirely chenin blanc a fascinating note of wild strawberries makes it taste more like a light rosé.

"I'm completely self-taught," he says. "I learned everything from watching [winemakers] work. I kept it all in my head." He grows only chenin blanc and pineau d'aunis on these southeastern-facing slopes of limestone shot through with varying percentages of clay and flint. The vineyards Jean-Pierre planted are now 14 years old, but the ones he bought boast some venerable vines, from 80 to 110 years old. While his reds offer compellingly nuanced experiences—he maintains that pineau d'aunis is as great a grape as pinot noir—his whites inhabit another level altogether. His reserve whites, many still in barrel after five or more years, make for extraordinary drinking, especially back-to-back where the differences between the vintages become crystal clear. These wines can effortlessly serve as an aperitif, accompany the meal, and either accompany or be the dessert on their own.

"In 2003, everyone else had problems with excessive heat, but this area didn't. All over they needed to acidify, but not here." And in fact the 2003, at twelve, tastes like a baby; there's still CO_2 prickling the tongue and a vibrant tartness. The 2005 spent forty-eight months in barrel; a bottle could stay open for three months without getting stale. At around 14.5 percent alcohol, matched with an equivalently extravagant viscosity, it shows a bit of truffle on the nose, as well as a whiff of the petroleum one finds in a great riesling. This is a wine to accompany the most luxurious meals: lobster, foie gras, roast chicken with truffles. Robinot still has a couple of barrels of the 2005 that he didn't bottle. "It tastes like vin jaune from Jura."

The 2009 fermented in barrels for five years. Harvested at 16.5 percent sugar, a bit still remains: 10–15 grams, but perfectly balanced by the acidity. It drinks like a botrytized Moulin Touchais from the late 1980s, with a nose like Sauternes but the taste of the Loire: oxidative notes of nuts and dried fruit wrapped snugly in just-picked acidity and an ethereal perfume of citrus and honey, with a finish that lingers like the final chord of "A Day In The Life." The 2010 is even better, if possible, with more details and an irresistible juiciness balancing the intensity of the concentrated, almost caramelized sugars. The 2011 is still settling into itself. "It's got the acidity, the volume," he says, swirling a glass reverently under his nose. "You can see how it will evolve; the aromas will come out." He adds, almost as an afterthought, "This one is at Noma."

100,000,000
years of accumulated oyster shells
80
year-old vines
3+
years in barrels

Mentioning that there will be fish for lunch, which they eat often, he gestures at the ground. "All my wines go with fish. Even my reds taste good with oysters, because they grow on millions of years of accumulated oyster shells. I tasted the sap from a vine; it tasted like iodine, like an oyster." Indeed the local soil, helpfully revealed by the cliffs flanking the caves, is limestone studded with fist-sized chunks of chalk; lumps of it litter the ground. This chalky limestone is part of the same formation that encompasses the cliffs of Dover and runs through the Loire to Burgundy and up to Champagne: the floor of an ancient subtropical sea that now flavors many of the planet's greatest wines. This rich and varied mineral matrix results in what he confidently calls "one of the greatest terroirs in the whole Loire valley. Wines from here will easily last one hundred years."

Continuing, eyes glinting with enthusiasm, he asserts that "The greatest white wines on the planet are riesling and chenin blanc," for their complexity and longevity. He places chardonnay third on the list, though he raves about the chardonnays from Jura and Auvergne. White Burgundy? Surely wonderful, he agrees, but almost all contaminated by chemicals. He dismisses chardonnay's most famous expression outright. "I don't drink champagne, it's too polluted."

"It's a swear word," finishes Noella. Walking up the hill to their car, he continues. "Life should be in harmony with nature. Chemical wines are not." The setting, superbly harmonious, looks more than a little Shire-ish: caves with doors set into verdant hillsides, immaculate spring weather, jovial locals toting crates of bottles for lunch. And such lunch: asparagus, rillettes made from a pig fed with their garden's potatoes, wild Atlantic trout with seaweed and sautéed zucchini from a friend's garden.

In 2013, Robinot cofounded Les Vins SAINS, an association of natural winemakers who adhere to the strictest definition of the term. SAINS stands for *sans aucun intrant*

ni sulfite (without any additive or sulfite), and it means just that: members must farm organically or biodynamically, use only wild yeast, never fine or filter, and above all add no sulfur (or anything else). "The greatest names are all full of chemicals now. Even organic allows fifty chemicals, including sugar and yeast." As a result, he refuses to put organic on the label; all he puts now is SAINS. The association, lacking the enforcement power of governmental agencies, relies on growers to adhere to the strict standards. Given the increasing marketability of organic agriculture, Robinot says that it's important to know the members and see how they work, not just take their word for it.

The ethos at the center of Les Vins SAINS derives from a belief that nature makes the best wine, and that human intervention should be kept to a minimum. Robinot speaks passionately about the magical transformation that water undergoes as the vines turn it into juice, and why it is that natural wines feel so much better in our bodies. "This kind of untreated wine is like water, plant water, enriched by the vines; one never gets tired drinking it, and the last glass is as good or better than the first." He believes that his job is to guide the process, making certain decisions, but never to interfere with water's natural trajectory from soil to fruit to wine. "If you fuck with the vines, they're unbalanced. If you leave them alone, they thrive and attain balance." And this balance, he insists, opens the door to life's essential pursuit: pleasure.

Spooning some rillettes onto crusty bread, he waves it in the air for emphasis. "Wine has to accompany the food, never dominate it. It must be a marriage. That marriage is the third dimension, the hardest part. The marriage between the wine and each plate becomes a unique experience, that is lost forever in time except for human memory." He's on a roll. "The whole point of life lies in accumulating these ephemeral experiences, in making pleasure—gustatory, social, aesthetic—our top priority." When your faithful correspondent mishears "eau végétale" (plant water) as "or végétal" (plant gold) and then explains the error, Jean-Pierre laughs delightedly. "Plant gold is even better! Write that!"

MENU

WEEK OF MAY 8

CONSOMMÉ

bass, pepper wort, ground ivy

PAGE 94

ASPARAGUS

rhubarb kimchi hollandaise

PAGE 95

HALIBUT

wild onion, oyster mushrooms

PAGE 96

SPAGHETTI

spelt, bantam egg, preserved chili

PAGE 98

PORK

marsh marigold

PAGE 100

GELATO

angelica, rye

PAGE 102

RICOTTA TART

blueberry, mint

PAGE 104

CONSOMMÉ

1

For the first course, Kevin made fumet consommé. Earth and sea intermingled beguilingly; their marriage made all the more impressive by the fact that most of the flavor in this dish came from fish bones and weeds.

2

A ladle of broth filled the bottom of a heavy cylindrical bowl, just covering some sprouted and simmered barley and a piece of grilled sea bass. This was topped with an assortment of raw foraged leaves on top: pepperwort, wild strawberry leaves, ground ivy, garlic mustard, moss, wood sorrel, and yarrow.

ASPARAGUS

Just in time for this menu, Samascott Orchards in Kinderhook delivered the season's first bushel of asparagus. Asparagus holds enormously evocative power as one of spring's principal signifiers, a poster child for seasonal food; around these parts, eating it after July and before April marks a clueless diner as being far more gauche than white pants after Labor Day ever could.

1

These turgid, verdant spears, briefly blanched, got lavishly slathered with a hollandaise made with rhubarb kimchi brine and cultured butter.

2

To complete the dish, rhubarb kimchi brunoise, shaved raw bacon—paper thin slices of cured pork, like belly prosciutto—and fried bread crumbs (actually more like shrapnel, coarse chunks bigger than crumbs and smaller than croutons) all brought their respective flavors and textures to the party: a rite of spring worthy of a riot.

HALIBUT

Wild onions, which look like dark, diminutive chives above ground and plump scallions below, and which reek like garlic, rank among the most useful of this region's wild plants. They far surpass ramps in their ubiquity and even reappear in the fall for extra credit.

1

This dish featured wild onions in broth form and thick slabs of halibut poached sous vide in the stock for 30–40 minutes at 122°F.

2

To buttress the fish with earthy umami, oyster mushrooms from Zehr Farm in Ghent sautéed in brown butter and deglazed with lamb jus sat alongside.

3

Finely minced wild onion tops embellished the meaty mushroom sauce, and a proud trout lily leaf finished the plate. This batch was gathered within feet of a new-born fawn, cowering curled against a fallen tree while Zak snipped the leaves nearby.

4

A bit more of the wild onion broth, poured tableside, contributed fragrant steam and tied the fish and mushrooms together.

SPAGHETTI

Spaghetti, made per the standard recipe (see p. 56) but with a 50/50 blend of white and spelt flours, served as the substrate for some quintessentially vernal flavors: ramps and egg.

1

The pasta, boiled to al dente, had an invigorating and lubricious toss in salted chili beurre monté with chopped grilled ramp leaves.

2

Each nest of pasta was topped with a sous vide bantam egg (148°F for 45 minutes) from the rapidly maturing hens at Fish & Game farm.

Amaranth sprouts made for a festive garnish.

PORK

A shoulder from a Large Black/Tamworth cross, slow roasted on the rotisserie and sliced thickly, offered a substantial piece of pork to anchor the dish. Porcine glory, presented in three forms—fatty, sticky, and crisp—was surrounded by slightly difficult spring greens: decadence and austerity spooning each other on a plate.

1

The meat sat atop quickly sautéed marsh marigold leaves, which are quite bitter, and marsh marigold bud "capers" (blanched, then salted), along with blanched fiddleheads.

2

A schmear of curried yogurt (seasoned with turmeric, ginger, coriander, fennel) on the plate added aromatic tang.

3

Each plate came to the table swaddled in a cocoon of frothy pig skin jus, foamed with an immersion blender, and garnished with a curl of chicharrón made from the same skin used to make the jus.

GELATO

The pre-dessert featured another foraged herb: fior di latte gelato (see p. 340) infused with angelica leaf. Angelica has an almost bready quality, a toasty undertone that makes it well suited to desserts. Its flavor carries particularly well in dairy, so the kitchen has produced several variations of this dessert including ice cream and a bavarois. Put the herb of your choice in cream and heat it to 140°F for two hours, then strain. A rye cracker dusted with cardamom sugar adorned the dish.

1

Walter makes his crackers a variety of ways, depending on their intended use. They're almost always very thin, brittle, and gently undulating. Most of the doughs hover around 40 percent hydration and should be about the consistency of pasta dough (though not worked as hard).

2

Sometimes he adds a little olive oil for richness. Adding seeds, spices, grated cheese, and the like can be excellent, but keep in mind that they will inhibit rolling the dough out super thin. Whatever you use, bake them until they're just colored.

RICOTTA TART

ABOUT 20 ¼-CUP SERVINGS

Finally, Kevin's ricotta-mostarda tart with blueberry syrup and wild mint tips concluded the menu. The ricotta balances milk's inherent sweetness with the vinegar used to curdle it, and the mostarda syrup, while sugary, retains plenty of citric acidity.

RICOTTA TART FILLING:

- 1000G RICOTTA
- 2 EGGS
- 4 EGG YOLKS
- 200G TANGERINE MOSTARDA SYRUP

1

Blend the eggs, yolks, and mostarda syrup together. With a rubber spatula, gently fold the egg mixture into the ricotta, making sure not to damage the curds.

2

Blind bake tart shells for 10 minutes at 325°F. Remove the weights and bake another 4 minutes. Leave to cool to room temperature before filling the tarts with the ricotta mixture and baking again at 280°F for 6 minutes.

RICOTTA:

MAKES ABOUT 6 CUPS

- 1 GALLON MILK
- 1 QUART CREAM
- 250G VINEGAR
- 23G SALT
- 5G CITRIC ACID

3

Mix together the milk, cream, and salt. Heat to 185°F while stirring with a rubber spatula to prevent the mixture from sticking and scorching.

4

Once the mixture has reached 185°, take the pot off the heat and stir in the vinegar. Cover the pot and let the mixture sit for 10–15 minutes.

5

Set up a hotel pan with a perforated pan inside and line it with cheesecloth. Pour the mixture into the cheesecloth-lined pan.

6

Refrigerate and let drain until thick (when the dripping stops). Reserve the whey for another use.

CITRUS MOSTARDA:

1000G WATER
600G CANE SUGAR
1500G CITRUS FRUIT

7

Dissolve the sugar completely in lukewarm water and test the brix to ensure it's at 38. Adjust if necessary.

8

Quarter and seed the fruit and lay in a single layer in a nonreactive (stainless, not plastic) container. Bring your sugar syrup to a boil and pour over the fruit. It needs to be submerged, so use weights if need be.

9

Let sit at room temperature for 24 hours.

After 24 hours, pour off the syrup. Check the syrup brix, increase it by 5 percent, and repeat the submerging, resting for 24 hours, pouring off syrup, and increasing the brix.

When you reach 50 brix, add glucose syrup equal to 15 percent of your total syrup weight (this keeps the result from crystallizing).

10

Continue step 2 every 24 hours until you reach 68 brix for home canning (water bath) method or 75 brix for shelf stability without sealing.

Once you reach your desired brix, hold everything for 2–3 days at room temperature before canning to ensure there's zero fluctuation in the brix. At no point in the process should this be refrigerated.

The Yawn of Time

ZAK

IN COLUMBIA COUNTY OUR DEEDS ARE DONE AND DONE AGAIN AS OUR LIFE IS DONE IN COLUMBIA COUNTY.

In Columbia County, spring trails into summer uneventfully. The powerful longing for sunshine and flowers that infects us all in that awkward month when winter turns to spring has already been rewarded; the disappointment of early morning frosts dissipates sometime around the end of April (in the most stubborn years, early June). Late June is subtly transitional: the mornings are comfortably cool, the green grass is soft from recent rains, moisture fills the air, and the green extends beyond the grass so powerfully that any hint of single digit days and frozen roads is long lost to the mysteries of what lies behind the foliage.

The valley is green: the green that rules all greens, jungle canopy green. You may well believe you're in a jungle when you get wrapped up in vines and bushes, blossoms and berries. It happens. When it does, the smells and the overwhelming fertility induce fantasies of growth never ending, ungoverned by trimming, pruning, clipping, or human intimidation of any kind. It is in those moments that I work to live in the daydream of the bounty growing around me, insulating me from sound and sight of anything other.

Alas, like all highs, it doesn't last. In fact, among us humans, the farmer, the gardener, and the cook are most acutely aware of the transition from spring to summer. Because before the time when grass browns, burnt by the sun, the rains failing to catch up, and before the interruptive moment when air-conditioned office towers are all that stand between the abstract productivity of the city's masses and the mad dogs of the noonday sun, the texture and temperature of the soil changes and with it so do the products that we love.

So while we skip into summer, we hold fast to the last fertile bursts of spring. We will away the oppressive heat for a little longer so we may continue to enjoy the pop of a sour cherry and the green sweetness of a shell pea. The beans begin to mature and we find ourselves sorting studiously through every leafy tangle in the strawberry patch, ensuring that not a single plump red berry goes unpicked... or uneaten. This transition, this time of year when it *is* summer but in our absentminded, contented haze we have forgotten to say goodbye to spring, is the span between the seasons I think of fondly as the yawn of time.

Summer

SUMMER GETS BUSY FAST, as various projects undertaken in the spring begin to bear fruit (or, more accurately, vegetables). The garden exceeded the admittedly low expectations people had for it in its inaugural year due to the expert ministrations of Jori and Zach Kalas plus some great weather. The first half of the season was meteorologically ideal for growing things: regular heavy rains alternating with long periods of scintillating sunlight. Everything flourished.

The second Labor Day weekend menu marked a milestone, of sorts. With the exception of some peaches featured in a dessert broiled under an almond streusel, all the produce came from Fish & Game Farm and Blue Heron Farm: beans, potatoes, okra, brussels sprout leaves, chilies, parsley root, and a bunch of herbs including lemongrass. The same weekend, as if to cloud this happy landmark, the vicissitudes of foraging unfortunately revealed themselves when the wild mushroom supply disappeared after a very dry August. Charred whole shishito peppers subbed handsomely for the chanterelles in a potato dish on Sunday after the mushrooms ran out, and Zak thinks they might actually have been better, what with the familial simpatico between potatoes and peppers.

Summer's greatest culinary glory comes during the second half in the form of nightshades; as tomatoes, potatoes, peppers, and eggplants ripen they provide some of the most satisfying and versatile food the plant kingdom can offer. Both eggplants and peppers can be made into silky-smooth purées but also offer pleasure in a less processed state: the slight bitterness and resistance of thick eggplant skin and seeds (in

the case of chilies, the seeds and membrane also hold most of their heat) provide a contrast to more refined textures and flavors. Zak likes to include these elements in certain dishes, both for their honesty and because he's fond of a slightly obdurate difficulty, an al dente assertiveness, that requires attentive engagement from the diner.

Though their season is fleeting, tomatoes and peppers preserve as well as anything from the garden. Jori's tireless processing results in all manner of pantry staples, and a significant percentage of those involve tomatoes and chilies. She preserves more than five hundred pounds of tomatoes a season, whole in olive oil and as paste and ketchup. The first potato harvest, a substantial two hundred pounds, got washed and stored in the root cellar. Subsequent years yielded still more.

No mention of summer food would be complete without corn, sweet corn, which when shucked right off the stalk needs neither cooking nor seasoning to delight with its succulence. Corn and tomatoes, corn and chilies, corn grilled over hardwood and slathered with cultured butter—there's no more compelling illustration of the "if it grows together it goes together" adage than high summer's incandescent bounty. Corn and chilies featured prominently in the food prepared by the crew when Fish & Game Farm hosted an epic feast to benefit the FarmOn! foundation, a Columbia County not-for-profit founded by Tessa Edick to promote sustainable agriculture that's fully integrated into the communities it feeds by teaching young people to become farmers.

COMMON HANDS FARM

Hudson, New York

3 miles from Fish & Game

Common Hands Farm was closer to the restaurant than any other producer, even Fish & Game Farm: about a minute outside Hudson by car. Presided over by business and life partners Tess Parker and Dan McManus, its ten acres divided into a patchwork of orderly row crops produced a wide variety of fetching vegetables to restaurants, to farmers' markets, and to their growing number of CSA customers. In their fifth year in business they obtained biodynamic certification after practicing the method since the beginning; McManus grew up in a biodynamic community in South Australia.

In 2016, Common Hands moved to a 150-acre site in Ghent. They're sharing the lease with a few other farmers—growing grain and raising animals—acting as joint stewards of the land. The tenfold increase in size opens the door for dramatic growth; New York City is an insatiable market. The move allowed them to raise chickens and to expand their CSA into eggs. They have added a full-time employee, bringing the

40

miles is the maximum distance traveled by most of Fish & Game's ingredients

total to six, and also have five apprentices helping as well as summer interns. Currently, their vegetable CSA has around one hundred members in Brooklyn and Queens. They plan on raising some pigs and hope to plant an orchard nearby on another rented plot where they also live.

While growing and selling primo produce takes plenty of time and effort, the couple clearly spend still more of both working to build a larger infrastructure for sustainable agriculture in the region. Seeing an opening, Parker created the Upstreet Market in Hudson, open every Wednesday afternoon and offering a welcome midweek exchange for growers and shoppers alike in summer. She embraces the trend toward bespoke farming for restaurants (and loves growing custom crops for Fish & Game) but the next essential step, she says, is better distribution and other cooperative practices where small farmers pool modest quantities to fill bigger orders. These and other developments are beginning to happen, as the Hudson Valley comes into its own as one of the country's preeminent agricultural and culinary regions.

These changes, driven by a dramatic increase in public awareness of food issues, have allowed Common Hands to prosper, beginning an exciting new chapter where the farm integrates fully into a larger community. Teaching young people to farm, always part of their core mission, has now become a larger and more polished facet of the project. Demand for high-quality local produce has never been higher, and the more people understand about their food and where it comes from, the easier it gets for farmers to earn a decent living practicing agriculture that builds soil rather than depletes it. In recent years, as consumers began steering more of their food dollars toward their neighbors, she concludes, "We've seen a proliferation of organic farms and CSAs. Food culture attracts more like-minded people; it's been immensely beneficial to farmers."

$200,000+

spent by Fish & Game at local farms in one year

80%

of the price of Fish & Game's food stays in the local community

A HOLISTIC ETHOS OF CONSUMPTION CAN EXTEND BEYOND THE TABLE TO INCLUDE YOUR WALLET AS WELL. Just as shopping at farmers' markets fills us with virtue (and delicious produce), so too does eating at restaurants that work closely with local farmers and producers.

When you eat at Fish & Game, you're enjoying the nexus of a complex web of supply chains, most of which begin and end in Columbia County. Picture the restaurant at the center of a spider web. Most of the radiating strands, each reaching to a farm, stretch less than forty miles, most about half that. In 2014, Fish & Game spent over $200,000 on food from local farms. All of those dollars—plus those spent on firewood, and a meaningful percentage of the utilities—flowed directly into the local economy. Factor in the staff's wages, which are mostly spent locally (at liquor stores) and something like 80 percent of the price of your food stays in the community.

Seeing a producer's name on the back of your menu means that the restaurant endorses their commitment and methods, that they're kindred spirits, with serious skills and a yeoman's work ethic. Zak, Jori, and Kevin are enthusiastic boosters for the region, but they have never chosen to buy something local that's inferior to a similar ingredient from farther away. If it appears on the menu, it meets their world-class standards; you will never be asked to take one for the local team by eating lackluster product just because it comes from nearby.

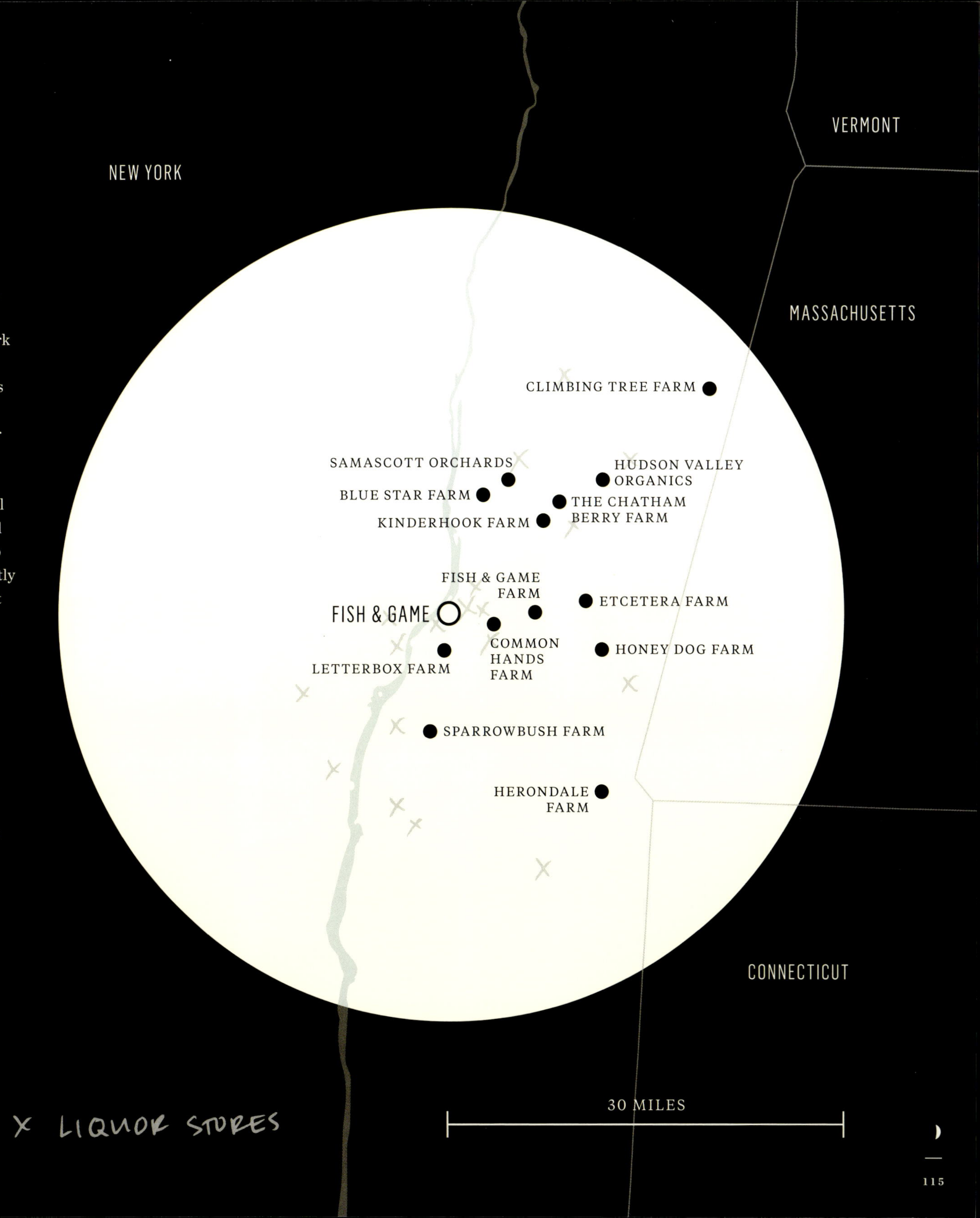

TOMATOES

Tomatoes, the poster children for homegrown produce, need no introduction. One reason for their iconic status lies in the fact that they contain all five flavors—sweet, sour, salty, bitter, and umami—in significant amounts, making them a culinary rarity. Columbia County's short growing season nonetheless allows for a big crop, provided the plants are started indoors a couple of months before the frost-free date (which is around mid-May).

Slicing tomatoes are grand, because a fat slab of still-warm tomato with a pinch of crunchy salt on it represents the distilled essence of summer bliss, but Fish & Game focuses on growing cherry and paste types because they preserve so well. In its first year, the garden produced enough that the restaurant didn't need to buy any tomatoes.

TOMATO PASTE

Jori makes tomato paste by cooking and blending plum tomatoes, then spreading the reduced purée on sheet pans and dehydrating it further in the oven. This allows for a much thicker result than the stovetop, where sticking and burning would be too likely. Then she vacuum bags the paste in roughly one-pound quantities and freezes them.

Her oil-cured tomatoes straddle raw and cooked; they retain the bright flavor of fresh fruit but pack the decadent, oily heft of confit. The oil they're packed in does not suck, either.

OIL-CURED CHERRY TOMATOES

1

Wash perfectly fresh cherry tomatoes thoroughly, then dry them completely. Pack them into half-gallon jars, up to the shoulder of the jar, taking care not to break or split any of them.

2

Pour about a quarter cup of sea salt over the tomatoes, gently shaking the jar so the salt falls through the gaps and dusts most of them.

3

Heat some good olive oil to 350°F (just below the smoke point of 375°) and carefully pour it into the jars until the tomatoes are submerged. Cover tightly and store in a cool place.

KETCHUP

ABOUT 6 PINTS

14 LB RIPE PLUM TOMATOES

4 LARGE WHITE ONIONS, CHOPPED

1 HEAD GARLIC, PEELED AND CHOPPED

6 SWEET PEPPERS, CHOPPED

2 TBSP SEA SALT

½ CUP CANE SUGAR

6 DRIED HOT CHILIES

1 STICK CINNAMON

1 BAY LEAF

1 FAT PINCH ALLSPICE

1 PINT WHITE WINE VINEGAR

1

Cook tomatoes, onions, garlic, and sweet peppers until soft, then mash and pass through the coarse screen on a food mill.

2

Tie the spices in a square of cheesecloth. Add the sugar, salt, and spices and simmer to reduce. Remove spices after 45 minutes.

3

When the ketchup begins to thicken, push it through a tamis. (Reserve the solids from the tamis and food mill for adding to kimchi.)

4

Return ketchup to the stove and add the vinegar, simmering until it tightens up into a paste.

A gram or so of xanthan gum may be needed to prevent syneresis (weeping) depending on the water content of the tomatoes. Blend on high until silky smooth. Can or freeze.

This goat tartare featured Jori's ketchup as well as shallots and pickled mustard seeds. Other accoutrements included a rye cracker, shredded *pan di zucchero* chicory, and turnip grated fine like wasabi.

When preserving food becomes part of your routine, those products exert significant influence on your cooking. Take this august course from a July menu, for example. A plate of ham and cheese and tomatoes, perfectly humble by many measures, also represents a quiet triumph, a Platonic ideal of peasant food: the season's first cherry tomatoes, along with the last of the previous summer's preserved tomatoes embellishing a plate of ricotta and delicate folds of thinly sliced slow-smoked pork loin.

This dish proved that the only thing better than a ripe, just-picked tomato is several of them basking in the sexy, savory glow of their older oil-cured peers sitting pretty in a puréed pool of their own embalming fluid and positively oozing umami. Thus a simple plate of food closes the tomato circle: the new crop ripens just as the previous year's canned supply is exhausted. That's the holy grail of tomato lovers everywhere. A little bit of pickled okra needed using up, and fresh nasturtium leaves garnish just about anything to great effect.

WEEK 2

The following week, more new tomatoes appeared as a delicate sauce for a byaldi, a savory expression of summer sunshine. Michel Guérard invented *confit byaldi* in 1976 as a nouvelle cuisine version of ratatouille: thin, unfried slices of squash and eggplant layered and baked with tomatoes and herbs. Thomas Keller refined it further, cooking the thin slices over a pipérade, then fanning out the cooked slices in a circle and dressing them with vinaigrette on the plate: the dish the eponymous rat cooked for Anton Ego in *Ratatouille*.

The Fish & Game version pared the preparation down further still: a light sauce of caramelized onions, thyme, and tomato sat under folded slices of lightly grilled yellow and green summer squash layered in the rectangular Staub pans, which slid into the wood oven to catch a bubbly browning and soften a bit more. Each pan served two, bisected tableside and served with a tomato's best friend, quenelle of fresh ricotta. Fresh cheeses like ricotta or mozzarella possess both sweetness and acidity, like tomatoes do, but also the density and richness that protein and fat contribute. Another nasturtium leaf added a verdant and peppery pop.

WEEK 3

Most som tum (green papaya salads) at Thai restaurants in this country include some green beans. The next week's menu used tomatoes in a riff on this classic in which barely blanched green beans subbed in for the tropical fruit. This first course, variations of which ran for weeks due to the presence in the garden of very many green beans, delivered a persuasive hit of hot, sour, and savory Thai flavors while remaining resolutely local. When there's a steady supply of perfect product, and a simple treatment shows it off handsomely, why take it off the menu? Soon enough, the pods start to dry out and get stringy; at that point they should be left to ripen their cargo so the beans can be dried for storage.

Slice a variety of fresh beans—like romano, soldier, and dragon's tongue, some skinny, some fattening with baby beans—into roughly one-inch lengths and then lightly pound them in a large mortar with blanched and peeled cherry tomatoes, salted chilies, thin slices of parsley root, and a dressing of maple syrup, herb vinegar, fish sauce, and fresh garlic. This menu's iteration included sardines and sea urchin, both lightly smoked, which tripled down on the fishy foundation of the dressing and added some luxe texture (the slippery tomato meshed marvelously with the uni) and protein. A garnish of fall pea flowers contrasted nicely against the orange urchin.

Nose to Tail

"NOSE TO TAIL" IS A COMMON AND WELL-UNDERSTOOD SIGNIFIER FOR A PARTICULAR APPROACH TO EATING ANIMALS, and one that any carnivore worth the name should enthusiastically embrace. Apart from the ethical imperative, there's a practical benefit to eating this way: by buying a whole (pastured, humanely slaughtered) animal, and doing justice to its life by eating every part of it, we understand our food in a deeper and more direct manner. Since each cut and organ responds differently to cooking and curing, one animal can constitute an entire semester's worth of lessons.

Learning how to treat each piece respectfully—and according to our taste—makes us better cooks and improves our diet. It also, paradoxically, leads to eating less meat; when properly processed into charcuterie (like prosciutto, sausages, terrines, and bacon), fresh cuts, and stock (from bones and skin), a pig will yield many more meals than an equivalent weight of chops. The quality, variety, and flavor of those meals will also be superior, so that less animal will be required to provide meaty satiety. Buying whole animals and taking responsibility for their transformation into food should be a condition of carnivory.

The same attitude must also apply to vegetables. As a country, we throw out about half the food we buy, a disgraceful statistic. When the food comes out of your own garden, though, or you know the farmer who grew it for you, the incentive to extract not just maximum flavor but maximum value becomes much greater. As much as anything else, Fish & Game is a think tank dedicated to this principle.

The kitchen's goal of wasting nothing is an admirable and easily imitable ethos in your own kitchen. Animal bones, raw or roasted, become a variety of stocks. Vegetable trimmings can be used to flavor vinegars (fermented right in the wine, or macerated in finished vinegars to add flavor) and also used in stocks. Various bready remnants—stale heels, orphaned rolls, and the like—if not soaked and fermented for pumpernickel, will be ground into crumbs and used to add flavor and texture to subsequent loaves, pasta, or desserts. The truly fossilized loaves go to feed the chickens.

This frugal approach to product gets a huge assist from Jori, who delights in extracting rich elixirs from the humblest of scraps. It makes a point, underscoring the restaurant's commitment to honor the ingredients, and also pleases Kevin's parsimonious attention to the bottom line; this approach keeps food costs low, since most product gives close to a 100 percent yield. But frugality, though a noble culinary influence, is not the main motivation; the scraps and trimmings provide some of the most valuable and inspiring ingredients in the crew's arsenal.

Nasturtium stems, which make up the bulk of the plant, hold as much flavor as the leaves. When cured in soy or fish sauce for a few months, they impart an herbal note to the liquid while receiving some salty stank in return. Strained out and used separately—the stems finely minced, like chives—each component brings added complexity and depth when it finally sees action on your plate. Turnip peels make an earth-deep and mustard-sharp vinegar. Corn cobs sweeten stocks as well as adding a starchy sturdiness. There's no limit to the number of ways in which value—both monetary and culinary—can be extracted from food that most people throw away.

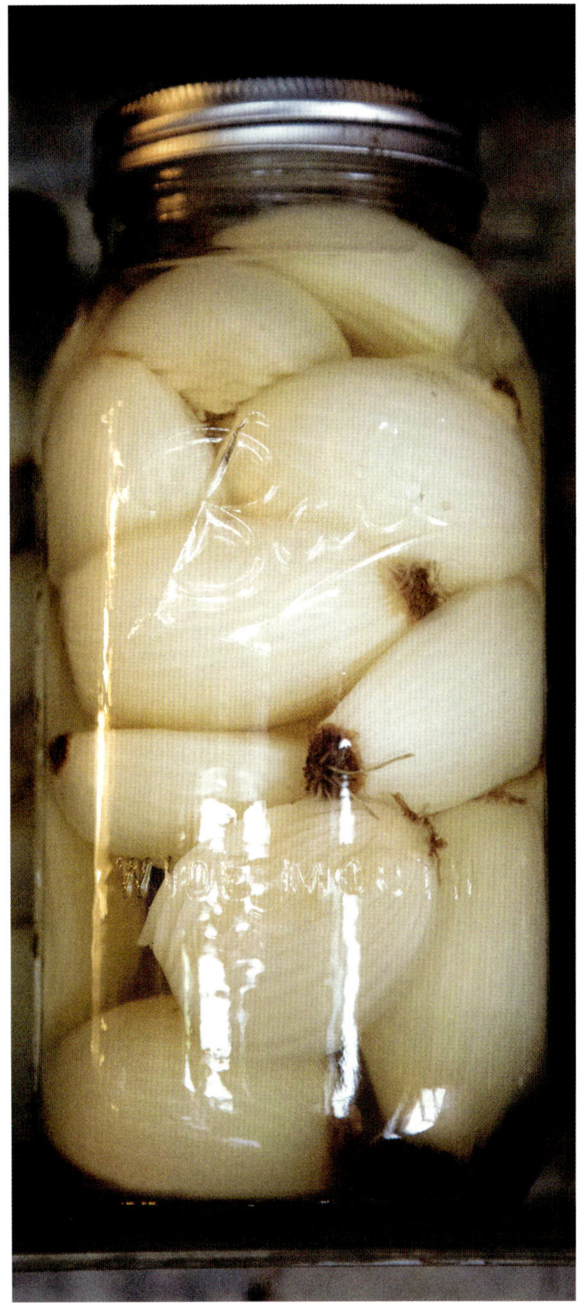

Thinking this way is half the battle; once you start channeling your inner peasant grandmother, you start to see the value and potential in even the humblest peels. There is a point, however, at which the returns begin to diminish pretty dramatically. If you're spending all your time pickling turnip peels, that's not efficient either. Some of it should go back to the Earth in the form of compost that will nourish the next crop; building black soil deserves mention among the loftiest of culinary aspirations.

Hewing closely to grandmotherly sagacity limns another important way in which Fish & Game's cooking differs from many restaurants: leftovers are not stigmatized. Not leftovers from diners' plates, obviously, but small amounts of sauces, purées, and other concoctions are always labeled, stored, and used up when the opportunity presents itself. Keeping track of this inventory and working out ways in which it can be deployed to excellent effect is another of Kevin's many talents.

The great gift of well-made leftovers cannot be overstated. Besides acting as reminders of recent meals, they represent culinary assets that accrue huge value over time. Many dishes, especially stewy braises, improve dramatically in flavor over the course of a day or two in the fridge. Leftovers exist in a culinary space between the pantry and fresh food: neither raw nor preserved, often fully seasoned, and combining a variety of flavors. At Fish & Game, some stray tidbits (usually quantities too small to use in a menu) end up embellishing family meal. At home, of course, every meal is family meal so there's even more latitude to incorporate less soigné remnants into dinner.

PORK

Pigs, the most culinarily useful animal, feature prominently on the menu in a variety of forms. Pork contains multitudes; it spans cultures, continents, and millennia, forming the base animal protein for some of the world's great culinary traditions, Chinese and Italian among them. Pork handles sweet and heat with equal aplomb, luxuriates in wood smoke, and offers a broad spectrum of textural experiences. This part of the world boasts terrain well suited to raising pigs, who thrive on land too rugged for pasture.

Pigs represent the gold standard for the nose-to-tail ethos; every part of them can be used to excellent effect in the kitchen. Their fat-to-meat ratio is naturally ideal for charcuterie, and the fat from different cuts possesses distinct culinary identities: back fat has a sturdy density, belly fat a succulent softness, and best of all the leaf lard from around the kidneys makes pastries of surpassingly flaky tenderness. Every part of a pastured pig tastes terrific, even the skin.

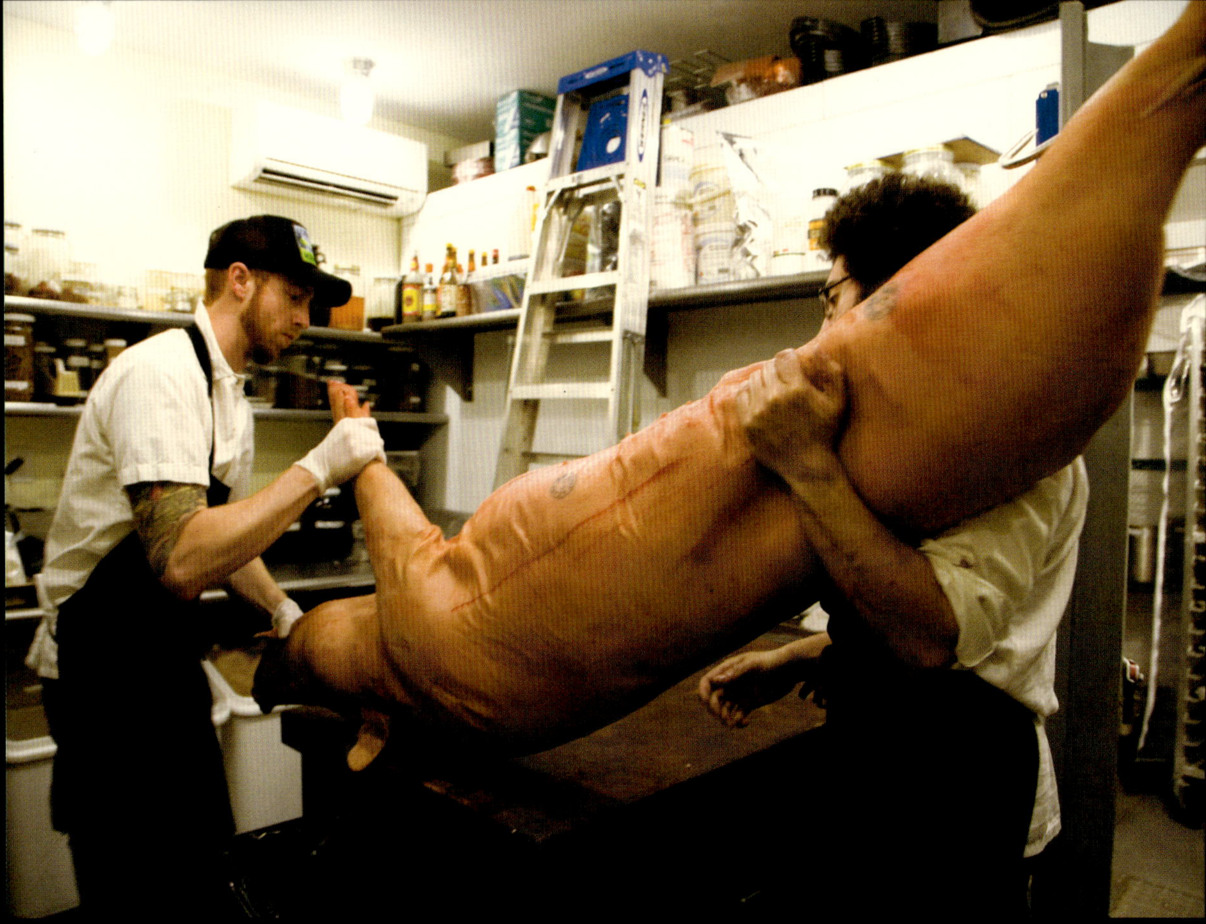

LOIN
HAM
SHOULDER
TENDERLOIN
BELLY / RIBS
HOCK
HEAD

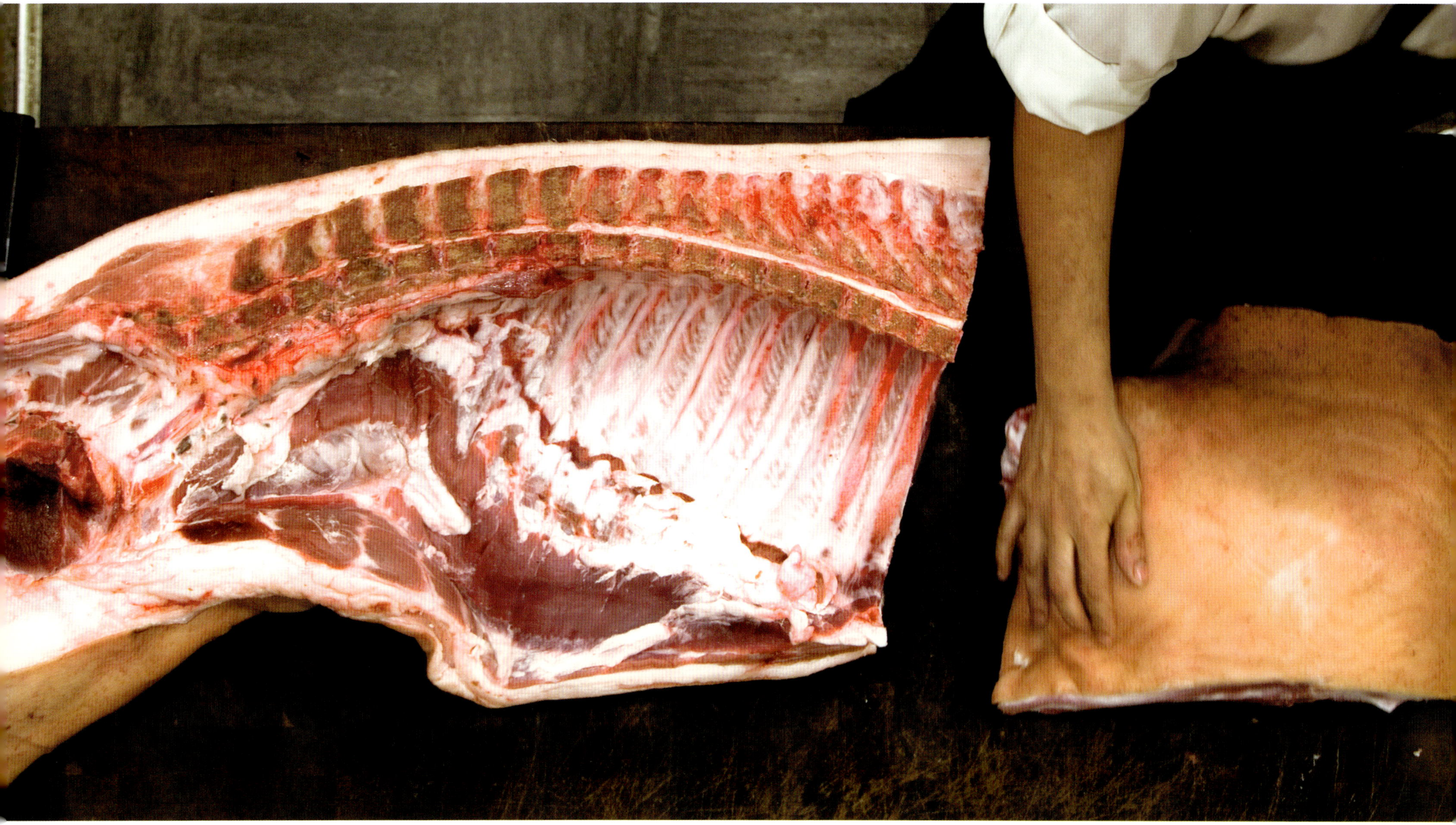

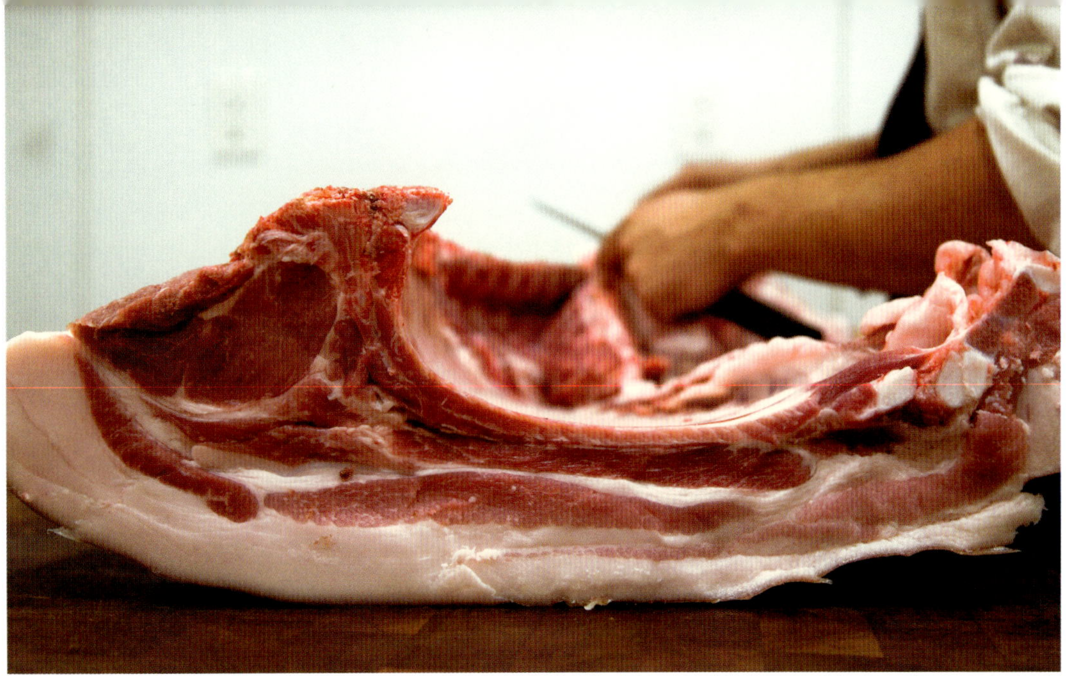

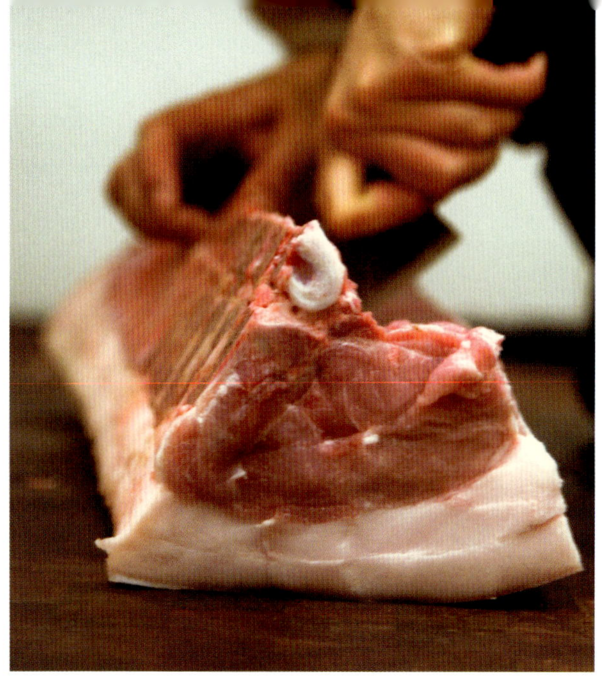

The pigs that Fish & Game buys, always whole, are heirloom breeds prized for their thick fat and profound depth of flavor. Every animal spent its life outside, rooting and grazing in fields and forests, eating whey, grain, and organic vegetable scraps as supplements. Pork raised this way possesses a deep red hue, closer to lamb in color than to the anemic pink "other white meat" found in factory-farmed products. Even to call those ghastly entities farms does the word a disservice; they're not farms, they're horrors. No ethical eater should have anything to do with commodity meat.

While making bacon—universally acknowledged as the apotheosis of meat—pork also encompasses religious restrictions; two of the world's three great monotheistic traditions enjoin its consumption. Three thousand years ago, this made sense; trichinosis is a nasty affliction. But today, courtesy of Modern Science™, that disease has become vanishingly rare when dealing with pastured pigs. This means, among other things, that we can enjoy our pork cooked to a perfect pinkness, not the shoe-leathery gray of yore. Fatty cuts offer more latitude, what with the onboard lubrication, but please, for the love of pork, let the meat stay pink.

Zak (or, more recently, Steve, whose knife moves with calm precision) takes the pigs apart basically the same way every time. Normally, pigs arrive at the restaurant with their heads separated and bodies halved lengthwise; the band saw in the upstairs prep kitchen is not large enough to handle a whole pig. Sometimes the head is still attached, and thus also cut in half. This makes it impossible to take the whole face off—something Steve enjoys doing, before curing and rolling it—but easier to cut off the jowls for *guanciale*. Whatever becomes of the faces, the heads always see the grill and then the stock pot.

Hocks come off first; they contribute copious gelatin to stocks. They can also repay some smoke and a long braise with glorious beans and stews. Shoulders, separated at the fifth rib, are often then bisected on the bandsaw for easier handling and preparation, whatever their final treatment will be. Bellies, separated from the loins with a hacksaw, either become bacon or smoke on the high grill. For service, the ribs come off and the belly is deployed as needed. The ribs themselves will appear on the bar menu or go—say it with me now—into the stock pot.

Prior to cutting off the back legs, the tenderloin needs to come out. Scraping it off the ribs is relatively easy, but chasing it all the way to the ends requires some deft knife work. More often than not, the tenderloins end up in family meal or are ground for sausage; unless the pig is enormous they don't provide enough meat for a menu. The tenderloin, being very lean, also lacks character as a cut. Just because something costs a lot at the store (hello, filet mignon) does not mean it makes the most compelling eating.

Normally, shoulders will sit in a brine for a few days before hitting the spit for a long, slow, rotational bask in the heat of the dining room fire. Loins, stretching from that fifth rib all the way to the hip where the ham starts, usually repair to the high shelf over the grill to set a spell after being cut in half crosswise for easier handling. These two methods—spit and grill—impart dramatically distinct results to the meat, despite involving the same pig, the same wood, and the same distance from the heat. The difference of ninety degrees in the food's orientation to the fire—in front of versus above—means that meat on the rotisserie catches a subtle whiff of wood while meat on the grill soaks up serious smoke. In either case, this beautiful beast comes to table with the fat on; trimming it would insult its provenance. More than that, though, eating it might make the best bite of the night.

Rear legs, cut generously to include the sirloin, go straight into the prosciutto cure. Having two legs cured and hung at the same time means they can be eaten in successive weeks or months, letting one get a little farther down the road, and offering a glimpse (for those lucky enough to taste both) of the difference a little more time makes to the same pig. The experience resembles nothing so much as opening two of the same wines from the same year a couple of years apart; our engagement with each bottle arrests its development and gives us a vivid snapshot of the effects that the passage of time has had on that juice from that place, but only on the day we drink it. Opening the wine and slicing the ham stop their movement through time and allow us to taste them, forming discrete understandings of their evolution: the culinary equivalent of Heisenberg's uncertainty principle.

Our menu tonight, any night, began years ago.

—ZAK

The rotisserie spit in front of the fireplace gets a lot of use. Ducks see regular rotation on there, two or three at a time, usually after their legs have been removed for other nefarious purposes like confit. One February found a couple of mulefoot pig shoulders making the rounds, dripping seductively onto peeled potatoes lined up beneath in the narrow steel trough designed for just such a use. It's always a good idea to brine shoulders first, in about a 2 percent salt solution for a few days, so they can hang out in the heat for a long time and stay juicy. Once the shoulder's interior has reached 135°–150°—around six hours in the restaurant, but your mileage may vary—it stays warm on a tray up over the grill until it's time to carve it for service. Lacking a rotisserie, a grill with indirect heat or an oven can yield good (if different) results. If using an oven, be sure to put the meat up on a rack with the spuds beneath it.

300

acres foraged by Climbing Tree Farm pigs

656

pounds of wild acorns eaten in a pig's life

6

hours roasted on a spit

CLIMBING TREE FARM

New Lebanon, NY

30.1 miles from Fish & Game

Climbing Tree Farm started by accident. A few free sheep, used to tame an unruly lawn on an old family farm in Berlin, New York, led Colby and Schuyler Gail down the path toward growing animals for meat. Now, on about ten acres each of pasture and forest sloping down a mountainside in nearby New Lebanon, they raise heritage pigs, sheep, and poultry (chickens, plus geese and turkeys for the holidays). All of their animals live outside all year and graze rotationally to allow the plants to recover between visits.

In both quantity and quality, the pigs are the stars of the Climbing Tree show. The soft-spoken, unassuming couple and their two young children tend heritage breeds and crossbreeds, some quite rare: Red Wattle, Berkshire, Gloucestershire Old Spot, and Mulefoot. Mulefoots are named for their non-cloven hooves; Zak loves the breed for their deep flavor—with a slightly metallic, almost briny complexity—and for their thick, sweet, easy-eating fat. They're prodigious foragers and often jam their whole heads into the ground to find food. The breed is currently designated as Critically Endangered, with only a few hundred purebreds in the world; the American Mulefoot Hog Association calls them "The rarest swine in America."

The stereotypical image of pigs on a farm shows them in a pen with a wallow. Seeing the Gails' pigs wander, root, play, and sleep in the forest, it's instantly clear that pigs are primarily woodland animals. Though they enjoy open spaces, it's obvious how much they love the trees for shade, back scratching, and above all for the nuts and fruit they offer. It's easy to spot the hickory and oak trees in these woods; they're all surrounded by moats of soil churned by pigs searching for fallen nuts. The Gails lease three hundred or so acres from a neighbor, who is selectively logging the property and leaving the nut trees to create what's known as sylvopasture, a hybrid of field and forest that offers a wide variety of food sources for the animals.

Forage makes up about half the pigs' diet, in season; in addition they get milk from High Lawn Farm in Lee, Massachusetts, whey from Berkshire Blue in Great Barrington (New Lebanon is just a few miles from the Massachusetts line) and non-GMO grain grown to order. Besides the pigs, Climbing Tree is also raising Bresse chickens for Fish & Game. This French breed, prized for its rich, gamy flavor and luscious yellow fat, is considered by many to be the best eating chicken in the world.

I HAD BEEN WAITING A LONG TIME FOR THIS.

I cut the ham from the pig's carcass sixteen months ago, in February of 2013. A Tamworth pig: mild-mannered creatures with red bristles, a fine marbling throughout, and a ratio of meat to fat that we presumed was well suited to the prosciutto we set out to make.

I had done my best to precisely cut the ham to include all the hind muscle groups while not cutting into the loin. The ham, once separated, was round, smooth and appeared truly prosciutto-worthy, so we buried it in sea salt. At a certain point, based on our somewhat loose calculations, we remembered to pull it from the salt, brush it off, and hang it up.

It's really quite simple.

CUT THE MEAT, SALT THE MEAT, HANG THE MEAT.

Just use quality meat.

ONLY USE QUALITY MEAT. ALWAYS. USE. QUALITY. MEAT.

More than a few variables exist between the salting and the finished product. We're working those out. Those are our secrets. I will say this: traditional methods, frowned upon by know-nothings and rhapsodized by the cognoscenti, seem to have a favorable effect. Yes, friends, there is no substitute for sweet country air.

Fifteen months after hanging in various spots in our verdant valley and only days after the one-year anniversary of our opening of Fish & Game, we cut into our ham. Older than the restaurant itself, this is one of several pre-opening projects that is teaching us how the ingredients that end up in the kitchen ready for the evening's menu are years in the making.

Jori provided more examples of this principle when I showed her this essay. She wrote back to me: "We plant garlic in October and wait patiently until June/July to eat it. We start seeds in February for a plant we won't harvest until August. We plant puntarelle and asparagus and wait three years to harvest them. We do these things because of the beauty and the reward of having the connection, even though in this day and age it seems like it takes too long."

We had to cut into this ham to determine if our curing and aging methods had taken the ham in the right direction—not because we were impatient, as impatient as we all seem to be in this age of immediate gratification—but because we have more hams hanging. Had this ham gone off, there was great likelihood the others were off as well. To date, all the hams had been cured and hung in the exact same method, only at different times. This ham was our test.

We have no ham tester (the little hollow point needle used in Parma and other famous ham regions throughout the world) to stick into the meat and pull out a core sample. We do need to buy one of those. Holding the ham, smelling it, touching it, we all—Kevin, Jori and I—shared the feeling that everything would be all right. But we had to cut it to know: to taste the salt, the texture, to see whether or not some unwanted bacteria had crept inside, quietly rotting the meat from within, giving us false hope.

The meat was fine. Better than fine. It was a deep pink, with a tight grain and perfectly *à point* in its saltiness. Fifteen months is approximately nine months shy of when I'd like to be pulling the hams; however, with more pigs queuing up for curing we felt it prudent to check our progress to aid in guiding our future efforts.

I will say this: traditional methods, frowned upon by know-nothings & rhapsodized by the cognoscenti, seem to have a favorable effect.

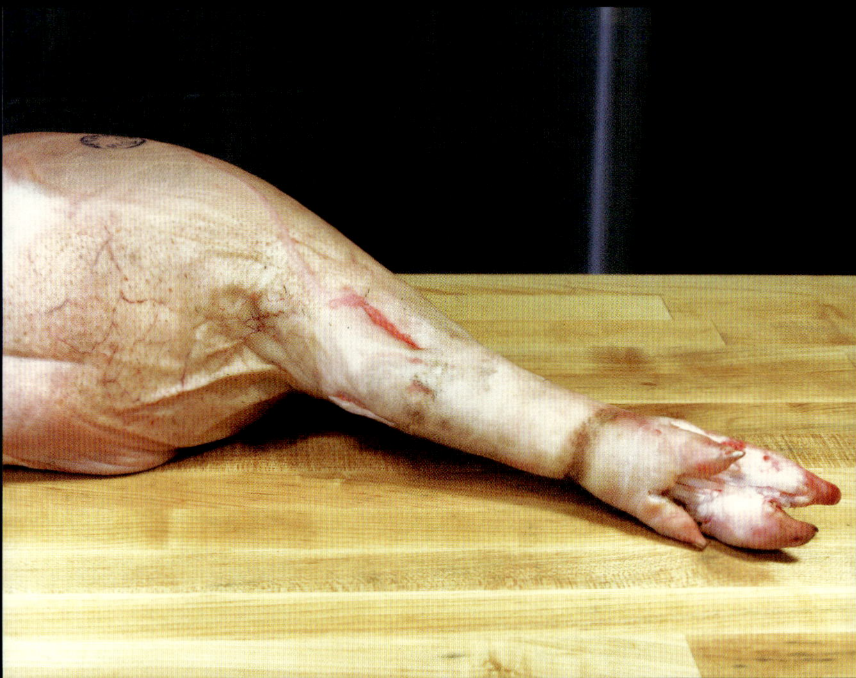

PACTIV

Yes, friends, there is no substitute
for sweet country air.

ALLOWING THE HAMS TO HANG FOR AT LEAST TWENTY FOUR MONTHS, I think, will afford them a more developed "nose:" greater complexity and a bit of funk in the aroma, adding greatly to the sensuous pleasure of consuming salt-cured, air-dried pig.

The ham into which we cut became a staple at the bar, served thinly sliced. Last week we also served it in the dining room wrapped around one of our eggs, soft boiled, and dressed with a ramp leaf salsa verde. Honestly, though, I prefer this kind of ham eaten on its own, perhaps accompanied by a glass (or two) of Malvasia from Emilia-Romagna... or perhaps even a dry cider, made nearby... or sherry, of course. With ham this good you can't really go wrong.

As Jori elucidated, the ham is only part of that for which I've been waiting. The ham is the ham. The waiting also pertains to the time, space, and mindset to make the ham and hang it in the manner we did: like having a garden and working the soil, allowing it to develop and knowing that what we do won't be truly great until the soil is rich with life. The waiting also refers to the spring that teased out its arrival following the deep freeze of this winter past. The waiting is what was and isn't anymore as I am here and definitely not there.

Waiting may not be the right word. I'm not sure that I or Jori or any of us immersed in this project were ever really *waiting*. I'm not one to pine. It's just nice to be here giving time and allowing for life to take time. Proper time. And I'm just conscious enough to recognize that. Cuisines are born of availability, necessity, and accident. Some actions, however, are simply intuitive. A dog will bury a bone and let it rot for a month before digging it up and savoring the putrid delicacy. Fish sauce, soy sauce, *salumi*, cheese, vinegar, and wine: we don't really make these things, we just set up the right conditions and allow them the time to occur naturally.

I am, however, also aware that the years, the winters, take their toll and, as Alvaro Mutis put it, on one's "face one could see the rigidity of controlled pain that is accepted as the price we must inevitably pay to go on being who we are." The spring eventually softens this hard existence but the lines remain, remnants of the absence of mercy in nature. We have no choice other than to be okay with this.

On occasion something will trigger memories of the time I spent working and living in the city. There were times of elation, moments of inspiration, collaborations with great talents, long hours, weeks, months, intense and engaging discourse, fucking in cars parked outside three-star Michelin restaurants, apartment and neighborhood hopping, intentional decadence, drinking and overeating, falling in love. Life happened. And as it did it brought memorable moments.

But for a good part of my time in the City after the turn of the millennium, there was a lingering discomfort: a dissatisfaction with the cynicism that surrounded the business, some bad partnerships, and the density, but most of all an unbridgeable disconnect with the product and conflicted feelings about the paradigm on which so many restaurants are built. That has changed. And now spring is here.

We at Fish & Game have created a unique situation in the Hudson Valley, the result of a fantasy shared by more than the people directly involved with the restaurant. What is being built—and what has already come to pass at and around Fish & Game—is part of a more general awakening. An attentiveness. A more considered style of living than I have ever witnessed or been a part of.

Being human and still very much a New Yorker, I find it challenging not to quip that this "enlightenment" is probably due to our heightened sensitivity that the waste of our rampant consumerism is close to consuming us. Such unchecked growth is perhaps partially a result of too much of the "Think Big!" mentality, the mantra of industry titans and self-proclaimed masters of the universe. I wonder if it was hard for He-Man to see beyond his muscles.

I've begun to think of it this way: we're not capable of much, yet the little bit we do can resonate far beyond our time. It is this small work, when done with great care and attention to detail—up and down the ladder of all the elements involved in our doing, before and after the doing is done—that is making this time more beautiful than any I have ever known. Witnessing this *and* being a part of it, has made the waiting—if only recognized after it has passed—worth it. And so I smile, knowingly, as I begin to understand that spring—the cutting of a ham amidst the growing green—is our annual reminder of the necessity of patience and its persistent beauty.

1

thirty-two-pound ham

15

days covered in salt

450

days hanging in the barn—gentle breeze, freezing wind, humid air, Columbia County weather

1

week for Fish & Game customers to consume the entire cured ham

PROSCIUTTO

1 HAM

Whole-muscle charcuterie works because salt (and sugar, when applicable) draws water out of muscle and fat cells as they bring in salt, equalizing their salinity with their environment. This osmotic pressure kills pathogens, rupturing them and quickly making the raw meat inhospitable to colonization by any bad bacteria, as well as drawing any flavors (herbs and spices) from the cure into the meat. The loss of water also begins the drying process, further protecting the meat from contamination and concentrating the flavor of all the acorns and apples that helped build the pig.

Prosciutto needs no sugar, herbs, or spices mixed with the salt. While other cures often contain bold flavors, a great prosciutto (or *jamón*, or *jambon*, or ham) uses pure salt* to concentrate the essence of an immaculately raised animal without diluting or adulterating it in any way. Where boiling maple sap reveals the seductive interaction between a tree and the earth, curing a ham shows the marvelous complexity with which an animal reflects and refracts the land on which it was raised.

**One notable exception to this rule is the Jambon de Bayonne, which is rubbed with powdered piment d'Espelette before drying, an admirable practice.*

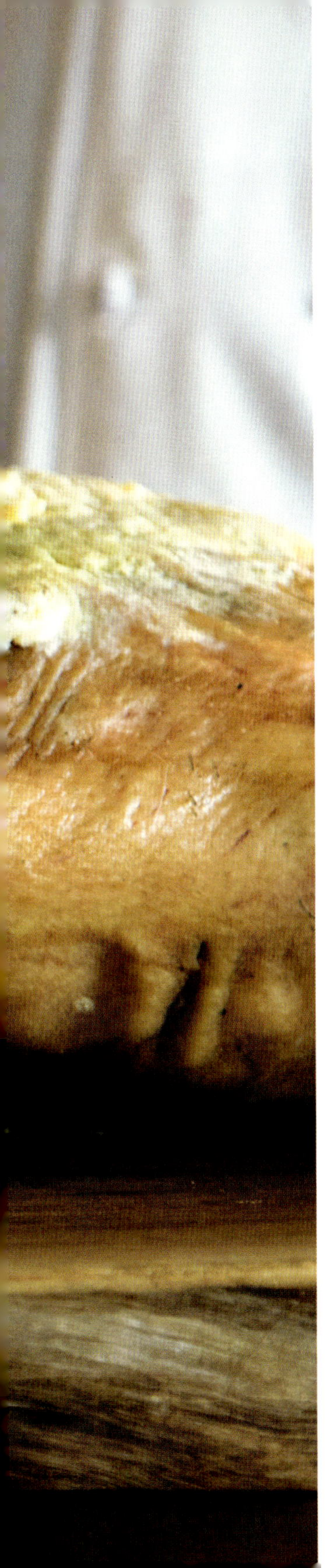

1 WHOLE, BONE-IN PIG LEG

SEA SALT SUFFICIENT TO COVER THE LEG

ENOUGH RENDERED LARD TO COAT THE EXPOSED MUSCLE

1

Shave any hairs off the leg with a razor or sharp knife. Wipe the skin all over with a damp cloth. Pour half the salt into a container large enough to comfortably hold the leg. Pour the rest of the salt on top, thoroughly rubbing it into the skin and especially into the exposed meat and around the protruding bone.

2

Let it sit, covered in salt, for one day per kilo in the refrigerator, then wipe all the salt off. Rub all the exposed meat with lard, covering it with a thick layer (this prevents the area without skin from drying out too quickly).

3

Tag the leg with the date and hang it (using the hole behind the hock where the carcass was hung) somewhere that is ideally basement temperature (55°F) and not bone dry, with good air circulation. Check periodically for mold, and use a ham tester if you have one to take occasional core samples from near the bone (smear lard over the resulting hole when you're done).

4

Somewhere around the fifteen to eighteen month mark, depending on temperature, humidity, and size, the ham should be fully cured. Slice as thinly as possible and take a moment to thank the departed animal for the gift you're about to receive.

GUANCIALE

4 JOWLS

4 PIG JOWLS

20G MACE

40G DRIED RED CHILI

20G CORIANDER

7G FENNEL SEEDS

700G FINE SEA SALT

A pig's jowls have alternating striations of muscle and fat, not unlike the belly, and a particularly concentrated flavor due to being worked so much. Sliced thinly, guanciale imparts a porky intensity to any dish, whether sautéed with mirepoix in a pot of beans or served on grilled bread to soften and melt like the divine love child of lardo and prosciutto that it most closely resembles. Of all cured pork products, guanciale may well be the one you never want to run out of.

1

Toast and grind all spices, then mix them together with the salt.

Trim any gray glands from the jowls, rub well with the cure, then pack the meat in the remaining cure.

2

Cover and leave in the fridge for five days, flipping once a day. Rinse off cure, pat dry, and hot smoke until the interior temperature reaches 185°F. Chill, wrap tightly, and store in the fridge, or cryovac sections of it to thaw as needed.

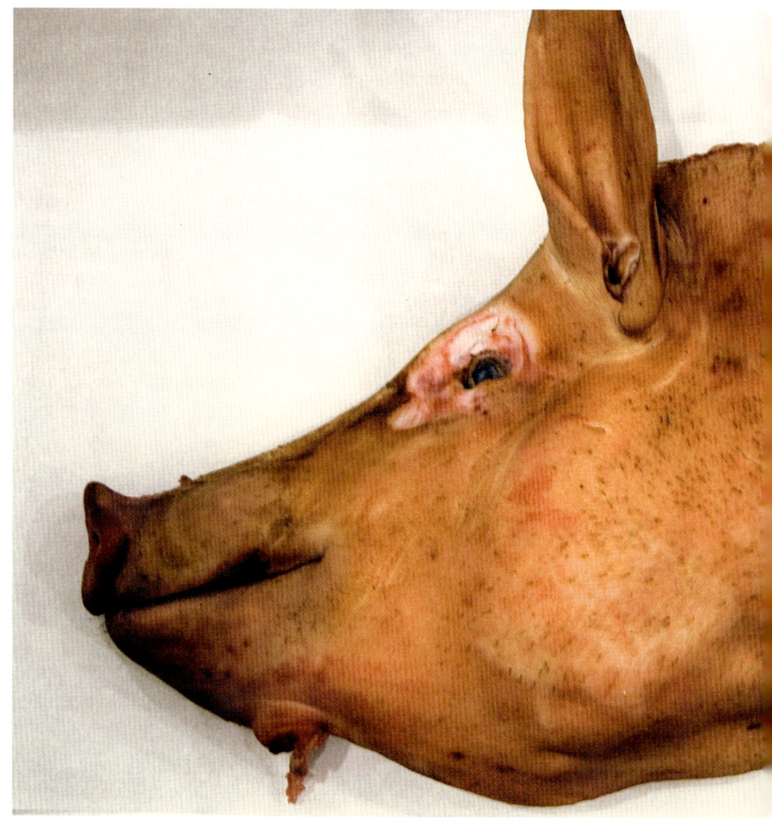

BACON

10 2-POUND SLABS

10 KILOS PORK BELLY, SKIN REMOVED

1 KILO KOSHER SALT

400G MUSCOVADO SUGAR

50G BLACK PEPPERCORNS

75G MOROCCAN CORIANDER

50G WHITE PEPPERCORNS

20G ANISE SEED

30G LONG PEPPER

Bacon needs no introduction; no food (not even, God help us, kale) has seen as much hype and been twisted to so many diabolical ends as cured, smoked pork belly. Fish & Game uses bacon as a flavoring agent and often slices it paper thin to drape over hot preparations so it can cling to them like shrink wrap made of salty, smoky meat.

1

Toast and grind all the spices, then mix them thoroughly into the sugar and salt. Rub the mix all over the meat, then place the meat in a container with half of the remaining cure underneath it and the other half spread on top.

2

Cover and leave in the fridge for five days, flipping once a day. Rinse off cure, pat dry, and hot smoke until the interior temperature reaches 185°F. Chill, wrap tightly, and store in the fridge, or cryovac sections of it to thaw as needed.

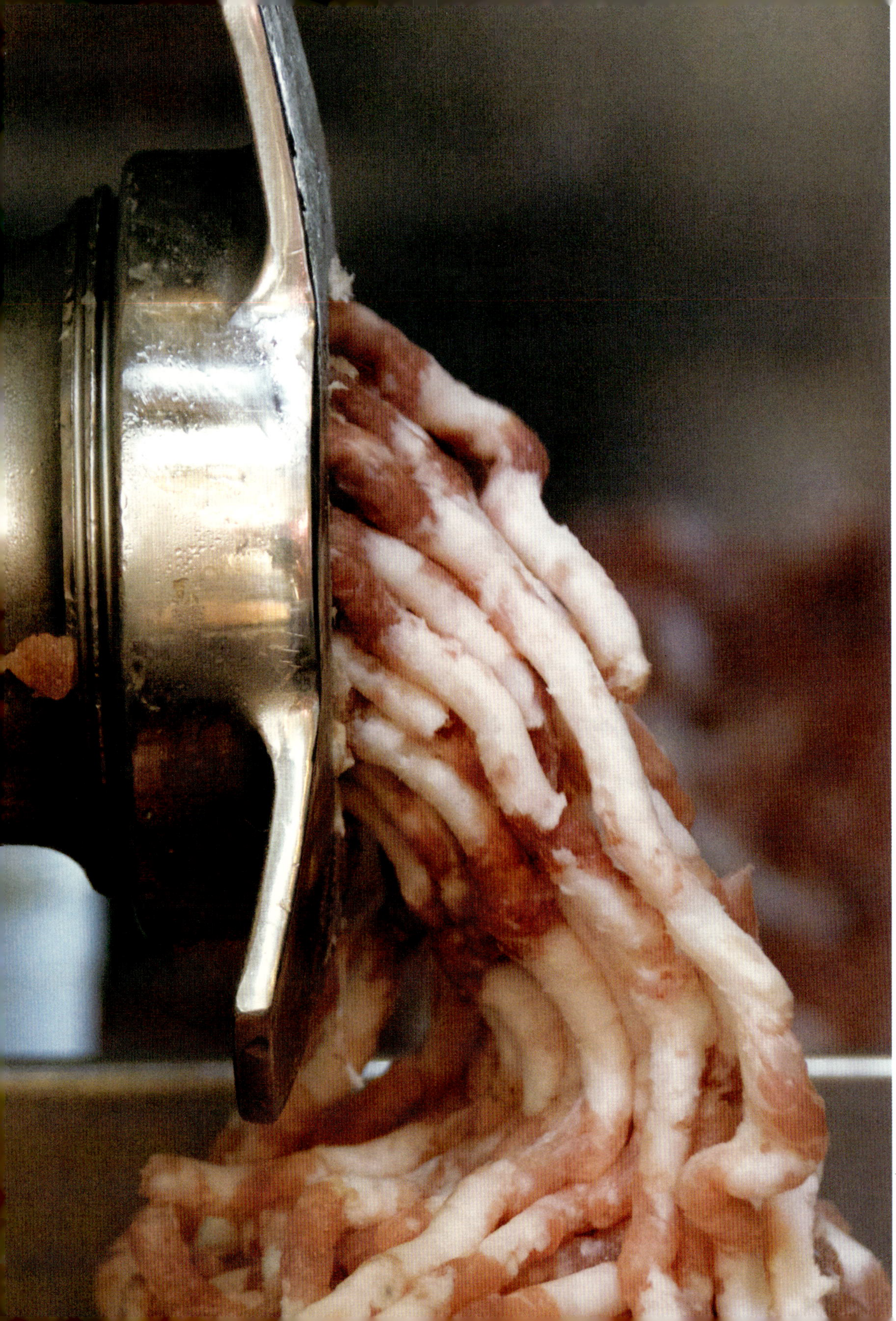

GROUND MEAT CHARCUTERIE USES SALT THE SAME WAY, BUT ALSO RELIES ON LACTIC ACID BACTERIA to lower the pH of the meat to the point where it kills any pathogens. Sausages prepared this way ferment in a warm place for a day or two to promote bacterial growth (and thus develop an addictively sour tang) before curing somewhere cool until firm. Because the inside of a cured sausage is an anaerobic environment, pink salt (sodium nitrate) must be used to prevent botulism.* Fresh sausages meant for cooking don't need pink salt.

All charcuterie involving ground meat requires a few specific conditions to ensure success. First, hygiene: all equipment, hands, and surfaces should be thoroughly scrubbed and rinsed. Meat should come from a trusted source, and ideally should not have seen a freezer. Second, cold: meat and fat should be half-frozen right before grinding for best results, lest the fat start to smear and become too slippery. Put the parts of your grinder in the freezer half an hour before beginning, and grind all meat into a bowl sitting inside a larger bowl of ice water.

Charcuterie is a complex subject, with specific health issues that require knowledgeable attention. There are a host of good books on the subject; buy them and read them. Beyond the quality that attends a comprehensive understanding of the subject, the safety of you and your guests depends on it.

**For cured sausages, #2 pink salt is required. Look for Prague Powder #2 or Insta-Cure #2; the #2 refers to the presence of sodium nitrate, which over time breaks down into sodium nitrite, providing ongoing protection against pathogens while the sausage cures and dries. Number one salt only has sodium nitrite and is thus used for things like bacon and corned beef by people who like that garish pink color and characteristic "cured" flavor. Fish & Game doesn't use pink salt on whole muscle cuts or anything that's cooked before service.*

FERMENTED FINNOCHIONA SAUSAGE

ABOUT 30 30-OZ SAUSAGES

4,422G PORK
884.5G PORK FAT
97.5G SALT
13.65G PINK SALT
58.5G POWDERED MILK
19.5G DEXTROSE
17.5G FENNEL SEED
13.65G WHITE PEPPERCORN
8G BLACK PEPPERCORN
6G GARLIC POWDER
1G KOJI
137.5G CHIANTI

1

Toast and grind all of the spices. Dice the pork and fat before mixing it with the spice mixture, powdered milk, and dextrose. Grind the mixture through the small die. Mix the grind with the pink salt thoroughly by hand.

2

Place in a mixer fitted with the paddle attachment and mix slowly while adding the wine. Increase the speed to emulsify everything together, stopping when the meat is pasty and sticky.

3

Let the mixture rest for an hour before casing, then pipe the mixture into bung casings. Tie them off with butchers twine and prick them all over with a cake tester.

4

Wrap the sausages in cheesecloth and place in the CVAP for 48 hours at 86°F. Pull from the CVAP and rewrap the sausage in new cheesecloth before hanging in the walk-in for twenty-four days. Cut on a deli slicer for service.

LIVER SAUSAGE

17 5-OZ SAUSAGES

16 OZ PORK LIVER
24 OZ PORK FATBACK
48 OZ PORK SHOULDER GRIND
35G SEA SALT
55G PINE NUTS
30G SUGAR
15G CORIANDER
5G BLACK PEPPER
20G FRESH GARLIC
13G TANGERINE ZEST
4 OZ DESSERT WINE

1

Toast and grind the spices. Mince the garlic and zest. Combine the spices and garlic with the sugar, salt, zest, and pine nuts before mixing in the dessert wine. Add spice paste to all the pork products before grinding everything through a large die.

2

Mix by hand after the grind to make sure everything is fully incorporated. Cover and let sit in the fridge overnight before piping into pork casings. Store in fridge or cryovac for the freezer until needed. Grill or fry for service.

FERMENTED THAI NAEM SAUSAGE

10 5-OZ SAUSAGES

- 1000G LEAN PORK
- 350G PIG SKIN
- 25 CLOVES GARLIC
- 2.5 TBSP SEA SALT
- .5 TBSP SUGAR
- 1 CUP COOKED RICE
- 40 CHILIES

1

Remove all fat and hair from the pig skin. Simmer the skin until it is able to be punctured easily, then remove and cool. Julienne skin into 1 × ¼-inch pieces. Grind together the pork, garlic, chilies, rice, salt, and sugar. Stir in the skin.

2

Let the farce sit one day before proceeding with casing. Pipe into pork casings and prick them with a cake tester. Place on a rack in the CVAP and ferment the sausages at 30°C at 90% humidity for 3 days. They should be good and funky, and pretty sour, when they come out. Grill or fry for service.

BREAKFAST SAUSAGE

70 3-OZ PATTIES

4,535G PORK

1,905G PORK FATBACK

137G SALT

1 QUART MAPLE SYRUP

14G SHATA PEPPER

40G CORIANDER

40G FENNEL

30G GREEN PEPPERCORN

29G GREEN CARDAMOM

This ran as the centerpiece in a breakfast sandwich of extraordinary sensuality. This masterpiece was to a sad and soggy McMuffin as Glenn Gould's Goldberg Variations (the 1982 version) are to George Winston.

1

Toast and grind all the spices, then combine them with the pork, salt, and fat. Run the mixture twice through the large die. Add the maple and paddle the grind in a mixer to emulsify it, then refrigerate it overnight before packing into a terrine mold lined with plastic and freezing until ready to use. Slice into ½"-thick discs (F&G uses the bandsaw) and grill or fry for service.

DUNDICUT AND PICKLED GARLIC SAUSAGE

30 5-OZ SAUSAGES

3,096G PORK

1,204G PORK FAT

155G PICKLED GARLIC PUREE

11G PINK PEPPERCORN

18G CORIANDER

14G SALT

9G DUNDICUT PEPPER

129G FISH SAUCE

1

Toast and grind all spices and then mix them with the fish sauce. Dice the pork and the pork fat and mix with the fish sauce spice slurry. Combine with the rest of the ingredients and run the mixture through a large-grind die twice. After ground, mix again by hand to ensure everything is fully incorporated. Let sit overnight before casing. Grill or fry for service.

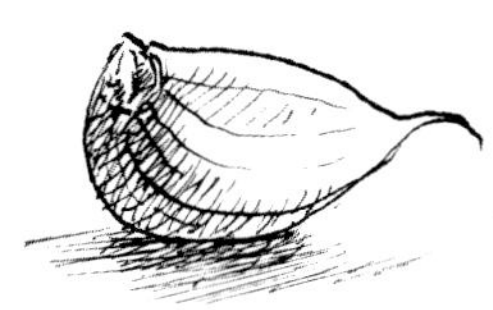

RAMEN PORK BALLS

ABOUT 150 1-OZ BALLS

3,500G PORK

750G LEAF LARD

55G CORIANDER

20G WHITE PEPPERCORN

35G GREEN PEPPERCORN

5G MACE

14G FENNEL

20G SALT

110G FISH SAUCE

Ramen makes a handsome repository for a variety of adornments: seasonal greens and roots, the obligatory onsen egg, and pork in several forms. These meatballs contribute powerful flavor to a bowl of soup—made with meat from the same animal whose bones made the broth—and add the archetypal visual pleasure of meatballs snuggling with skinny noodles.

1

Toast and grind all of the spices, then combine all ingredients in a mixer bowl and paddle briefly to incorporate. Let sit overnight, covered, in the fridge before rolling into small (1") balls and poaching in stock for service.

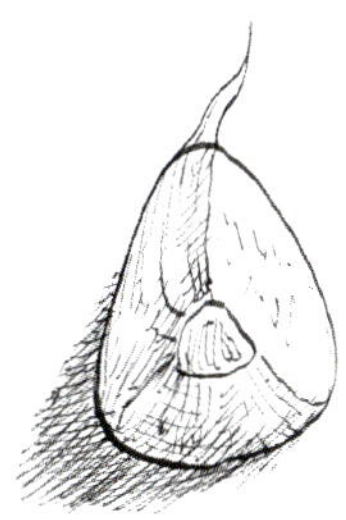

EGGS

Pastured chickens lay the best eggs. The Fish & Game flock of about sixty hens—a mixture of Delaware, Dark Cornish, and Barred Rock—lives in a coop that the kitchen crew built on an old trailer chassis that had been left by the side of a country road. Besides some organic corn, stale bread, and well water, the Fish & Game chickens eat grass and weeds and scratch in the dirt for bugs, doing exactly what they would do if left to their own devices (because they are) except that they're protected from predators by a solar-powered electric fence by day and the friendly confines of the coop at night.

It's been exciting for the cooks to have access to a steady supply of the best eggs they've ever worked with. These eggs, with their vivid orange yolks and deep flavor, get featured frequently on the menu as the main component of a dish. When eggs are this perfect, the key is to cook them just so and serve them with complementary garnishes that don't overpower their flavor: some cured meat, a pickled cabbage leaf, a dollop of ramp pesto. The most austere example, barely cooked *en cocotte* in the fireplace embers with slivers of squid and pickled daikon, was almost confrontational in its audacious underdoneness; everyone loves a runny yolk, but wiggly whites intimidate.

In an age where any texture imaginable can be achieved through the use of hydrocolloids and other additives, it's important to remember that eggs are the original hydrocolloid, capable of creating a huge variety of gels, foams, and emulsions, not to mention giving sexy richness to all manner of baked goods. And those magic powders, despite their remarkable powers of transformation, impart no taste of terroir. These eggs embody it.

3

pounds of creepy crawlies eaten by the Fish & Game hens each day

44

eggs laid per day

4.5

minutes for the perfect soft-boiled egg

Immersion circulators allow the full spectrum of viscosities to be easily achieved; half a degree can make a difference in the consistency of yolks and whites alike, so the specific textural or aesthetic needs of a particular dish (say, a yolk that stays put so a sliced half egg can adorn a duck dish) can be easily accommodated. More often than not, though, the kitchen simply simmers them for four and a half minutes, plunges them into cold water to stop the cooking, and then holds them in a warm bath until service.

Finely grated, hard-boiled yolks are simultaneously dry and lubricating, almost like graphite. Walter grates yolks into some of his biscuit dough to add another facet of fat, complementing the already copious butter. Sieved eggs, served as a classic caviar accompaniment, have also accompanied anchovies on toasted brioche. Zak is fond of a dish he originated at Five Ninth: a buttery soft scramble, whisked by hand on the flat top, for the resulting silky texture and because it's a bit of authentic old-school cooking, requiring constant attention for a sublime result. The resulting golden goodness provides a quivering and receptive substrate for cured sausage and sriracha, resulting in a comfortingly breakfasty vibe. The sausage is shaved thinly on a mandoline to mimic the fluffy consistency of the eggs.

Eggs may reach their luxe apotheosis—in conjunction with butter, that other central culinary miracle and prodigious emulsifier (and, happily, something else that this region excels at producing)—as the hollandaise that appears on roast or confit potatoes, smoked beef, or broiled oysters. What's better than a pastured egg-cultured butter hollandaise enlivened with homemade vinegar instead of lemon? Nothing, that's what.

HENS ARE MEAN AS FUCK.

It's a Hen-Eat-Hen World

JORI

Spending the season working the gardens with the hens roaming around me gave me some solid time to watch them closely and observe their behavior. I'll just get straight to the point here: hens are mean as fuck! I mean, they're not mean like they run after you and peck you, but they do run after each other and peck each other. They form cliques and the cliques tease the weaker hens and cause such intense stress for those teased hens that the stressed hens slow down their egg production or even stop laying altogether. If the situation gets bad enough, a stressed hen will start to lose weight, quickly followed by losing feathers. Then the clique will peck at her exposed flesh until sores form, at which point we (the farmers) have to remove that beat-up hen from the flock and isolate her or the clique will literally peck her to death.

We spend time integrating the healed hen back into the coop, hoping her restored health will give her a chance. It's a crapshoot. Even if the now-healthy hen is doing well and seems to have integrated back in, we can only tell if she's really in or not when it rains. When it rains, the hens in the clique all run together and huddle under some sort of shelter. On our farm, it's a stone bench. They pile on top, all smooshed together and wait for the rain to stop, all while constantly clucking to each other. The clucking during this time honestly sounds like "Ooooooo...oh no she didn't." The hens outside the clique are left scrambling in the rain, pacing in front of the clique, auditioning, desperately hoping to get in. I won't get in to the stupidity of them doing all this right in front of the open, available, and dry shelter of the coop.

Experiencing all of this brought back a memory from the fifth grade. You see, I was teased a lot as little child, so I was used to it, but when my family moved from Houston to Austin in my fifth grade year, I experienced a different kind of teasing. I remember trying to integrate into this preppy public school and it didn't go so well at first.

Having not been accepted into the "cool" clique, I made the mistake of telling some girl that I had a crush on a popular boy. Then recess came. The clique was huddled on the top of the hill, all smooshed together, looking down the hill and waiting for me to come out of the building. I saw them as I passed the window in the corridor heading out. I pushed the door open and the clique, as if they were one solid mass, began walking toward me, clucking to each other... all clucking at the same time. They approached. I cowered and looked up at them through the top of my Coke-bottle glasses that NASA once asked to borrow

to try and find a distant planet. The head girl made some mention about how I couldn't have a crush on the popular boy because he had a girlfriend (who of course was standing in front of me and was part of the clique) and the clucking grew louder until one girl remarked that the popular boy would never like me anyway because I was a "dog." They all clucked a hurtful, haughty cluck and the clique mass moved on, making a sound eerily similar to "Ooooooo… oh no she didn't."

When I had this memory, I started thinking more about social tendencies of females. When you're in the clique and one member of the clique gets mad at you, the rest of them get mad too. They alienate you. You're teased, left out, and verbally abused. It affects your grades and you never want to return to school. You fake being sick and miss a few days, and then your mom makes you go back. Sometimes, it's like "poof!" they're not mad anymore. Other times, it has only gotten worse, the incessant teasing, the clucking, and it compels you to start looking at other schools because maybe you'll have a better chance to be part of a clique somewhere else. So you too can cluck with the clique.

This doesn't always stop at school either; it can continue into adulthood. Competitive cliques of females in the workplace trying to displace or remove a weaker colleague, all working to sabotage or break her down… pecking at her sores every day. Some women keep auditioning for cliques all their lives as if it's better to be clucked at than not at all. I kept thinking about these situations and how they related to scenarios throughout my life. And I've been on both sides: being teased and teasing.

So, standing there in the rain in the garden, watching these hens huddle and audition, I couldn't help thinking: do hens mimic social tendencies of females, or do females mimic the social tendencies of hens? Or are we all just a bunch of stupid birds? Whatever the answer may or may not be, I do know that a roasted hen tastes good and mean females suck.

Mean hens still taste good.

FRIED CHICKEN

Fried chicken is a quintessential summer dish. The Fish & Game version of it offers a few refinements to the traditional method.

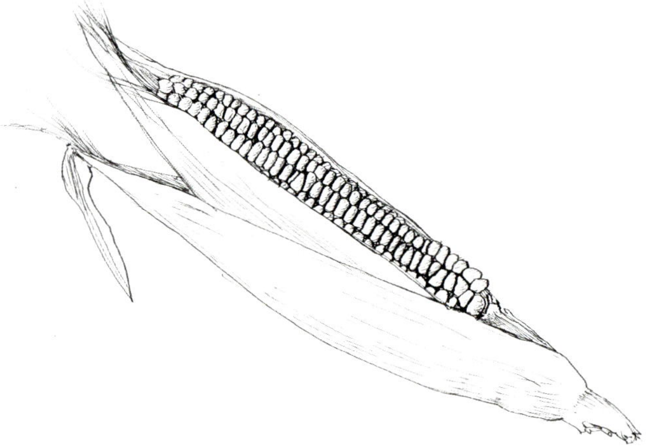

1

All frying oils are not created equal. This batch was a mixture of rendered lard, grapeseed oil, garlic oil, and onion oil. To make onion oil, Kevin burns sliced, skin-on onions in hot grapeseed oil (until they're verging on black) to infuse the oil with flavor, then strains out the solids. Garlic oil, a byproduct of making garlic confit, should be infused with whole cloves at a much lower temperature, about 160°F, for six hours, then strained. Garlic confit should only be used in food that you want to taste really really good.

2

The chicken came from Yellow Bell Farm in Elizaville, an offshoot of Feather Ridge Farm, whose eggs are ubiquitous in better stores throughout the Hudson Valley. There were some birds left over from an event, and this seemed like a worthy way to use them. After marinating overnight in buttermilk (the liquid left after making cultured butter) flavored with savory, chilies, salt, and pepper, the chicken breasts were poached sous vide (135°F for one hour) with butter, chicken stock, and herbs before flouring and frying.

3

A simple corn salad accompanied the chicken: wheat berries fermented for a couple of days in water with a little buttermilk, fresh corn kernels, diced chili, garlic, and onion, dressed with the barrel-aged fish sauce and Jori's herb vinegar. Its bright, clean flavors nimbly complemented the chicken and offered a quieter crunch than the crisp carapace of fried flour.

4

Tableside, each plate got a generous spooning of a thick, sticky sauce: cultured cream (what the butter is made from, a lot like crème fraîche) and honey, with fresh spilanthes flower buds broken up and sprinkled in. Spilanthes, commonly known as toothache plant, has a bright citrusy tang combined with a powerful numbing property similar to Sichuan peppercorns. As individual filaments distributed throughout the sauce, the effect was subtly mouthwatering rather than overwhelming.

5

Lots of beverages would pair brilliantly with this dish: nice bitter beer, an earthy white, herbal rosé, or tangy and transparent red. But to honor the product and technique in such a refined rendering of iconic comfort food, and to flatter all the flavors within—dairy in marinade and sauce, bright sweet and sour salad, gentle heat and addictive umami of the meat—Champagne is the only way to go.

SOUR CHERRIES

Sour cherries, as stone fruits, rank among the best food that trees know how to grow. The Hudson Valley, rich with orchards, in a good year provides a staggering amount of this glorious fruit during the short season that begins roughly mid-June and lasts a month or so. People refer to them as pie cherries for good reason; tart cherries possess an addictive acidity, much like cranberries, that remains sharply delineated even when sweetened (unlike sweet cherries' slightly lazy, too-easy flavor that doesn't cook well).

Fish & Game brings in flats of them, shiny and gleaming, and the kitchen turns them into a variety of more durable products, since any celebration of the season must also include preservation. Cocktails, condiments, desserts: there's nothing this fruit can't become. If you pit the fruit before using it, be sure to macerate those pits in booze with a bit of sugar for a month or six to make a delectable cordial.

SOUR CHERRY KIMCHI

ABOUT A HALF GALLON

10 LB SOUR CHERRIES, PITTED
(reserve pits for cordial or vinegar)

1 BUNCH CHIVES

2 BUNCHES BOLTED CILANTRO
(with seeds a plus)

1 BUNCH NASTURTIUM STEMS

5 OZ FRESH YOUNG GINGER, CHOPPED

8 CLOVES GARLIC, PEELED

1 MEDIUM WHITE ONION, CHOPPED

8 OZ SEA SALT

1

Pick the nasturtium leaves off of the stems and set them aside. Cut the chives, nasturtium stems, and cilantro (including flowers and/or seed heads) into ½" lengths.

2

Mix the cherries with the herb stems in a large bowl. Put the nasturtium leaves, ginger, garlic, onion, and salt in a blender or food processor with enough water to just cover everything, then blend until smooth.

3

Pour the salty herb slurry over the cherry mixture and toss well to combine. Pack into the fermentation vessel of your choice with a weight on top of the fruit and put somewhere cool to ferment for 2–8 weeks.

SOUR CHERRY KETCHUP

Follow the recipe for ketchup on p. 120 but substitute pitted cherries for the tomatoes. The result makes a superbly useful condiment in any situation where ketchup seems like a good idea. One of its more splendid deployments involved a lamb tartare, where cherry ketchup, pickled mustard seeds, and minced shallots seasoned the raw meat famously.

QUARTERBACK SLING

At the beginning of one sour cherry season—and it wasn't a great season, what with all the rain, which bloated and split the fruit—Kat was preparing to make a cherry cordial when Steve walked by. She proudly proclaimed "I'm popping more cherries than a high school quarterback!" And thus a cocktail was born.

From "High School Quarterback," the name swung over to Jori's suggested "Three in the Pink," at which Kat, against all expectations (including her own) that there's no such thing as too lewd for her, balked. Because the drink derives directly from a Singapore Sling, Quarterback Sling was the moniker that stuck. It also evokes images of dumb jocks with broken arms, which is appealing because fuck those guys.

It's worth mentioning that this drink owes its inception to another venerable drink: Brigham's raspberry lime rickey. Brigham's, that hundred-year-old Boston-area ice cream franchise, invented a drink made with seltzer, raspberry syrup, and plenty of lime. It remains the quenchingest virgin drink New England has ever produced, and Kat, being a wicked nostalgic Masshole, has that flavor profile in her DNA. As in a rickey, the extra lime in this sling gives it an addictive acidity, and the falernum adds herbal complexity that elegantly weds the sweet fruit to the savory gin.

1.5 OZ LONDON DRY GIN

.5 OZ SOUR CHERRY CORDIAL

.75 OZ LIME JUICE

.25 OZ FALERNUM
(recipe below)

2 DASHES LADY JAYNE'S GINGER BITTERS

1

Combine all and shake gently, then pour into a highball or tiki glass full of crushed ice. Mound more ice on top, then garnish with a generous grating of fresh lime zest.

FALERNUM:

1 OZ WHOLE APRICOT KERNELS
(optional)

2 OZ WHOLE ALMONDS, CRUSHED

12 CLOVES

12 ALLSPICE

1 STAR ANISE

ZEST OF 8 LIMES

JUICE OF 3 LIMES

2 OZ FRESH GINGER, CHOPPED

COLD PRESS SIMPLE SYRUP
(1.5 cup sugar to 1 cup water just warm enough to melt sugar)

16 OZ OVERPROOF RUM

1

Toast the almonds, cloves, and allspice. Break up the nuts and allspice in a mortar. Add everything except the syrup to a mason jar and circulate loosely covered for 2 hours at 78°C. Strain and squeeze out all liquid. Combine with syrup while hot and allow all to cool at room temperature. Bottle and label with date.

SOUR CHERRY CORDIAL:

2 POUNDS OF WHOLE CHERRIES

1 LITER OF BRANDY

1 CUP OF SUGAR

1 CINNAMON STICK

While the somewhat cheesy, redolent-of-Trader-Vic's original sling calls for cherry brandy, this version uses her homemade sour cherry concoction.

The recipe calls for gin that's lean enough not to overpower the drink but that can stand up to the brandy. Properly balanced, they yield a stellar result: the individual components disappear and the combination becomes a sweet, sour, cold, and delightfully gulpable summer treat.

1

Mash the whole fruit up in a jar big enough to hold everything with plenty of room, then put the jar in a water bath at 60°C for an hour with the water deep enough to equal the liquid level inside the jar. As with the coriander cordial on p. 65, leave the lid a bit loose so evaporating alcohol can escape.

2

Strain out the solids, separate the cherry pits and return them to the brandy, and return the jar (lid still loose) to the bath, now heated to 75°C, for 45 minutes. This extracts more of the magic almond flavor that hovers at the core of all stone fruits and softens the alcoholic heat by evaporating a bit more of it; the result ends up about ten proof gentler than the original brandy.

As a March break concluded, Jori and Madison emailed back and forth about the bar's depleted inventory and the lamentable lack of any fresh herbs for garnishing cocktails. Madison had been thinking about something with lovage cordial and gin, but Jori suggested sour cherry because there was more of it in stock. Made with Beefeater, an early attempt at this combination tasted too much like a martini. Ransom's Old Tom gin, however, worked famously with Ransom's vermouth—almost as if they were made to go together—and meshed beautifully with the previous summer's fruit cordial.

Because smudging the glass purges it of evil spirits, banishing the bad juju, Jori named the drink Queen Julia Jax after Julia Jackson, a famous New Orleans voodoo queen in the 1940s and a character in Dr. John's "Jump Sturdy" from his immortal debut album Gris-Gris. Dr. John features prominently in playlists at Fish & Game and Zak and Jori's place as well; Jori shortened Jackson to Jax because it sounded drinkier. The faint whiff of sweet smoke gives the drink a little extra flavor, and it makes for an entertaining ritual every time Madison makes one.

1.5 OZ RANSOM OLD TOM GIN

1

Light a bundle of dried sweet grass, wild thyme, and clover. Invert a coupe over the burning end and fill the glass with smoke.

2

Combine all with ice and stir. Strain into the glass and serve.

SOUR CHERRY SORBET

ABOUT 30

620G CHERRY JUICE
182G SUGAR
92G GLUCOSE POWDER
4G STABILIZER
52G LEMON JUICE

1

Heat the sugar, glucose, and stabilizer in a small amount of the juice just until they dissolve, then add the remainder of the juice and freeze in canisters. Process in a Pacojet before serving (see p. 339).

CLAFOUTIS

ABOUT 20

3 EGGS

16G MAPLE SYRUP

220G PITTED SOUR CHERRIES

60G CREAM

230G MILK

60G PASTRY OR CAKE FLOUR

10G COGNAC

This classic came to table piping hot in little iron Staub dishes and got a festive grating of a sharp sheep cheese to finish it, providing a little cheddar-on-the-apple-pie vibe.

1

Whisk the eggs and maple together thoroughly, then add the flour and continue whisking until the mixture is smooth. Add the cream, milk, and cognac, stirring to incorporate them fully. Rest the batter for 12 hours in the fridge.

2

Butter and sugar the inside of a shallow ovenproof dish no more than one inch tall. Arrange cherries in the dish, almost covering the bottom. Pour custard mix until it comes halfway up the cherries. Sprinkle sugar on top, then bake at 182° C for about 12 minutes. Finish in the wood-fired oven or under a broiler until hot and beginning to brown on top. Grate some tangy hard cheese on top if you like.

UMEBOSHI

AS MUCH AS YOU LIKE

While not technically a sour cherry preparation, this is too good not to include. In Japan, ume plums (little apricot relatives) are lacto-fermented and then partially dehydrated to make plump, purple, sour, and salty little orbs that garnish a multitude of traditional dishes. The plums, pitted, also make a purée that goes wonderfully with chicken, and the liquid by-product of the fermentation, called *umeshu* (ume vinegar) packs a fruity, saline punch. In the restaurant, plums and their liquid enhanced a roast duck dish; the liquid seasoned the jus and the pitted fruit garnished the plate. The last of the liquid lifted a sour and spicy Malaysian-style fish soup. Some of it may even have found its way into a cocktail. Jori used Mount Royal plums; look for smaller and firmer fruit for best results.

SMALL PLUMS

BEE BALM LEAVES

SEA SALT

1

Rub fresh leaves of bee balm with sea salt to bruise them slightly.

Take whole firm fruit and toss them in Everclear, then strain and air dry them. Weigh the plums and put 10 percent of that weight of salt in a separate bowl.

2

In a wide-mouth jar large enough to hold all the plums with an inch at the top to spare, sprinkle a layer of salt on the bottom of the jar, followed by an even layer of the salted leaves, followed by an even, gently packed layer of plums. Be sure not to split the fruit. Repeat these steps until the jar is full and all the plums are in. Top off with any remaining salt and/or leaves.

3

Put a weight (like pie marbles in a sealed bag) on top, cover the jar mouth with cheesecloth, and hold in a cool dark room until liquid covers the top of the plums. Reduce the weights by half and return the jar to it for another two weeks.

4

Remove the plums and leaves from the liquid, reserving both in separate containers and reserving the liquid in the jar. Spread the fruit on a woven bamboo mat so they're not touching and lay the leaves out in a single layer. Dry the fruit and leaves in the sun, protected from pests, turning them daily. Let them dry until the fruit is completely wrinkled but still yielding to pressure like prunes. Once dry, return the plums and leaves to the liquid and store in a sealed jar in a cool, dark place.

MAI TAI

Fish & Game runs a mai tai every summer. This storied tradition goes back all the way to 2013 when the restaurant opened. As part of the pre-opening preparations, Jori found some awesome vintage tiki glasses at a thrift store in Austin, complete with rhinestone eyes. Endeavor to find similar glasses or your mai tais will be lackluster.

Last year's iteration far surpassed the first version, due to Jori's brilliant invention of chanterelle orgeat. Orgeat is, of course, a sweet and flowery almond syrup (originally also made with barley, which is *orge* in French; be sure to ask for "orgy syrup" if you want to impress people with your worldliness) that's a crucial ingredient in mai tais. Presented with a bumper crop of plump chanterelles in June 2014, Jori had a flash of inspiration and whipped up this concoction on her first try. It's gorgeous.

While using mushroom syrup in an updated umbrella drink might sound bizarre, in fact chanterelles share a flavor compound with apricots. (In Japan, chanterelles are called *anzutake*: "apricot mushroom.") And apricot pits are pretty close to almonds; like other stone fruit, they're in the same genus (*prunus*) and share that marzipan-y benzaldehyde molecule.* Only a supertaster like Jori would ever guess that there's something unusual happening in this beverage. It drinks like the classic, but better.

**Another cool benzaldehyde factoid is that it can be synthesized from cinnamaldehyde, a major component of cinnamon's distinct perfume. Science!*

2 OZ RHUM J.M. PAILLE

1 OZ CHANTERELLE "ORGEAT"

.5 OZ DRY ORANGE CURAÇAO

.5 OZ LIME JUICE

1

Combine all, shake, and serve over crushed ice. Float .25 oz Ron Zacapa 23 on top. Garnish with a mint sprig in a vintage tiki glass.

CHANTERELLE ORGEAT

400G FRESH CHANTERELLES, WASHED

300G SUSHI RICE
(or any short-grained, glutinous rice)

16 CUPS WATER

2 CUPS SUGAR

1 CINNAMON STICK

PEEL OF ONE ORANGE

2

Make a sachet with the cinnamon and orange peel. Boil the mushrooms and rice in 12 cups of water until completely soft, then blend on high with 4 more cups of warm water until smooth. Pass through strainer.
Add the sugar and sachet, then heat gently and stir to dissolve the sugar. Remove the sachet, cool, and store in the fridge.

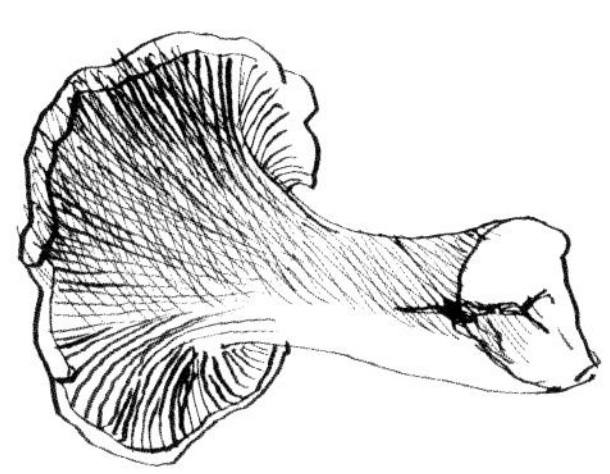

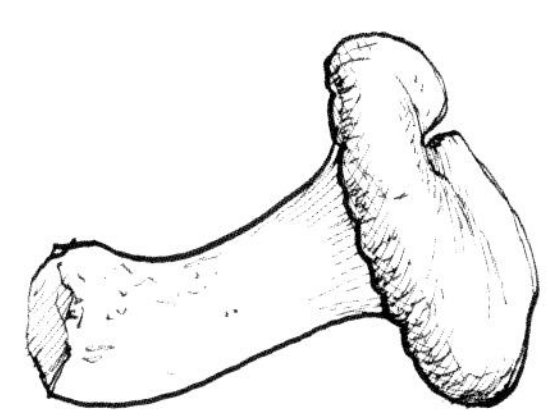

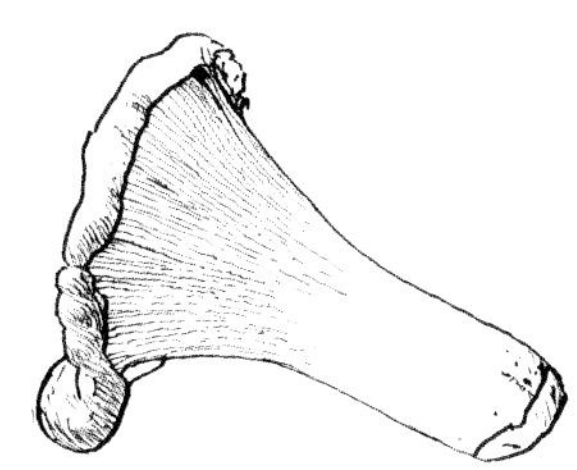

DOMAINE DE L' OCTAVIN

Arbois, France

3,760 miles from Fish & Game

Descending into Paris across the flat expanse of Northwestern France in spring, one sees fields of three colors out the airplane window: light green (wheat), dark green (corn), and yellow (colza). Driving from Paris to Burgundy, the landscape remains much the same: gently undulating tricolor fields punctuated by occasional forests. Shortly before Beaune, the ground rises, becoming irregular; the highway begins to curve and climb. This geological formation, a northern spur of the Massif Central, forms the great côtes of Burgundy.

The other side of the Saône valley, though—less than an hour's drive farther east—is geologically distinct. Starting at the broad arc of Lake Geneva on the Swiss border, the precipitous ridges that terminate around Arbois represent the outermost ripples of the Alps' influence: the Alps begin in Arbois. These cliffs, much younger, sharper, and steeper than Burgundy's cap-rock scarps, lend Jura's topography a wilder character and a distinct terroir. Clay, limestone, and marl, a mixture of the two that darkens according to the proportion of clay, gives the earth in this region the nickname "terre noir." Poulsard (also called ploussard) and trousseau populate most of the red vineyards, with some meaningful pinot noir; savagnin and chardonnay dominate the whites.

The prime vineyard area extends between the farthest reach of the mountains' thrust sheet (which defines the western edge of the Arbois appellation) and a huge rampart of Jurassic limestone that runs roughly parallel a few miles farther east. The village of Arbois sits nestled against this frontal scarp, a maze of red-roofed ochre stone punctuated

with a couple of particularly fetching bell towers and bisected by the Cuisance River. Arbois hosts some exemplary natural winemakers. Domaine de l'Octavin, owned and operated by Charles Dagand and Alice Bouvot, occupies the leading edge of winemaking in the region and produces some of the most joyously drinkable juice in France.

Bouvot, a petite and charming brunette, speaks in a lilting alto that quiets and quickens when she wants to emphasize a point. Standing in one of their vineyards outside town on a warm but rainy day in early May, she explains that any winemaker worth the name considers herself a farmer first. "If the grapes are healthy, they make good wine." Domaine de l'Octavin is certified biodynamic, she continues, because organic farming, though admirable, ultimately is not enough; biodynamic farming principally concerns itself with the life and vitality of the soil, with nurturing biodiversity on both micro and macro scales, and with timing all significant activity in vineyard and cellar alike to coincide with the phases of the moon. "It takes humility and a lot of time," she continues, shrugging in that particularly gallic manner that requires mouth and shoulders simultaneously, but the result expresses both terroir and a contagious *joie de vivre* not found in chemical wines.

Eliminating synthetic treatments and fertilizing the soil with compost promotes the growth of beneficial bacteria, which covers the fruit. This diversity of microflora, she explains, makes it harder for acetic acid bacteria—which produce volatile acidity and its logical extreme, vinegar—to flourish. Although, she corrects herself, even volatile acidity, a bête noire for winemakers, has its place; she says she's grown to love a little bit of it, provided that it does not dominate. And their wines can possess a funky edge to their acidity, a savory tang that flirts with acetic overtones, but that contributes an addictively mouthwatering quality when balanced against the juicy fruit.

Jura's oenological reputation centers on *vin jaune*, an oxidative savagnin aged for years under a layer of mold called a *voile* (veil). Those wines, sherry-like in their complexity and nutty umami, rank among the world's best food wines. Octavin's version, a viscous and cloudy potion the color of a Turner painting, manages to whet an appetite and satisfy it at the same time. Their other wines mostly sit at the other end of the spectrum: transparent, quaffable marvels with astonishing vitality and focus. Their whites mostly ferment in fiberglass or stainless steel after pressing, except for the Pamina, a chardonnay that ferments and ages in old oak for two years before bottling. Foutre d'Escampette, a *pét-nat* chardonnay, is bottled with residual sugar and sealed with a crown cap to trap carbonation. The result makes for delightfully fizzy sipping free from Champagne headaches.

The reds undergo carbonic maceration for varying lengths of time. Whole bunches of grapes (still with stems) go in the vat and ferment under the carbon dioxide produced by the fermenting juice released by the weight of all that fruit crushing some bunches at the bottom. This juice ferments normally and releases the gas that protects the rest from oxidizing or rotting.

Bacteria ferment the juice inside the whole grapes, while their skin stays intact; a bunch of fruit pulled out after eight months looks as fresh as one just picked, but the fruit tastes like wine, with little sugar left. Then the fruit is pressed and continues to ferment until all sugar has been consumed.

Many of their wines' names come from their love of Mozart operas: Dorabella, Don Giovanni, Pamina, Commendatore. Their name represents a synthesis of octave and vin; their logo is a stylized treble clef. They enlist friends to provide art for the labels and hold strong affection for gnomes; besides the two colorful, grinning statues flanking a stainless vat in the garage, they appear on the label of their vin jaune as well as their Corvée du Trousseau, nicknamed "le nain" ("the gnome"). The text on the bottle says "Drinking trousseau is never drudgery." It's true; the wine tastes alive, with bracing acidity and playful syncopated layers of fruit and funk that dance around that tart axis like druids around a menhir.

The Don Giovanni comes from a vineyard of old pinot noir vines intermixed with some chardonnay; the resulting

field blend becomes the wine. The great Burgundy grapes perform well in the region; the terroirs, though different, can be considered cousins. Octavin's trousseau and poulsard both possess a rubescent translucency, practically glowing in the glass, and revealing an intense saturation when held up to a light: suitable visual analogs for the vibrant flavors within. The pinot in the Don Giovanni gives it a darker hue, but the chardonnay dilutes it to an incarnadine glow. These wines look lit from within (so can you, if you drink enough) and while garnet serves well as an adjective in Bordeaux, here the wines are pure ruby, lacking even a hint of brown to tarnish their luster.

All vinification takes place in an anonymous garage a few blocks from their house, which is not climate controlled but which stays pretty cool, especially in the chilly Arboisian winters. The couple own one of the 3.5 hectares (8.5 acres) that they work and rent the rest, though they hope to acquire another hectare to grow more savagnin. They employ one helper, "but that's the limit for what we can work by hand. And we want to do it ourselves," she emphasizes.

Bouvot does want a horse to help in the vineyards, since they compact the ground much less than a tractor and need no diesel. Much of their soil contains a high proportion of clay, so it becomes treacherous when wet and hard when dry; a tractor's wheels can dig muddy furrows or compress the already dense dirt if moisture levels sit too close to either extreme. Crouching down, she grabs a rain-dampened handful and squeezes it to show the clay; it forms into a sticky clump. Compost helps—they add it every fall after harvest—but a horse can mow tasty weeds and fertilize the soil while also pulling a tiller.

They got off to a sluggish beginning. "The locals didn't understand what we were doing; everyone just wanted savagnin *sous voile*." The first few vintages, 2006 through 2009, sold slowly, and then exports kicked in and they sold out. Now business is better. Bouvot laments her country's inherent conservatism but does see a gradual increase in local demand for their wines. "France is stubborn, but now that the Scandinavians, Americans, and Japanese want natural wine the French are catching on. We still only shipped a pallet and a half to Paris last year, though." Does she ever see the domestic market embracing their work? She pauses as a pair of low-flying Rafale fighters whip past in tight formation, letting the roar of their engines fade before continuing. "People are opening their eyes, but most conceptions of quality still focus on the labels, not with how the wine is made. It's changing, though."

Because their methods are still largely frowned upon by officials and peers alike, the couple recently removed their wines from the Arbois appellation; as a result they all simply bear the designation *Vin de France*, the lowliest label in the land and a common refuge for similarly minded producers fed up with bureaucratic intransigence. This retreat may be strategic, though. Tides ebb, tastes change. Burly behemoths may topple before scintillating jewels. Stranger things have happened.

For a name to cover the field in which they toil so fruitfully, she prefers *vin vivant* ("living wine") over *vin naturel* since, just as in this country, the word "natural" on a label means nothing. Working without the institutional support of the greatest wine-producing country on earth poses significant challenges. They want to expand the garage, for example, but have been thwarted by the town government. "It's frustrating, because we're one of only two producers actually vinifying in the village." But the status quo is not so bad, she hastens to add; the family works together (their two children are too young to toil in the vineyards but love to tag along), and they live their lives on their own terms. "What we love is working with the land. We're free; we do what we want, we assume all the risk, but we're not stressed. We don't worry."

MENU

WEEK OF JULY 3

MUSHROOM AND ONION-TOP BOUILLON

spicy garlic paste

PAGE 186

BLUEFISH

cucumber, cherries, kimchi

PAGE 187

PORK BELLY

strawberries, sprouted fenugreek

PAGE 188

PEAS

onions, basils, garlic scapes

PAGE 190

LAMB AND RICE PORRIDGE

sprouted wheatberries, leaves

PAGE 192

BEET CHIPS

shiso cream, chicory, chocolate

PAGE 194

ANISE HYSSOP CAKE

toasted sweet oat milk

PAGE 196

MUSHROOM AND ONION-TOP BOULLION

1

With green onions, the unbalanced ratio of glowing white bulb to vividly verdant leaves does not lend itself to featuring both in equal measure in a given dish. The solution is to make stock out of the greens, especially after grilling them well so they pick up some of that marvelous charred scallion mojo.

2

The only trick, apart from dousing them liberally with good olive oil and then salt, is to let them char pretty thoroughly. As with peppers, even when the outer layer is black, the layer just beneath that is slick, succulent, and sweet. When simmered into stock, that burnt outer layer acts like an *oignon brulé*, giving color and a caramelized sweetness to the resulting liquid. There's not a little satisfaction to eating them fresh off the grill too; the balance of burnt bitter outside with juicy layers underneath makes for deep pleasure. Charred scallions (and leeks, and ramps) feature frequently in Fish & Game dishes.

3

The soup, a pork stock enhanced with onion greens and chanterelles, also contained fat morsels of the orange mushrooms and copious slivers of onion bulb and green alike. To quadruple down on the allium flavors, the soup came with a bright-green condiment in a small bowl: a paste made from onion soubise, garlic scapes, and salted green chilies all mashed together in a mortar. You're looking for a slightly chunky, slightly stringy texture, not a smooth purée.

BLUEFISH

1

Oily bluefish likes an acidic counterpart (think escabeche) and also handles sweetness with aplomb. A sauce of cherries and their juice, simmered gently and lifted with a little maple and fish sauce, provided a brilliant embellishment to this underrated Atlantic fish. These were sweet black cherries, not the more common sour type, but a few leaves of crunchy kimchi provided whatever acidity the fruit lacked in addition to adding a pleasant textural contrast.

2

A grill does wondrous things to a bluefish—it takes smoke as well as salmon—but in order to fully crisp the skin one must finish it in a hot pan, basting it with bubbling butter.

Some silky sliced cucumbers, dressed with olive oil, fish sauce, vinegar, and dill, completed the dish.

PORK BELLY

FENUGREEK EMULSION

FENUGREEK SEEDS

FRESH WATER

GRAPESEED OIL

The pork belly dish, light enough not to cloy on a humid evening but packing sufficient heft to satisfy, continued the fruit and flesh combination from the fish dish but with a dramatically different feel. Tiles of slow-smoked belly layered with slices of fresh strawberry sat atop a schmear of sprouted fenugreek emulsion. Like bluefish, pork loves fruit. Nothing speaks summer as fluently as an heirloom strawberry, too tender for trucking. In the immortal words of William Butler, "Doubtless God could have made a better berry, but doubtless God never did." Chewy, fatty, smoky meat alternated with immaculate slices of heavenly fruit, undergirded by an intensely herbal purée.

1

Soak fenugreek seeds in fresh water, draining and changing it twice a day until they sprout.

When the rootlets are a quarter of an inch long, strain the sprouts and put them in a blender with just enough fresh water that the blade spins freely.

2

Make a smooth paste, then add grapeseed oil in a thin stream with the motor running until you achieve an emulsion with the consistency of mayonnaise. Salt to taste and serve.

PEAS

Fresh peas need little ornamentation; improving upon their just-shelled state can be a challenge. These peas, along with some snap pea pods, got the barest blanch, just enough to brighten and set their color, and then had a quick tumble in a buttery skillet before being tossed in a little fish sauce and herb vinegar with some tempura-fried haricots verts and a variety of basil leaves. The onion soubise returned as a sauce of sorts, a pale purée that added a bright oniony jolt and also served as an adhesive, keeping those peas and leaves from rolling all over the plate during its harrowing trip from the kitchen. Pea flowers made an appropriate garnish.

TEMPURA BATTER (FOR iSi GUN)

1 LITER

400G CAKE FLOUR

20G CORN STARCH

10G SOURDOUGH STARTER
(see p. 231)

1 EGG

591G ICE WATER

1

Combine cake flour, corn starch, starter, and the egg. Using four chopsticks in one hand, incorporate the ice water into the mixture (don't let the ice cubes fall in). Some lumps are fine as long as a majority of the batter is smooth.

2

Place batter into the iSi gun and charge once with nitrous before letting it rest. Test before service to see if additional charges are needed.

3

The siphon fills the batter with tiny bubbles; the result thinly coats vegetables but still offers an appealing crunch when bitten. Dispense batter as needed into a bowl and dip sections of beans into it before frying them quickly; they should not color beyond a light buff. This batter has also been used to great effect with segments of asparagus.

LAMB AND RICE PORRIDGE

1

The lamb course featured smoked loin sliced over a porridge made of Etcetera Farm rice cooked in lamb stock until al dente, whereupon sprouted wheat berries and roasted carrots joined the fray to offer textural contrast and earthy sweetness.

2

Sprouting grains, as with legumes, increases their nutrition (their endosperms break down into digestible compounds) and sweetens them as they begin to metabolize their own starch into sugar to feed the growing sprout.

3

A scattering of leaves and flowers—chard, mizuna, daylily, and nasturtium—partially obscured the slices of dark red meat fanned across the puddle of grains.

4

The lamb dish carried over to the following week, where the meat—braised shoulder this time, finished on the grill—was served in a separate bowl alongside the porridge so the crisp brown roasty edges didn't get soggy in the broth.

BEET CHIPS

ENOUGH CREAM FOR
AT LEAST A DOZEN SERVINGS

BEETS

1 PINT CREAM

1.5 OZ 10× SUGAR

3 SILVER GELATIN SHEETS

1 OZ POWDERED MILK

The pre-dessert, an elegant combination of beets and shiso, took these two sweet-savory fence straddlers and pulled them firmly toward confection territory. Earthy beets and spicy shiso always retain their savory side, though, even when treated so sweetly. But cold, creamy foams positively coo dessert, showing that texture and temperature often speak as clearly as taste when it comes to telling our brains what we're eating.

1

Slice beets thinly on a mandoline, then poach them in beet juice simple syrup for six minutes at 160°F. Dehydrate the slices for 12 hours until crisp. Invent a cocktail with the syrup.

2

Whisk together the cream, sugar, and powdered milk. Heat the mixture to 110°F and blend in an ounce of fresh shiso leaves. Bloom the gelatin in cold water, then dissolve in the hot cream. Strain the liquid into an iSi siphon and charge twice. Refrigerate until service.

3

Squirt a little green rosette* of shiso cream into a small chilled bowl, then top with a few beet chips and a pinch of cacao nibs. Garnish with slivers of shiso leaf.

**Red shiso has a more pronounced cinnamon note than its green sibling; that tends to make it more compatible with sweet applications. It does not, alas, allow for making Zappa references in your recipes.*

ANISE HYSSOP CAKE

ABOUT 45 1×3" CAKES

145G PASTRY FLOUR

3G BAKING POWDER

2G SALT

50G EGGS

158G SUGAR

113G WHOLE MILK

100G ANISE HYSSOP LEAVES

79G OLIVE OIL

OATS

MAPLE SYRUP

1

Preheat your oven to 350°F. Sift flour, baking powder, and salt together. Blend the anise hyssop and olive oil together in a food processor until the leaves are shredded into tiny pieces: like pesto.

2

Whisk the eggs and sugar together until the mixture thickens and the sugar has dissolved. Combine the milk and olive oil. Add half the dry ingredients and then half the wet ingredients to the egg, fully incorporating them before adding the rest.

3

Pour mixture into a sheet tray lined with a silpat, making sure the batter is spread out evenly. Bake for 15 minutes until the top is golden and a cake tester comes cleanly out of the center. Let cool, then cut into desired portions.

4

OAT MILK

Toast whole oats. Soak them in the fridge overnight in milk, then blend furiously for two minutes. Finely strain the liquid and season it with a pinch of salt and a bit of maple syrup. Pour some oat milk over each piece of cake at the table.

Anise hyssop stands out among the many perennial herbs that thrive in this climate. Besides its beautiful flowers, which bees positively adore, its dark, serrated leaves have a lovely licoricey flavor that carries a noticeable sweetness. A few leaves provide a perfect conclusion to any grazing one might do while gardening, so using it in a dessert made perfect sense. This recipe is for an olive oil cake that has seen use with various flavors, notably fresh turmeric. Substitute grated turmeric for the anise hyssop, or try something else. The following week, the oat milk was replaced with milk jam, so the dish came to table on a plate.

Eating Through It

ZAK

I've always felt a more acute understanding of summer's departure than its arrival. Perhaps my sensitivity to its approach is deadened by the seemingly endless waiting through spring for those long, hot, languorous days, awareness calloused by an unyielding impatience for fruit so ripe that I don't notice summer's here until the juice is already dripping down my chin. Maybe. By the time the fruits are all picked and I'm eating the best tomatoes of the season, I try not to notice that the morning light, my alarm clock, has become a bit lazier, showing up later than the time to which I have grown accustomed, seeming exhausted and disinterested. And I'm groggier, aware of what's happening but reluctant to admit that it must end.

Delusion, one of the mind's major achievements, keeps us waking up, pulling ourselves out of bed to own the moment, all the while knowing we're powerless against the rotation of the seasons. And yet we always try to dodge the end.

With heads down we cultivate the garden, cognizant of Voltaire's dervish and the farmer and the futility of idleness or

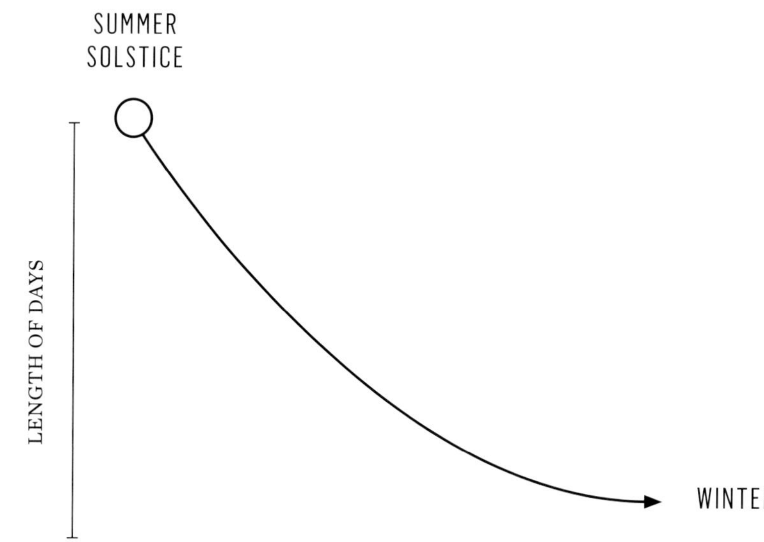

wondering why. The changing seasons rarely make us cry, even when a warm fall day, redolent of summer, turns us on like an apparition of lost love. We are quick to find comfort in routine, the beat to which we dance. We all find routine; even the proud who eschew it disdainfully are only circumnavigating the more generic definition of the word. Routine finds its way into the work and work weaves its way along the routine.

Nothing wakes us from this comfort like change. The summer, no matter the rain or our busy lives, is always a long, wonderfully easy jam session that ends too soon. It all ends too soon. It ended too soon. And winter feels endless. Adjusting to less light and brisker mornings is one of the more jolting shifts, an abrupt segue that leaves you on the dance floor swaying awkwardly, uncertain how to move your body to the new beat that's emerging from the fugue that is change. But it comes, it always comes, until we become compost. So now we wait for a new beat, the next beat... the next thing to eat.

The leaves have begun flaming out, giving their green to the acorns and ripe shells of black walnuts: departing gifts. And the brilliant leaves falling off the trees are wildly beautiful: the oranges and reds, yellows and purples, electrified with a drama far different from the whisper of a more reserved morning light, quietly heralding summer's departure. Soon the swirling winds will whisk the colorful leaves by my face as I stand happily powerless in the middle of the grand rotation, reminded of all that summer gave, its bounty growing over fences and into the roadsides, the early mornings filled with so much to do to manage the aggressive growth.

And I'll remember being wine-drunk late at night as I rested in the soft grass, still warm though the sun had gone, and I'll remember the juice and the sticky hands and the perfume of the delicate flowers whose scent belies their fragility, and I'll also remember the tomatoes that never made it into jars, but fell, rotting in the garden, an unused offering. The fruits and greens, the berries and herbs that summer pushed upon us and yet we could not get to all of them even though the days were so long. The days were long and for a moment, lost in the dance, I thought it would never end.

The summer, no matter the rain or our busy lives, is always a long, wonderfully easy jam session that always ends too soon.

Fall

THE NORTHEASTERN UNITED STATES HOST THE BEST AUTUMN ON THE PLANET. After Labor Day, summer's languid finale quickens and sharpens, becoming drier and leaner, ushering in seemingly identical days of resplendent clarity. This creates an illusion of timelessness: nature stuck on repeat, offering up day after day of cool, clean brilliance. Tired of summer's sticky heat, we're grateful to add another layer and light fires to push away the evening chill when we sit outside. The food, marrying the bounty of summer's end with the lower temperatures that inspire heartier fare, reaches a pinnacle. Fall is the most culinarily powerful season, with ubiquitous harvest imagery and the only secular holiday specifically devoted to a meal.

Two Dutch Belted cows arrived around Halloween of the second year, along with a pair of goats. The goats are Lamancha/Boer crosses; the former give great milk and the latter make good meat. They live in a newly sided barn with a view across the valley to the chicken coop and garden. The gregarious goats are always keen to meet visitors, jamming their soft noses into hands and camera lenses alike, looking for food and love (in that order). The cows, however, were skittish and took some time to become comfortable with people. Kalas began milking them the following spring.

Zak and Jori hosted a garlic planting party in November of year two at Blue Heron Farm, so the whole crew gathered on an auspiciously gorgeous day to stick a few thousand cloves of garlic into the ground; Kalas had tilled long beds near their garden, which quickly got filled with orderly rows of Red Chesnok, Red Inchelium, and Georgia Fire cloves. The ultimate goal was to produce 500 pounds of garlic for the restaurant plus enough extra to plant for the following year. The planted cloves, totaling about 75 pounds, yielded about that amount. A jeroboam of Frank Cornelissen's excellent Contadino made the rounds and kept everyone fueled. The planting finished just as the sun dropped behind the ridge, which subtracted about twenty degrees from what had been a balmy afternoon. The group quickly repaired to Zak and Jori's house and built a big fire in the steel firepit/grill that Zak designed.

A couple of weeks later, Thanksgiving brought fifty or so people to the restaurant for a traditional dinner: spit-roasted turkeys, stuffing made with Walter's bread, cranberry sauce, brussels sprouts with lardo, potato purée, and gravy. As a homey respite from the regular set menu format, guests could ask for seconds of anything they wanted more of. Then came Jori's pies: pumpkin (actually made with red hubbard squash, plus her ginger bitters) and pecan, courtesy of a care package from her mother in Texas. Home cooks take note: even professionals suffer holiday stress in the kitchen. The dough for the rooster confit tortellini (an appetizer) was dried out, necessitating another batch on short notice; Zak was folding and pinching the pasta right up until the first customers arrived. Then the rotisserie broke. Though the staff had to scramble, the guests never noticed. Service!

Autumn has a uniquely powerful identity. But like its opposite, spring, it also begins as one season and ends as another. Fall often starts with an exceptionally long run of glorious weather: bright sun, unusual warmth, and cerulean skies that set off the blazing foliage to great effect. Then, usually around mid-November, the weather shifts dramatically. By the time December arrives, the leaves have fallen, the ground is frozen, and fresh vegetables are limited to sprouts and a few hardy greenhouse crops. It's fully dark before 5:00. Then the pantry raid starts, as the kitchen works its way through Jori's vast arsenal of preserves, pickles, and condiments. Late fall ushers in a time of slower, more comforting food—food containing all the enhanced tastes that those ancient processes impart—prepared, and, ideally, eaten a bit more deliberately.

Portland, Maine

BROWNE TRADING

Portland, ME

262 miles from Fish & Game

Any restaurant with "Fish" in the name should probably walk the walk (and swim the swim) when it comes to immaculately fresh, sustainably caught seafood. While it's easy to obtain seafood from anywhere in the world, Fish & Game deals exclusively in North Atlantic species; Hudson is located in a spot roughly equidistant from Boston and Montauk, making a big swath of sea fair game for fish that, while not exactly local, stays at least regional.

The Gulf of Maine, a chilly expanse of ocean stretching from Cape Cod to Nova Scotia, has historically been one of the richest regions in the Atlantic; Georges Bank, the most accessible of its great fisheries, defines its seaward border. Portland, Maine, is in an ideal port to land the diverse bounty of delectable species that swim, crawl, or just kind of sit there in the frigid, fertile water. Browne Trading, a small family-owned business in Portland, supplies fine restaurants on the East Coast—including Fish & Game—with superior finfish, shellfish, sea urchins, and crustaceans.

Browne runs a retail shop in a storefront in their building, but the real action happens out back. Right next door to Browne's waterfront building sits the Portland Fish Exchange, the clearinghouse for all the seafood that day boats bring in most weekday mornings. They tie up right alongside and unload, using a wide piece of pavement behind the building to untangle their nets so the huge winches that sit astern can coil them back up. Their catch, stacked in iced totes, boxes, and bins, shunted and scooted around the Exchange's warehouse by fleet forklifts—which do not take particularly kindly to

wandering photographers—is all visible from an adjacent room, where buyers bid on the fish in person or over the phone. Browne is ideally placed to buy the freshest and best, and they pay for it.

It's a short trip—about 200 feet—for the fish they buy to their processing facility, a refrigerated warren below the offices where huge tuna get butchered, halibut get filleted, and orders are packed in fresh ice for shipping. More often than not, this means that product arrives at the restaurant less than 24 hours after it came out of the water. A stack of boxes in the center of one room, each one bearing "Le Bern" scrawled in marker, offers a potent endorsement; when Eric Ripert is buying the fish, that's pretty much all you need to know.

And that's the point of a restaurant like Fish & Game: a team of experts aren't just preparing the food for you, they're obtaining the ingredients from scrupulous purveyors who, as with the meat, produce, and wine, care as much about the method of production and harvest as they do about the taste. The oceans are in trouble, and understanding which species are still fine to eat can be challenging. A good restaurant makes these choices on your behalf, so you don't have to grill your waiter about the provenance of your grilled squid. As Nick Branchina, director of marketing at Browne, succinctly puts it, "These fisheries are some of the most carefully managed in the world. If we get it, it's sustainably caught."

BANGS ISLAND MUSSELS

Portland, ME

263 miles from Fish & Game

Matt Moretti holds a master's degree in biology, so his knowledge of the Casco Bay's ecosystem is as deep as his desire to grow food within it. Though it floats in the ocean, and entails much of the same exertion and equipment one finds on a dayboat, the Bangs Island Mussel Company is most assuredly a farm. A prolific farm: annual production fluctuates, and they harvest less often in winter, but Moretti aims for 450,000 pounds every eighteen months from their seven rafts moored in two spots northeast of Portland.

The rafts—galvanized steel I-beam frames spanned by wooden joists, all bobbing on foam-filled plastic floats—sit on about 50 feet of water, depending on the tide. Beneath each raft, spaced a foot or two apart, heavy nylon ropes cluttered with mussels hang down from the joists into the water column. The ropes stop about 15 feet short of the bottom so that crabs and other predators can't reach them and climb up; each raft is also wrapped in netting to keep ducks out. Ducks dive, so the nets hang down to the bottom. Mussels filter plankton out of the water to grow, and when they reproduce, their spat attaches to the ropes to begin growing more mussels. It's a farm that buys no seed or feed.

Mussels, unlike oysters, sell by the pound. They're shiny blue-black coins of the sea, and extracting them is serious business. The crew starts early, loading the biodiesel-fueled boat with plastic tubs and ice from their facility on a wharf in downtown Portland. It's about four miles to either of the leased spots, so they cast off about half an hour before dawn; this puts them out at the rafts at first light, and they

Bangs Island Mussels

HONDA

get straight to work. Everyone on the four-man crew has his role, and they all do the same jobs, in the same order, on every day that they go out. This makes for a remarkably speedy, well-choreographed routine that pulls two thousand pounds of slimy, crusty, densely clumped mussels from the sea and sees them bagged, immaculate and gleaming and ready for sale, in less than eight hours. They work hard, fast, and fluently, hardly speaking to each other all morning. Time is mussels, and mussels are money.

Moored near the rafts, the processing barge houses all the equipment for harvesting and sorting the crop. The morning's work consists of a strenuously linear process that begins under a raft, wends through the barge, and finishes back in the water again. While the rafts float in peace most of the time, with the only sound coming from lapping waves, crying gulls, or the plangent lowing of a foghorn, when the crew arrives it gets loud. A little gas generator, noisy as hell, sits on a shelf against one wall inside the shack. It powers everything on the raft—water pump, winch, declumper, socking machine—and with no amps to spare; when the winch is engaged the shrill pitch of the engine's whiny roar dips momentarily as the motor strains to meet the sudden demand.

While one man works the winch control, another whacks each length of tense rope with the handle of a plastic shovel—they're ubiquitous at every stage of the operation—to clear it of mussels so it can coil around the spool. The mussels, shoveled into a pile, receive a quick rinse courtesy of a thick red hose that spews seawater for the duration of the day. Then they're fed into the hopper of a declumper, where blunt vanes revolve and break the clusters apart into individual shellfish before sending them sluicing through a revolving cylindrical cage and onto a stainless steel sorting table where mussels below market size fall through the slats. The crew's gloved hands massage the slippery, clattering shells around, applying vigorous pressure, and then push the survivors off the table through two holes at one end. Plastic totes below those holes get schlepped onto the boat and packed into insulated tubs with crushed ice as quickly as possible.

Those too-small specimens that fall through the table do not go to waste. By means of the socking machine, a Mad Max-looking cross between a wheelbarrow and a loom that binds the juveniles back onto the just-pulled ropes with tubular netting and a revolving bobbin, the undersize mussels reunite with the ropes after their brief separation; they quickly reattach themselves and the cotton mesh biodegrades. In a reverse echo of the first step, each rope is deftly clambered out onto the raft and tied off to hang in its allotted space, back down into the chilly water from which it emerged just a couple of hours earlier.

Although Moretti has 3.6 acres leased, the seven rafts, at 40 by 40 feet each, add up to just over a quarter acre of total surface area. Even allowing for a raft's breadth of sea between rafts for access, that means half an acre of ocean produces twelve tons of food, every month, all year round. Moretti, summing up his satisfaction between bites of sandwich on the trip back to shore, grins widely, a noticeable shift from the no-nonsense demeanor that abides on the barge. "What other kind of farming can produce 200 tons of food [with shells, but still] from a quarter acre in eighteen months?"

4
men

8
hours

2,000
pounds
of mussels

BASKET ISLAND OYSTERS

Falmouth, ME

275 miles from Fish & Game

Before about one hundred years ago, New York City was synonymous with oysters. People of every class consumed them by the literal boatload. New York Harbor, by some estimates, contained half of the world's oyster population in the nineteenth Century; the lower Hudson River was practically carpeted with them. Pollution and over-harvesting (sound familiar?) put an end to the era, but those ugly, lumpy shells might just hold the future of seafood. Those shells contain one of the most virtuous bites of ocean life that someone in the Northeast can enjoy: it wasn't trucked too far, it cleaned the water, it put no pressure on wild sea life—quite the opposite, in fact, since oyster beds provide habitat for other species—and it supported hard-working farmers. Increased demand only means that more of these beneficial businesses can thrive That's wins across the board, with no downside. It is not possible to eat too many farmed oysters.

Every oyster growing from New Orleans to Nova Scotia is the same species: *Crassostrea Virginica*, the American or Eastern Oyster. All the many names they're given have only to do with where they grow, and thus how they taste; oysters represent remarkably eloquent expressors of terroir (or merroir, more accurately). Many of Browne's oysters, including their flagship Browne's Point variety, come from the mouth of the Damariscotta River, about 30 miles up the coast from Portland, past Bath; the brackish waters of that estuary produce bivalves possessing a particular sweetness. The Basket Island Oyster Company's spot, however, is in open ocean, where the salinity is closer to 3.5 percent. This makes for a concentrated, briny hit of pure Atlantic essence on the half shell.

Basket Island owner Mark Green has a PhD in oceanography. While he still teaches ecology, oceanography, and aquaculture courses every spring at a nearby college, his main gig and consuming passion is oyster farming. He came to his new vocation in the lab: "I realized I was more interested in keeping the oysters alive between experiments than I was in the experiments." (His thesis was on ocean acidification, the unhappy result of too much carbon in the atmosphere that climate-change deniers don't like to talk about because it's indisputable.) Now, pursuant to financial backing from a couple of friends, he has two acres of sea floor leased in a secluded cove north of Portland. From the surface, his farm looks like a placid piece of bay dotted with a haphazard grid of buoys surrounding a shabby raft piled high with wire cages and plastic buckets. Underwater, however, stacks of cages teem with oysters.

"You need three things for great oysters: clean water, cold water, and a good food supply. We have all three, in abundance." He gestures out at the expanse of Casco Bay on a mild October morning as his white fiberglass Carolina skiff scuds toward the farm, voice raised over the noise of the outboard and spray. Fitted with a small electric crane for hauling up the cages, and with a crew of Green and one helper, the boat is small but efficient. The cages, hoisted onto the raft and opened, spill out a muddy cluster of shells mixed with a few sea squirts, crabs, and little fish. They get sorted, rinsed, sorted again, and packed for return to shore.

The tumbler, revealingly similar to the apparatus Farmer Ground (see p. 237) runs their grains through prior to drying them, sorts the oysters by size, with smaller ones falling through the mesh and larger ones making it to the end. A few trips through the grading wheel over the two-plus year lifespan of an oyster also chip bits off the lips' leading edges; the result of this minor damage is that new growth comes in at a steeper angle, deepening the cups for a plumper and more desirable product.

Shellfish leave the water cleaner than they enter it; as filter feeders that's pretty much their job description. The result, Green continues, is both ecologically beneficial and a sound business: "I pay myself and my workers a fair wage and offer benefits." Sustainability, after all, is a meaningless term unless the people working the land (and the water) can make a good living by doing it. With the help of some new backers, he is starting a new farm on another two-acre plot; within the next couple of years his target is a million oysters from each parcel every year. At about 80 cents per oyster wholesale, that adds up to a lot of clams.

Green buys seed from a company in Walpole, up on the Damariscotta River. The seeds, slippery pips a millimeter wide, spend the first few months of their lives in upweller silos: plastic containers through which fresh seawater is constantly pumped, ensuring a constant supply of phytoplankton to promote maximum growth. After two or three months, they're moved into rectangular fine-mesh plastic bags that fit inside the cages on the farm until they're large enough—about the size of a quarter—not to fall through the cages' wire mesh, at which point they come out of the bags. Then they sit on the bottom of the bay, feeding on the tides, growing, for another year or so until they're market size.

In principle, the concept is straightforward. In practice, however, it can be tricky; these are still wild animals, living in the ocean, and there are many variables. Besides predation—sea stars love oysters, for example—sometimes they just die, often en masse. As shorthand for these issues, Green uses an aphorism someone told him back when he got into the business: "There are two kinds of oyster farmers: those who have killed a million oysters, and those who will."

PORTLAND
BOSTON
FISH
&
GAME
MONTAUK
NYC

WOOD OVEN-ROASTED OYSTERS

As one of life's pure pleasures, raw oysters on the half shell will never go out of style. Cooked oysters don't suck, however, and oysters roasted with hollandaise "are almost too good," according to Zak. He's right. The combination of salt, fat, acid, and umami makes this dish the haute equivalent of your favorite guilty-pleasure potato chips: a pupil-dilating rush of highly addictive flavor. Two is not enough. A bucketful would not be enough. The dish was originally created for Lavinia Mitchell; one night, in the very early days of Fish & Game, she was craving oysters but didn't want to eat them raw since she was pregnant. Kevin whipped up some hollandaise, Zak grabbed some kimchi and popped a few oysters, and into the wood-burning oven they went.

Not long after, the dish returned as a menu supplement and bar snack. And there it stays, a signature treat that everyone who walks in the door can enjoy. Playing a crucial supporting role in this perfect bite (as so many of her concoctions do in so many dishes) we find Jori's daikon kimchi: fat rounds of radish fermented with their greens and the traditional accoutrements of ginger, garlic, chilies, and scallions. It's not hard: shuck the oysters, leaving them in the lower shell with their liquid. Arrange the shells in a pan or skillet on a bed of coarse salt to hold them steady. Put a fat pinch of finely minced daikon kimchi greens on each oyster, top with a generous spoon of hollandaise, and cook in a wood oven or under a broiler until the sauce is nicely browned. Garnish each oyster with finely diced daikon root and serve immediately.

On the decadent emulsion spectrum, Hollandaise holds pride of place at the very top. Butter and egg yolks, two of nature's most magnificent fats—and both with extraordinary emulsifying powers—whisked together with some tart acidity (while tradition calls for lemon juice, northern climes require vinegar or kimchi brine) make for an embellishment of great succulence. The restaurant uses an iSi siphon, charged with two canisters of nitrous, to dispense the hollandaise; it sits in a bain marie or on the edge of the flat top keeping warm until an order comes in, at which point Steve snaps out of his existential crisis du jour and shucks a couple of oysters. If you're making these all at once, a spoon will suffice to apply the sauce.

HOLLANDAISE

2 EGGS

6 YOLKS

1 LB BUTTER

1 CUP KIMCHI BRINE, STRAINED

2 FAT PINCHES SALT

In the event that there's hollandaise left over when the oysters are gone, having it in a siphon turns out to be super convenient; it makes squirting the rest of it directly into your mouth (or the mouth of someone you love) extremely easy. For extra credit, you can try a hollandaise whip-it, where you inhale the nitrous while simultaneously eating the sauce. This is a really good idea and not at all dangerous.

1

Put the eggs and yolks in a blender. Combine the brine, butter, and salt in a pot and whisk them together over medium heat.

2

Once the butter is fully melted, pour the mixture slowly into the running blender until it visibly thickens.

3

Strain into siphon or saucepan and keep warm until needed.

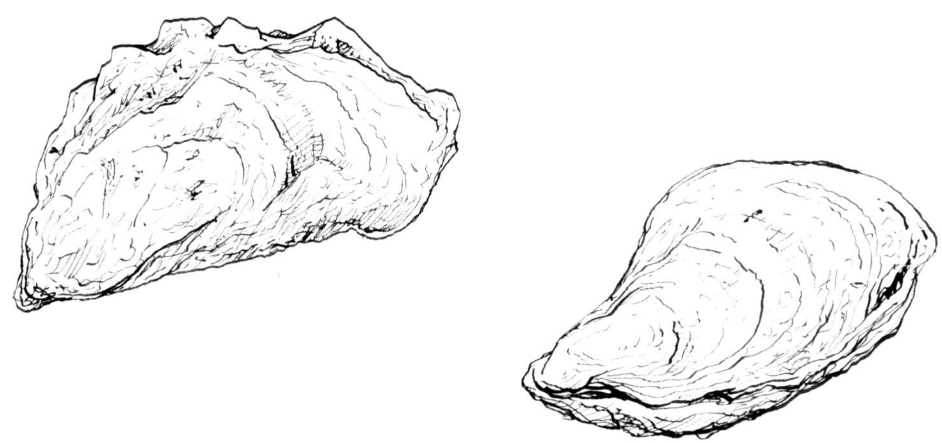

BUTTER

This region is rich in superb fats. Duck, goose, lamb, and pork all shine brightly and convey deep flavor, each imparting its own particular inflection to the sexy embrace that fat bestows upon food. But butter is a miracle. Only butter arrives fully formed as an emulsion; ironically, it looms largest among lipids because of the water that it contains. That hidden liquid offers the ability to poach as well as fry, to emulsify and enrich at the same time.

The kitchen uses 20–30 pounds of butter a week, both for cooking and to serve with the bread baskets in the dining room and bar. Most of the cooking is done with Plugrá, a national brand with a high fat content (the name comes from *plus gras*, "more fat," since it averages around eighty-two percent fat as opposed to regular butter's eighty percent). It sits, in glistening one-pound blocks, snug in 1/9 pans as part of everyone's mise en place, from whence the cooks scoop shiny dollops to brush on smoky lamb loins, thicken sauces on the flat top, or lubricate a pan going in the wood oven to finish. Walter almost always has a hunk of butter on his table; he's either cutting it up to make pastry or using the back of his beautiful Damascus steel bread knife to spread it on slices of whatever he has just pulled out of the oven. (Strictly for quality control purposes, of course.)

From the beginning, Fish & Game served cultured butter from the Vermont Creamery, which tastes very good and comes in neat cylinders. About a year before opening, the crew began aging these logs in the walk-in at Zak and Jori's, either rolled in ash or horseradish leaves, so they would taste even better. As part of the bread service, this butter gets mixed with yogurt (one pint per pound of butter) for tangy flavor and effortless spreadability, then served in substantial, flanged brass cups that would look right at home in a pipefitter's toolbag. If the butter was aged in ash, the ash is blended into the mixture.

After opening, the ash from the wood-fired oven provided an inexhaustible supply for subsequent batches, whether purchased or made in house. As the aged butter got used up, however, the reality of the gap between supply and demand became evident. Even in the best weeks, the kitchen crew was only able to make about half of what they needed, and that got used right away so aging was no longer an option.

With the goal of eventual butter independence for the restaurant, over the course of the first year Kevin worked out a reliable method for making cultured butter using cream from Hill-Over Healthy & Fresh in Copake. The technique involves inoculating the cream with a little buttermilk ($1/16$ of the cream weight) and holding it at 100°F for 32 hours in the CVAP to culture into something close to crème fraîche. It's then chilled overnight before getting paddled into butter in the stand mixer. After pressing out the liquid, it gets formed into bricks and refrigerated. The yield is approximately two thirds; a third of the cream's weight is water, most of which separates out as buttermilk. This is sometimes used for culturing the following week's batch, and Walter includes it in a variety of baked goods to add a lovely sourness and supplement the bacterial cultures that teem within his starter.

Finding enough cream has been an obstacle; most farmers aren't interested in producing so much skim milk. The ultimate goal is to take butter production off site and have it made according to Kevin's specifications.

BREAD

Bread, an ancient technology intimately intertwined with the roots of civilization, signifies home and hearth more than any other food. Walter's mastery, combined with the excellent grains, both whole and ground, from Farmer Ground and Champlain Valley Milling, make Fish & Game's bread program an essential component of each meal.

The first thing Walter does every morning when he arrives at the restaurant is make a pot of coffee, followed immediately by checking the oven temperature and feeding the starter. On Wednesdays, when the restaurant is not open for service, he lights the oven in the afternoon to heat it up. Before he leaves that evening, he stokes it with a few logs and leaves the door open a crack so they burn slowly into the night; the goal is to have it at about 600°F the next morning when he comes in to bake.

Once he has shaped and proofed the day's doughs, the oven will have cooled a bit, descending through the 500s by the time he shoves scored loaves off the peel onto the deck. Since most home ovens can reach 500°F, with a good stone one can achieve fine results; if your dough is well made, great bread can be baked in mediocre ovens.

OVEN:

600° — 8:00AM Walter arrives at Fish & Game; 8:01AM make coffee; 8:10AM feed starter; 8:20AM remove dough from fridge, proof

550° — 9:00AM check oven temp

500° — 10:00AM start baking; 11:00AM; 12:00PM

450° 400°

1:00PM

2:00PM
finish baking

3:00PM
build and light fire in the oven

4:00PM
make dough for next day

5:00PM

6:00PM 7:00PM 8:00PM 9:00PM 10:00PM

THE SECRET TO BAKING, WALTER EMPHASIZES, LIES IN USING YOUR SENSES AND STAYING AWARE of the ways in which seasonal changes in temperature and humidity affect the outcome. Baking may be the most measurement-sensitive culinary discipline, but the importance of this intuitive comprehension cannot be overstated. A *levain* is a living thing, so when and how often you feed it will dramatically change how it performs. Different flours have different protein content, and yeast reproduces dramatically faster on a hot, humid summer day than it does in the chilly winter.

He is always tweaking his recipes to compensate for these variations, and you should too as you develop your own style of baking (and learn the quirks of your oven, and the flours you use, and the feeding schedule that works best for your starter). When working, Walter touches the dough constantly, feeling its texture and elasticity. There's a lot of muscle and sense memory involved in making great bread, and that can't be taught; it must be learned through attentive and regular baking.

While baking at home involves less stress than restaurant cooking (one hopes), knowing your starter, oven, kitchen, and microclimate remains essential. Walter also thinks of the oven as being closer to a sauté station than a place where you leave things alone for a given period; loaves need to be turned, and shifted, and moved from hot spots to cooler ones if they brown too quickly. He understands the different temperature zones inside the wood-fired oven, and how quickly it cools down over the course of a morning, and how those factors differ depending on the season.

11:00PM
coals and ash removed,
oven door closed
12:00AM
1:00AM
2:00AM

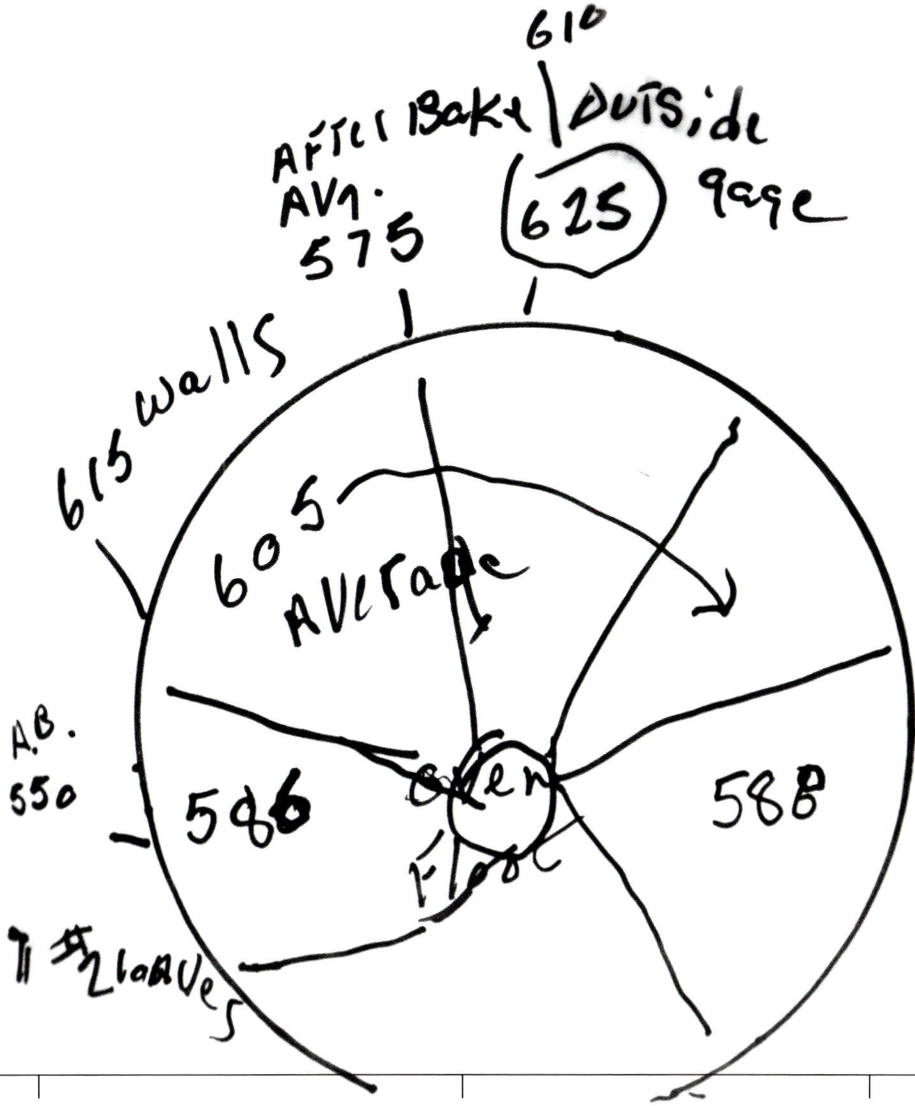

3:00AM 4:00AM 5:00AM 6:00AM 7:00AM

Pain au levain is the classic French peasant sourdough. Walter's version possesses all of the chewy, complex, and deeply satisfying character that the loaf is prized for—an addictive reminder that bread and water are in fact sufficient to sustain life for a long time. Schmear on some butter (and swap in a glass of wine for the water) and it's a complete meal. *Levain*, the French word for sourdough starter, derives from the Latin *levare*, to raise, and is the origin of the English word leaven. (Also lever, as in Archimedes's "Give me a lever and a place to stand, and I shall move the earth." Think of your wild yeast pets as millions of tiny levers, raising your loaf together like an Amish barn.)

600°

8:00AM
Walter arrives
at Fish & Game

PAIN AU LEVAIN

FIVE TWO-POUND LOAVES

4.25 LB HALF WHITE FLOUR

.5 LB WHOLE WHEAT FLOUR

.25 LB RYE FLOUR
(for flavor, but also great starter food)

4 LB WATER
(.5 GALLON)

1 LB STARTER
(15%–20% ratio depending on season; more in winter)

2 OZ SALT

This recipe makes ten pounds of dough, enough for five two-pound loaves. Scale up or down as needed, and remember that all flours and microclimates are not created equal. When making the dough, it's better to err on the side of dryness; it's always easy to add water but not flour, which can form dry pockets in the dough.

1

Mix the flours and water together in the bowl of a stand mixer fitted with the dough hook and turn it on low for about 5 minutes.

2

Let it sit about 30–40 minutes to hydrate, then mix in the starter and let it sit another 30–40 minutes for the "autolyse," which develops gluten, before adding the salt and mixing it in well.

3

After salting, ferment the dough in the refrigerator overnight (12–14 hours). Remove the dough, divide and shape, then proof it at room temperature for 2–3 hours before baking.

4

Preheat oven to 500°F an hour before baking. Score the loaves, then bake for 30–35 minutes, lowering heat to 475° after 20 minutes.

PORRIDGE BREAD

FIVE TWO-POUND LOAVES

This variation on *pain au levain* uses fermented whole grains to add more complex flavor and texture, as well as nutrition; as the grains begin to sprout, they release enzymes that digest the anti-nutrients in their endosperms that protect them during dormancy. Soak your grains (like wheat, spelt and rye berries, and coarse cornmeal) in water, alone or in combination, at room temperature for 48 hours.

Add a spoonful of whey, buttermilk, or yogurt if you like; they will jumpstart microbial activity. When you strain the porridge to weigh it out, be sure to save the tangy water to use as part of the water in the dough.

It's worth noting that Walter often uses a fair amount of spelt flour (both white and whole) in this bread. Play around with various percentages of flour within the 5-pound total, depending on what you prefer or have available. If you use chunks of stale bread soaked for a few days like the porridge, that soaker (blended into a slurry) plus a high percentage of rye flour in the dough will get you into pumpernickel territory pretty quickly. Experiment. You can treat your porridge and soaker like your levain, feeding them regularly with whatever grains and stale breads you have on hand. Develop a feel for these types of bread and you'll never waste anything again.

TO MAKE PORRIDGE BREAD, START WITH THE LEVAIN RECIPE AND MAKE THE FOLLOWING CHANGES:

Subtract ¾ lb water and 5.5 oz of starter

Add 2 lb 3 oz of strained porridge

Proceed as with the levain recipe, adding the porridge when you add the starter.

STARTING A STARTER

Combine equal weights (start with 4-6 ounces of each) of flour and unchlorinated water in a bowl, and mix them together thoroughly. If you have an unsprayed apple from a local orchard, add the peel (that pale haze you buff off onto your shirt is wild yeast). Leave it out on your counter, uncovered, and every day add another couple of ounces of fresh flour/water mixture, stirring well. (You can remove the apple peel after the first day.) Within five to seven days, give or take your microclimate and other variables, the mixture should begin to bubble gently and smell appealingly fruity and yeasty. It should not smell like cheese or feet; if it does you might want to chuck it and start over from the beginning.

Once established, feed your starter a little 50/50 mix every day to keep it happy. Two feedings a day will ensure the best performance. If you miss a few days, no worries; be sure to feed it the day before you want to bake and then again the next morning to bring it back to vitality. If, as a result of regular feeding and infrequent baking, you end up with a ton of it, fear not: it makes great pancake batter. It's also a good idea to give excess starter to all your baking friends; besides confirming their assessments of your kindness and generosity, it's also excellent insurance against killing your batch if you're away

The genius of brioche lies in its in-between status: half bread, half cake, it tastes like the former and eats like the latter. The secret to great brioche involves perfecting the ratio of butter and eggs to flour; at its best, brioche is a suspension of those two fats in a delicate matrix of starch and protein. It should melt in your mouth. Fish & Game uses brioche in a variety of ways, both sweet and savory.

BRIOCHE

FOUR TWO-POUND LOAVES

2 DOZEN EGGS

3 LB BUTTER

2 LB 8 OZ AP FLOUR

2 LB PASTRY FLOUR

2 OZ YEAST

14 OZ SUGAR

14 OZ MILK, WARMED

⅓ OZ SALT

1

Bring the butter to room temperature; it should be malleable but not soft. Cut it into walnut-sized pieces. Pour the eggs, milk, sugar, yeast, and flours into the bowl of a mixer set on low until the dough comes together.

2

While still churning, add butter one chunk at a time, waiting until each is incorporated before tossing in the next. Pour in the sugar, then salt, letting them fully integrate.

3

Proof the dough at room temperature for two hours, then portion and bake for 20 minutes at 350°F (This presupposes small, roll-sized loaves or a long loaf baked in a pullman-type pan.)

Walter often uses spelt in addition to all-purpose and half white flours, depending on what the final use will be. More often than not, thick slices of brioche spend a few minutes on the grill picking up some fetching diagonal char marks for even more flavor before plating.

PRETZEL BREAD

40 QUARTER-POUND LOAVES

2 LB 12 OZ SPONGE

3 LB 12 OZ WATER

2 LB HALF WHITE FLOUR

2 LB 4 OZ WHOLE WHEAT FLOUR

2 TBSP YEAST

2 TBSP SALT

6 OZ SOFT BUTTER

1

Place everything except the salt and butter into the bowl of a mixer equipped with the dough hook. Mix on the first setting for 4–5 minutes until the dough feels springy and fleshy, neither dry nor wet. Water can be added to adjust the hydration, but keep in mind that the butter will add moisture as well.

2

Add the butter and mix until it is fully incorporated, then add the salt little by little until it is mixed in. Place the dough in a Cambro with a lid to cover and let rest at room temperature for an hour.

3

Form 4-ounce pieces of the dough into little torpedo shapes, then brush them with a solution of 4 teaspoons of lye dissolved in a quart of water. Wear rubber gloves and goggles, and be careful of splashing; the lye solution is a strong alkali and can burn your skin and clothes. Sprinkle the loaves with coarse salt and score them with three diagonal slashes, much like a baguette. Bake for 15 minutes at 450°F.

A SPONGE, A MIXTURE OF YEAST, FLOUR, AND WATER LEFT TO FERMENT BEFORE USE, functions like a sourdough starter but with commercial yeast and a shorter fermentation time (between a couple of hours and overnight; Walter likes to let it ripen overnight). A sponge adds a bit of sourdough complexity and some highly developed gluten to a dough. Walter uses a sponge frequently in rolls and pastries; in the latter it contributes an appealingly savory tang that balances whatever sweet components come along for the ride.

Walter's sponge ratio is 1.5:1 flour to water by weight, so to get the 44 ounces needed for the pretzel bread, for example, thoroughly mix 27 oz of flour (half white or AP) with 18 oz of water and a fat pinch of yeast and leave it out, covered, at room temperature overnight. That will yield a little bit more than you need; store the remainder in the fridge for a day or two and add it to your next sponge to give it some extra depth and sourness.

GLUTEN

Celiac Disease, a serious and painful intolerance to gluten, is a real and debilitating ailment that affects about one percent of the population: roughly the same percentage of people who stutter. That should provide a good metric for how common it is. The gluten-free diet, however—another in the seemingly endless series of elimination diets (remember fat in the 1980s?)—represents widespread and unfounded bandwagon-jumping by an awful lot of people, many of whose issues with food may be psychological rather than physiological.

Fish & Game's breads, made from whole, organic grains fermented slowly, are the sort of breads our ancestors ate before commercial yeast, white flour, synthetic pesticides and herbicides, chemical additives, and genetically modified grains transformed bread into the appalling simulacrum of food that most people eat today. The domestication of grains made civilization possible, and their fermentation created leavened bread. (And beer and whiskey, for those of you keeping score at home.) Microbial metabolism makes grains more nutritious and easier to digest; this is why traditional cuisines around the world include some form of fermented grain as a staple. If you want to eliminate something from your diet, start with industrial foods and see how that treats you before you grab hold of the fad du jour.

PARKER HOUSE ROLLS

ABOUT 60 ROLLS

2 LB 1 OZ SPONGE

3 LB 13 OZ AP FLOUR

2 LB WATER

10¼ OZ EGGS

½ OZ YEAST

2 OZ SALT

5 OZ SUGAR

5 OZ POWDERED MILK

1

Place the water, yeast, milk powder, and sponge into a mixer equipped with the dough hook and spin on the second setting. Add the flour, and when the dough forms add the eggs in two batches.

2

When the eggs are fully incorporated add the sugar, then the butter. Once fully blended, let the dough rest in the bowl. Add the salt then work the dough again until it begins to pull away from and clean the sides of the bowl.

3

Let the dough proof for an hour, then cut it into 3-oz chunks. Roll each chunk into a ball, then flatten it into a disc. Dunk each disc in melted butter, fold in half, and nestle into a baking tray so each roll touches its neighbors. Bake at 375°F for 12–15 minutes.

FARMER GROUND

Trumansburg, New York

186 miles from Fish & Game

Walter's extraordinary gifts as a baker make Fish & Game's bread program a highlight of the dining experience, both in the bread basket and featured in various courses during the meal. It should come as no surprise, then, that the flours he uses are grown and milled by passionate New Yorkers in ways that benefit the land and the people who live on it in equal measure. Farmer Ground, based just outside Ithaca, is a collaborative partnership with two sides: a grain-growing operation, focused on producing ripe, organic, high-protein grains ideal for baking, and a milling plant designed to grind these carefully grown grains into flours well suited to a variety of culinary applications.

Thor Oeschner (pronounced "Tor") is the farmer in Farmer Ground. Besides the 1200 acres he either owns or leases, he contracts with other farmers to grow various grains to his specifications. Many of these farmers, like Oeschner himself, got into grain by growing animal feed. Grain for human consumption, however, especially flour, demands more exacting standards for ripeness, moisture levels, and protein content. Bread flour needs gluten, that much-maligned (mostly spuriously) protein, for its elasticity and rising power. Farmer Ground pays a premium for high-protein grain. Sprouting degrades baking quality, so wheat must be harvested at about 16 percent water and quickly dried down for storage to ensure peak performance. It's a steep learning curve: "While we're figuring out what conditions make for good food-quality grains, they're figuring out their businesses, how to harvest and dry grain quickly. Wheat is not as easy as corn, which dries fast."

Oeschner's farm, about fifteen minutes from the mill over some damn scenic roads, houses the cleaning and drying machines that process the grain for storage and eventual grinding. The principle, the same since agriculture was invented, is simple: clean off any dirt and detritus (careful work with the combine does a good job threshing away the chaff) and then dry the grain so it's shelf stable and won't sprout or grow mold during storage. They still use a cleaner built in 1910, which does a handsome job—that diligent harvesting makes for pretty clean grain to begin with—and the technology hasn't changed much since then: a series of screens, from coarser to finer, and a fan to blow lighter matter away. All the chaff, and the hulls from the mill, are sold as animal feed. There's no waste.

After cleaning, the grain travels through a slanted cylinder of two concentric spinning screens that separate out hulls and weed seeds. From there, it's a short trip to the dryer. Drying temperature varies according to each type of grain, and precise control is crucial; buckwheat must be dried below 100°F or the groat (seed) darkens and the germ is damaged. Grain saved as seed for the next crop must be dried even more gently. Buckwheat, by the way, is not related to wheat; it's actually a broadleaf plant that produces a high-protein groat with plenty of flavor but no gluten. The grains, which look like fat black little tetrahedra out of the combine, reveal plump beige groats once hulled. A lot of buckwheat flour's dark color comes from the hull; how much is left in the grind influences the shade, from dark grey to pale dun, in the finished product.

Greg Mol has years of experience as a farmer, including significant time spent at Roxbury Farm in Kinderhook before he moved to the Finger Lakes. He runs the milling half of the business, and it's a handful. Managing the grain orders requires planning two years in advance: "We're planting now [October] for harvest next August, which has to last until following August when we grind it." This long lead time can be an impediment to growth; initially they didn't contract for enough grain and couldn't meet the demand. Lining up supply has been the main challenge so far, since there's not a lot of high-protein grain being grown organically in the region. The increasing number of small distilleries also compete for grain, and they can pay more for lower quality. After supply, the main limit is milling capacity; they have more or less hit the ceiling on quantity without an equipment upgrade.

The mill, surrounded on three sides by fields, is housed in an anonymous beige metal-sided building with a cluster of shiny silos at one end. When the machines are running, on three floors that open onto the warehouse space, it's good and loud inside, full of ducts and chutes and shuddering hoppers of grain slowly emptying into hungry milling machines. Dust collectors, like you would see in a woodworker's shop, keep the air largely free of flying flour, but a film of it still coats every surface. Leading to the bulging canvas bags of one such unit, two lengths of flexible duct are spliced together with heavy wire and a worn piece of old denim cut from a pair of jeans.

Farmer Ground's mill grinds between a quarter and a half ton of grain per hour, which sounds like a lot until Mol explains that the next larger size mill in the region grinds 4–5 tons per hour, which is still very small in today's world of industrially grown and processed commodity crops. Above that loom facilities that grind ten tons an hour, 24 hours a day. That's a tractor-trailer every couple of hours. And there are bigger facilities out in the Midwest. Much bigger. To illustrate the scale of the operation, Bread Alone, a Hudson Valley-based organic bakery, uses a trailer full of flour every week or two. At its current capacity, Farmer Ground could just about supply them, using their entire output, leaving nothing for anyone else.

Their product line includes cornmeal, buckwheat, all-purpose, white, whole wheat, half white, and both white and whole wheat pastry flour. The half white—ground with the germ intact, thus possessing an appetizing buff color—is most interesting, with the flavor and nutrition of whole wheat but the versatility and rise of white. The half white forms the basis for Walter's sourdough starter and many of his loaves and rolls. It's also easier for the mill to produce: everybody wins!

Farmer Ground has no trucks of its own. Their not-so-secret weapon, Mol says, without which they may never have gotten off the ground, is Regional Access, a homegrown business specializing in organic products from the Finger Lakes, headquartered only five miles down the road and distributing throughout New York State. "It's tough to say if this ever would have worked without them. Now we're big part of their lineup."

After mentioning plans to install solar panels on the roof, Mol describes their ideal goal as finding a sweet spot where they're small-scale enough to ensure artisanal quality but large enough to remain viable in a world dominated by giants. Oeschner finds himself motivated by more than simple numerical measurements of quantity and quality. Enlisting his fellow farmers to grow organic grain and seeing that they're paid a fair price for it drives him as much as the ongoing challenge of producing the best grain possible: "If I can make a living and help others to do the same, then I've done my job."

№ 27

Farmer Ground's high protein flour is designed for sturdy peasant loaves like the *pain au levain*. Making airy, tender laminated doughs with it, therefore, requires advanced baking chops, a light touch, and plenty of time. Walter's croissants and Danish, which he's been making on Saturday mornings for sale at Rubiner's in Great Barrington, possess all the qualities that the great flour imparts, but conveyed within a flaky matrix of buttery decadence. The trick is to let the dough rest for significant periods at several stages of the process.

DANISH AND CROISSANTS

12 SERVINGS

This dough is essentially brioche, which is then layered with butter and folded to create many thin layers of dough separated by equally thin layers of butter. The yeast in the dough produces carbon dioxide, creating bubbles of gas that make the dough rise, and the water emulsified inside the butter boils, creating steam, which causes the thin layers of flour to expand away from each other.

DOUGH:

2 LB AP FLOUR

12 OZ MILK

2 OZ EGGS

5½ OZ SUGAR

1 OZ SALT

½ OZ YEAST

1½ OZ BUTTER

22 OZ SPONGE

SPONGE:

13½ OZ AP FLOUR

8½ OZ UNCHLORINATED WATER

1¹⁄₁₆ OZ YEAST

1

To make the sponge, dissolve yeast in water, then mix flour in well. Leave out at room temperature, covered, overnight.

2

Combine all dry ingredients except the salt, and whisk all wet ingredients except the butter together. Add wet to dry and mix well, then add salt and butter and mix again.

3

Turn dough out onto lightly floured work surface and pat it firmly into a rectangle about 1½" thick. Wrap tightly and refrigerate overnight.

LAMINATION

4

For lamination, the butter's temperature is crucial; it needs to be the consistency of modeling clay. If it's too cold, it will puncture the dough. If it's too warm, it will be an ungovernable disaster. Dough and butter should both be 60°F. If you feel any hard lumps, use your hand to warm the spot with a bit of pressure, smoothing it out.

5

Between two sheets of parchment, roll butter out into a rectangle the same size as the dough. Place dough on floured surface, put the sheet of butter on top, and fold the rectangle in thirds along the short axis like a letter. Roll it back out to the original size and return it to the fridge.

Rest it in the fridge for 30–60 minutes between foldings; too long and it will get too stiff to roll out smoothly and need to sit at room temp for a bit.

6

Bring it out and fold it two more times, but these folds should be double: again folding along the short axis, fold the top and bottom quarters toward the center so they meet in the middle. Roll the slab back to the original size after each folding, then wrap and refrigerate overnight.

7

TO SHAPE THE DANISH, roll the dough out into a sheet between 1⁄8" and 1⁄4". Cut it into 3-inch squares and fold the corners in toward the center so you end up with an octagon. For extra credit, and to really let the dough attain maximum coherence, cover the shaped pastries and rest them overnight in the fridge one more time.

Fill the little wells in the center with the fruit, jam, or cheese of your choice, brush the top of the dough with an egg wash, and bake in a pre-heated oven for 5 minutes at 400°F. rotate the baking sheet and lower the heat to 375° for about 10 more minutes. This recipe yields about one dozen 3" × 3" squares.

8

FOR CROISSANTS, use a croissant cutter on the sheet after rolling it out. Take each triangle, point facing away from you, and pull the two close corners gently apart. Roll the wide end away from you, toward the point, pressing slightly on the roll so the layers bond together. Bake as you would the Danish.

MATFER
MADE IN FRANCE
G 01

HONEY

Early October 2014 saw the first honey harvest. Beekeeper Steve Melnyk and Jori suited up, pulling frames of comb from the hives and stacking them in plastic tubs. The six hives yielded five gallons of honey, a healthy amount but less than half the quantity required for honey autonomy. The bees actually produced much more than five gallons, but it's vitally important to leave plenty of honey in the hives so they have sufficient food to survive the long winter. Steve believes strongly in no chemical treatments—many keepers use antibiotics and pesticides to prevent foul brood and varroa mites, two common afflictions—so the honey is raw and organic.

The following week, after carefully cutting both ends off all the hexagonal cells that make up the comb, Steve fired up the extractor. A fat drum of stainless steel about three feet across and the same height, it stands on legs so a bucket can fit below the spout at the bottom. The frames of comb sit vertically in slots that radiate out from the central shaft like spokes, and the motor spins them hard to pull the honey from the cells. It takes several hours, increasing the speed gradually, to pull all the sticky liquid gold from the frames. The honey quickly found its way onto the menu, most noticeably in the form of a thick and fiery hot paste made with lemon drop chilies and cider vinegar that has appeared in dishes as diverse as goat tartare and a new cocktail that also uses honey syrup to sweeten a rather tart and unusual beverage.

CHILIES

After the essential trio of fish sauce, vinegar, and maple, chilies represent another key component of Zak's touchstone flavor architecture. Besides their heat, which can range from a subtle tingle to an outright emergency (though not so much in Fish & Game's food compared to the Fatty fare of yore) the many varieties of chili each add their own flavor to condiments and finished plates alike. While the food is not overtly Southeast Asian anymore, a dish or two on every menu will jump up and bite you back with some insistent, lingering heat.

JORI'S SAMBAL

ABOUT 8 PINTS

10 LB SWEET CALABRIAN CHILIES, GRILLED

1 LB RED CAYENNE CHILI, FRESH

1 HEAD FRESH DUG GARLIC

2 LARGE SWEET WHITE ONIONS

½ CUP FISH SAUCE

APPLE OR PEACH PECTIN

The first year, Jori made a sambal with grilled Calabrian chilies, puréed with garlic and onion. To thicken it, she used pectin from apples from the trees in the yard: cooked, mashed, and hung in a jelly bag for 48 hours to extract the juice. She then reduced the juice by half, poured over the chili paste, added fish sauce to taste, then boiled and canned the mixture. The following year was a terrible year for apples; she used peaches instead.

1

Grill the Calabrian chilies and get some nice roasty blisters all over them. Remove the stems and coarsely chop the peppers along with the onions, garlic, and cayenne chilies. Add all the chopped ingredients to a food processor and pulse until it looks like chunky salsa, then transfer to a mixing bowl with the fish sauce and allow the flavors to marry at room temperature while you reduce the pectin (step 3).

2

Add the fruit pectin to a pot and simmer to reduce by half. Add the chili mixture to a large pot and while stirring constantly, bring to a boil and allow to simmer for 10 minutes. Pour the hot pectin in the chili mixture and stir all together. Adjust seasoning with fish sauce and transfer to an airtight jar in the fridge.

3

PECTIN:

Gather around 10 pounds of unripe peaches or wild apples. Remove the pits or seeds and roughly chop the flesh. Add to a large stock pot with enough water to half cover the chopped fruit. Simmer the fruit, mashing it down and stirring every now and then. Once soft, transfer the mash to a damp cheesecloth and tie up to make a sack. Hang the sack over a bowl for 24 hours. Reserve the liquid for the sambal and make apple or peach butter with the mash... don't be a dick and waste it.

CIDER MASH

One fall, Zak gathered all the ugly old apples from their property and threw them in a big whiskey barrel to ferment under a weighted lid. By the end of the following summer, they had reduced to a thick and pungent goop that Jori and Kalas squeezed through a burlap sack. (The broken cider press lurked nearby, mocking their exertions.) The 50-gallon cask of apples yielded about 25 gallons of a cloudy brown liquid roughly halfway between cider and vinegar in flavor. This they bottled in carboys, with airlocks, for further fermentation.

The same barrel, still with about five gallons of the apple mash in the bottom, then got promptly crammed with 90 pounds of assorted fresh hot chilies, mostly from Honey Dog Farm in Hillsdale: jalapeño, cyclone, red flame, cayenne, chimayo, Georgia flame, red rocket, and padrón, plus five percent salt by weight, and then topped up with newly pressed cider from Vermont. By the time this chili mash is ready, it will have been two years in the making.

Fermented mash is much more useful than dried chilies. The chilies' significant heat becomes amplified: sharp with vinegar and rich in funk. A concoction prepared thus brings multiple useful qualities to whatever dish it touches: spice, acidity, and that whiff of controlled decomposition that adds a hint of the sublime to every meal. Fermenting chilies in cider also results in three marvelously useful products: the mash, which gets blended into a smooth and fiery paste; a salty chili vinegar, a profound hot sauce that needs no further embellishment; and hot and tangy powder made by dehydrating the seeds and skins caught by the food mill. This is the embodiment of one hundred percent yield and of adding enormous value through microbial metabolism.

LITTLE MISS MUFFET

This complex drink began with a simple error. Madison came in early one day, by mistake; she thought she had a meeting. Zak mentioned an idea about combining husk cherries and mezcal. They got to work.

The initial combination needed more body and acidity, so they added ricotta whey from the kitchen; Jori had preserved fennel in it, so that herbal anise note lurked around the edges of the sour, cloudy liquid. To make it a bit thicker, they blended some of the poached fennel into the whey and added a dab of the viscous (and vicious) lemon drop chili purée made with some of the newly harvested honey. (Not realizing that the chilies in question pack serious heat, Madison, upon first seeing the jar enticingly labeled “Lemon Drop,” took a big swipe on her finger and tasted it. Hilarious discomfort ensued.) The drink took shape over a couple of weeks: that first session with Zak, then the following week with Jori, and then final refinements a few days later.

The problem with using the preserved fennel whey was that opening a jar meant the fennel also had to get used somehow, and Kevin didn’t want to run fennel for the whole time the drink was on the menu. To solve this, they began blending fennel fronds in with fresh ricotta whey to achieve the same flavor. As the season progressed, the husk cherries ripened and lost the slightly green, vegetal taste they had at the drink’s inception. To compensate for the fruit’s uncomplicated and slightly flabby sweetness, they added a little bit of tomatillo—a close relative, but avowedly savory—to bring back that tight delineation of flavor. (Husk cherries, also known as ground cherries, are actually nightshades like tomatoes and peppers.)

While the ingredient list is mostly different, this drink has much in common with Where There’s Smoke There’s Fire, the restaurant’s signature drink for the first year and a half and itself a descendant of the Fatty-era Chupacabra. Besides the smoky mezcal (and it’s the same one) there’s a savory, saline profile with a sharp chili edge that hones one’s appetite in an unexpected fashion. This is the green curry to that other cocktail’s red, the starboard to its port: a fascinating manifestation of the fundamental flavors that undergird a menu asserting themselves quite handsomely in a glass.

1 DAB LEMON DROP CHILI PASTE

1 BAR SPOON HONEY SYRUP
(1:1 honey and water)

.75 OZ FENNEL WHEY

1 OZ HUSK CHERRY JUICE

1.5 OZ VIDA MEZCAL

2 DASHES FENNEL BITTERS

1

Combine all and stir with ice. Strain into a rocks glass with a 2 × 2" ice cube and garnish the top of the cube with fresh calendula petals.

2

LEMON DROP CHILI PASTE is easily made by stemming, seeding, and weighing a quantity of chilies. Steam them for half an hour at 212°F, then purée in blender with proportionate weights of the other ingredients, using the ratio of 32 oz chilies : 8 oz honey : 16 oz cider vinegar : 1 tablespoon salt. Put in jars and freeze.

ETCETERA FARM

Hillsdale, New York

15.4 miles from Fish & Game

Subtropical crops like ginger, turmeric, and rice normally fall within the list of standard exemptions that even devout locavores allow themselves. Though the hills of Columbia County sit a world away from the terraced paddies of Asia, some enterprising local farmers are growing these and other products with remarkable success. Since so much of Zak's culinary DNA involves spices and rice, the fact that a source—an organic, hand-harvested source—for some of these staples exists just up the road is a pretty big deal.

Yung Yuk and his wife Jeana Park live and farm on a ten-acre parcel in Hillsdale, between the Taconic Parkway and the Massachusetts line. About three acres are cultivated, while the rest is forest and wetland. They began farming in 1998; before moving here, the couple were businesspeople out in Los Angeles. Burned out on office jobs, they wanted to farm. They chose this spot specifically for the four seasons and bountiful water: very unlike LA, but not so different from their native Korea.

It's tough soil, strewn with rocks: far from the archetype of soft, black bottomland dirt. Though those rocky obstacles make for difficult digging, the clay content of the soil and high water table courtesy of their pond and marshland make for excellent water retention, which is ideal for rice paddies. By adding lots of lime and mineral powders, plus copious compost, they produce exemplary vegetables as well: garlic, salad greens, lots of cabbage for kimchi, minari (water dropwort, a popular herb in Korea) and a field of soybeans. Two large greenhouses provide an ideal climate for tomatoes, peppers, ginger, and turmeric.

Because they must be flooded to specific depths at different times, rice paddies need to be absolutely level: no more than a half inch of difference in altitude between one corner and its opposite. Yung does it all, with little help, using a pick, shovel, wheelbarrow, and hose level. The strains of short-grain rice they grow are adapted to a northern climate and perform well; each fall they harvest

MAY 1
soak rice grains

5 days
plant germinated grain, flood paddies to 2 inches

60 days
flood paddies to 5 inches

700–800 pounds of rice from the three paddies—roughly an eighth of an acre total—which adds up to about 500–600 pounds once hulled. They hull it in small batches, with an old machine, to order or as needed. Fish & Game buys just about all the rice they don't keep for themselves.

Because their land lies so far from the regions where rice is traditionally grown, weeds that are unknown in Asia, like sedge, present a problem. Yung tried floating peat moss in the paddies, and his wife tried growing duckweed—both strategies intended to block any light from reaching weeds below the surface of the water. These experiments failed, so he uses a Korean-made device that resembles a pontoon boat for the business end of a weed whacker, allowing it to float between rows of rice. While effective, he bemoans the fact that it's motorized, and precludes any conversation while working: "It's kind of loud; it ruins the sense of community."

Unlike other farms the restaurant buys from, Etcetera Farm is first and foremost a subsistence operation. The couple, assisted by their two children (and Jeana's parents in the summer) grow the bulk of this food for themselves. What they don't eat, they sell at their roadside stand, to restaurants, and at the Berkshire Co-op in Great Barrington. A farm like this is self-limiting without extra labor, Yung says, because "quality comes from hand work." They pick produce twice a week in season, harvesting everything manually, making repeated passes and only taking what's perfectly ripe on a given day. They keep the blemished product for themselves. With no walk-in or big cooler, and just one small chest fridge for delicate mesclun, everything must be delivered the morning after it's harvested.

They plan to add another paddy; rice is a profitable crop and there's room to expand. But more production means more work, and he says life is "more relaxing without employees." Part of the project consists of trying to find the perfect spot on the work/rest continuum, where they have enough to live on but don't have to toil all the time. One gets the sense, listening to him, of being privy to portions of an ongoing inner monologue as he ruminates on his seemingly constant state of doubtful contentment—pleased in that he wouldn't have it any other way, yet resigned to the permanent difficulties of the lifestyle. His notion of subsistence extends to mind as well as body: a desire not only to live off the land but to have a life defined by obstacles, by challenges, and to have their manual removal or pragmatic solution supply the satisfaction necessary for fulfillment.

Winter, while the farm is dormant, is a time for paperwork (which certified organic farms often find themselves buried in) plus felling and chopping trees for the following winter's firewood, and for fermenting denjang (the Korean version of miso) from their soybeans. Standing on frozen ground, pointing out a marshy spot at the edge of the woods, which looks to a layman like the perfect spot for the new paddy, he says "I want to keep the marsh. it's a good buffer, and we get so much wildlife: frogs, birds." Turning to indicate a sloping strip of meadow between the wetland and the chicken yard, he continues: "I'm going to dig here instead."

140 days
begin drying paddies

160 days
harvest, drying

180 days
hulling begins, continues through winter

CONGEE

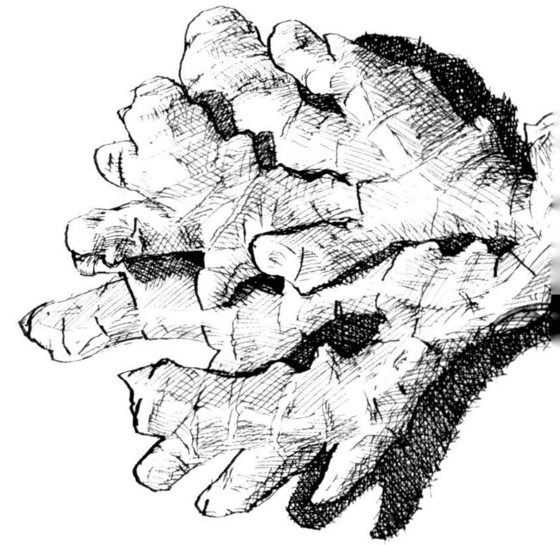

Congee is Chinese soul food: rice cooked in lots of water until it breaks down to a mushy porridge. Versions of rice porridge exist all over Asia, with as many variations of toppings and condiments as there are people cooking. Wherever it's eaten, though, it is renowned as healing food: easy to digest and deeply nourishing.

Zak likes to eat congee for breakfast, usually made from leftover rice and topped with bits and pieces of dinner: some refried pork belly, a few brussels sprouts, a grip of pickles, a spoon of fiery sambal. It appears regularly on the menu as well; the comforting texture and infinitely malleable flavor profile make it an excellent showcase for Yung's rice and other choice ingredients.

1

There's a setting on the rice maker for congee; it requires cooking rice in twice the regular amount of water one would normally use. For Etcetera's short-grain brown rice that would be a 4:1 water to rice ratio. Using brown rice instead of white allows more grain flavor and al dente character to remain in the finished dish; Fish & Game's congees, though soupy, still offer a grainy bite.

2

On pickup, the soft rice gets quickly simmered in an equal amount of stock, flavored with whatever the dish requires—like ginger, also from Etcetera—then topped with a piece of protein, often crispy fish or steamed clams (or both) snuggled up against a fermented vegetable and topped with a garnish of some fresh herb or sprout if available. When shellfish are steamed, the wine or brine they're steamed over will be stirred into the rice before plating.

PIERRE FENALS

Saint-Aubin, France

3,376 miles from Fish & Game

Many natural wines possess a particular funky, cloudy, or otherwise obvious quality that marks them as having been made that way. For aficionados, these attributes are features, not bugs; those unusual flavors, colors, and occasional effervescence mark the juice as authentic. Pierre Fenals's wines bear none of these marks. Crystal clear, tightly focused, and deeply expressive of their various terroirs, they show no signs of having been made without any chemical interventions whatsoever.

Tanned, bald, with a closely trimmed silver mustache and an avuncular demeanor, Pierre Fenals grins broadly and often: the smile of a man who has found his calling, and who pursues it with a thoroughgoing passion and diligent attention to detail. He farms biodynamically and uses no sulfur, no commercial yeast, no chaptalization, no additives, and no fining or filtration. He makes 35,000–40,000 bottles of Burgundy annually from ten different appellations, ranging from a humble Bourgogne Aligoté to grand cru Corton-Charlemagne. His wines, all bottled under the Gothic arch of his Maison en Belles Lies label, can be found on the lists of two dozen Michelin-starred restaurants.

Though his degree was in molecular biology, Fenals's first career was in fashion, in Paris, on the business side. At fifty-two, he quit. "Fashion is difficult, and superficial, especially once you get older. I had enough and left." He earned a degree in oenology, moved to Burgundy, and went to work laboring in various vineyards, learning with his hands for four years. In 2008, he bought his winery, a former warehouse with a huge basement, and a few vineyards. Now he owns four hectares and rents another three. The vineyards he owns, he works almost entirely by himself; the parcels he rents are tended to his exacting specifications.

His facility sits on a hill near his house in the tiny village of Saint-Aubin, tucked into a curving rift near the southern end of the Côte de Beaune, a couple of miles up the D906 from Chassagne-Montrachet. The main floor, where fruit is juiced and initially fermented, is populated by presses and vats: stainless for the whites, old oak for the reds. Each parcel gets its own vat, though the bigger ones require two. The lower level, a vast subterranean concrete vault, houses long rows of oak barrels, where the cool temperature makes for long, slow fermentations averaging about two years. By the time he bottles, he says, there are hardly any lees left; "it's all eaten by the wine."

The resulting clarity is one of his many priorities. "I want wine to be natural, but I want it to look good too. We consume everything with our eyes first. I want it water-clear, and full of vital energy." He launches into an enthusiastic demonstration of the ways in which he imbues wine with this energy. Explaining a method he developed with a colleague, adding a tiny amount of wine from a strong earlier vintage to each barrel before adding the new juice "to give it information," he uses a tiny pipette to count out 18 drops into a small vial before shaking it vigorously. "That's what I put in each barrel" He then takes small crystalline flakes of dried solids from the bottom of the barrels, shakes them vigorously in the vial with a bit of water, and adds that as well. The crystals help dissolved solids to form similar aggregates, he says, which precipitate to the bottom and clarify the wine.

Whether or not these methods make a meaningful difference, it's plain that they do no harm; his wines are as limpid as the most ruthlessly sterile-filtered industrial versions. A better explanation for the purity of his offerings might simply be the extraordinary combination of passion, skill, and fastidious attention to detail at every stage that he brings to his craft. He uses natural corks, for example, but has them branded with a hot iron instead of printed with ink; he says that the ink changes the flavor of the wine.

Biodynamic agriculture places great importance on the moon and its tidal pull on the water in living things. Fenals lets his red grapes macerate whole for one lunar cycle before pressing them, picking them during a rising moon and then pressing when it sets. He macerates whole bunches, never destemming his reds; besides increasing the aromatic complexity of the wines, this method keeps plenty of space around the fruit for gas to fill, producing excellent results. "C'est nickel," he beams, "nickel" being slang for perfect, immaculate.

In keeping with his meticulous nature, during vinification he tastes every day, at the same hour, in the same order, using the same glasses. Once the wine is in barrel, he follows the same method, but weekly. Approaching harvest, he will crush a few glasses' worth of juice to test for brix and pH so he can harvest at the optimal time, but otherwise his only tool is his tongue. He says that natural wine self-regulates when it comes to alcohol, "but you must pick when it's ripe, even if that means waiting until the first week of November to harvest sometimes. I'm not looking for alcohol, but the fruit must be ripe. It can be twelve percent but still not ripe." Like most natural winemakers, Fenals never crops his vines. "Biodynamic vines produce the correct amount of fruit; if you cut fruit it throws the whole plant out of balance." Because they're fertilized only with compost, the vines do not produce more fruit than the soil can support (as they do with synthetic fertilizers).

His Aligoté, at just eleven percent alcohol, is a simple melody of fruit braided around a bright acidic backbone. Not unlike a Muscadet, it calls for oysters: a reminder that the whole region sits on limestone and that limestone is, after all, nothing more than many millennia of molluscs. His Monthélie, at twelve percent, balances calcareous austerity with a nose of bright fruit. He describes the vineyard: 350 meters high, cool, chalky. The chalk, the altitude, the low yield of about 42 hectoliters per hectare: "It's all there, in the wine." The Santenay packs more punch, literal and figurative; a bit more body, and pronounced mango, banana, and pineapple notes. One can taste the depth of the roots as they penetrate deep into the marl and limestone: almost more of a soil for reds. The result wants to lie down for five or ten years to reach maturity.

He says the soils in Maranges, his largest appellation, are particularly hard to work: clay studded with decomposed grey marble, rock hard when it's dry and treacherous when rainy.

Both his Maranges initially possess an appropriately rustic character, which develops dramatically in barrel, losing their angularity and revealing dark fruit, especially black cherry. His premier cru Maranges "Les Clos Roussots" is notably finer and deeper than his Maranges "Le Saugeot." "The vineyards are just a few hundred meters apart from each other, and they're completely different," he remarks, swirling the glass under his nose. "Burgundy's geology and history are the most complicated of any wine region in the world. Only two grapes, and so much variation: even fresh from the press the juices taste incredibly different. It's paradise."

Burgundy, more than any other wine, communicates time as well as place, showing them to be the same thing. All Fenals's vines, owned or rented, are populated with old vines: most over fifty years old, the grands crus more than seventy. So his Corton-Charlemagne contains juice from vines planted before World War II, in a vineyard named for the king who became Holy Roman Emperor in the year 800, pushing their roots deep into the shells of a hundred million years' worth of oysters. The wine delivers complex layers of minerality entwined with elegant acidity and richly detailed fruit, especially in the mid-palate that distinguishes a great wine from a merely good one. The finish lasts and lasts.

An amphora, recently arrived from Italy, sits at the end of a long row of barrels. He doesn't know anyone else in Burgundy using amphoras and is keen to age some Maranges in it. "Clay imparts no flavor, keeps the wine very cool, and the shape of the vessel gently circulates the wine" by convection. Enjoying the notion that such ancient technology can slowly churn its contents using ambient temperature as an engine, he pats the terra cotta approvingly. "It's the industrial processes that I hate." He looks forward to its maiden voyage in the fall.

Transparency, the quality that differentiates his wines from so many of his natural peers', sets his work apart from much Burgundy as well. Handled properly, grapes speak fluent geology; the weather in a given year is merely an affected accent. Let the fungi run the show, as they do in vin jaune, and those flavors dominate. Let bacteria rule, like they do over Beaujolais, and maceration can bigfoot the terroir. Contaminate with commercial yeast, poison the vineyard, filter out the life: every intervention blurs the focus of the grapes' portrait of the soil. Fenals's significant accomplishment—in the planet's greatest wine region, no less—is wines that articulate the variations in geology without distortion; with nothing added to or subtracted from the grapes, their fermented juices become liquid lenses showing what lies beneath the ground, like vivid red and gold x-rays of the Earth's very bones.

Standing among chardonnay vines as the sun drops toward the wooded ridge across the road, he points out the variety of plants and wildflowers that thrive alongside the vines and the beehives he keeps in the overgrown strip (where rabbits, foxes, and birds also live) that wraps around three sides of the vineyard. Then he indicates the chemically treated vineyard immediately adjacent, where everything but the vines is brown and dead. "I can't drink sulfured, chemical wines anymore; they're too heavy, they give me a headache." Though, he admits, pushing a cork back into the Aloxe-Corton to take it home for dinner, "The other day a friend opened a 1986 Saint-Julien, and it was delicious." He smiles. "We finished it."

MENU

WEEK OF SEPTEMBER 27

LAMB TARTARE

This dish opened the meal with minced lamb, hand-cut into a medium dice. Lamb makes a much more interesting tartare than beef, and it can take more seasoning without losing its character.

1

Perfectly cooked meat is an easy sell, but eating it raw offers an atavistic experience, harkening back to the prefire dawn of humanity. Any savagery was well assuaged in this instance by a cohort of highly civilized seasonings: shallots, Jori's sour cherry ketchup, lemon drop chili paste, and pickled mustard seeds. Slices of grilled brioche, which accompany so many dishes at Fish & Game, provided an excellent substrate for the silky meat.

2

Alongside, a jumble of fermented fava beans added a requisite note of microbiological vitality. Jori made these favas by inoculating the beans with *Bacillus subtilis*, bacteria used in Japan to ferment soybeans into a pungent, stringy delicacy. She kept them in a warming drawer at 100 °F for a few days, then let them sit in the fridge.

3

The result was exciting—funky, spicy, and cheesy—but she wanted to experiment some more. Sadly, favas did terribly the following year so she didn't have enough to play with. Stay tuned for project number 712.

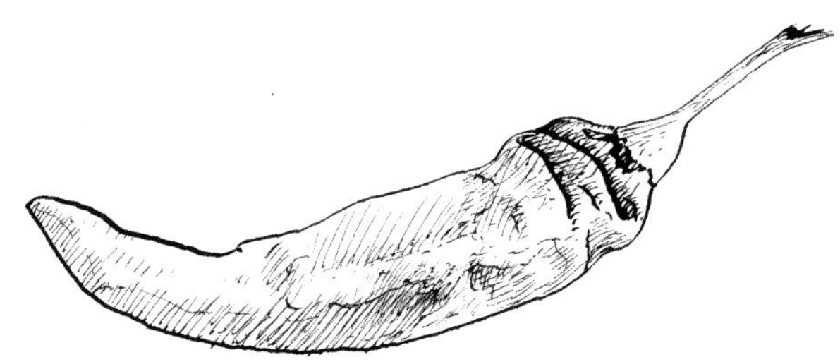

TUNA

A small rectangle of red watermelon looks a lot like a piece of tuna sashimi, and tuna likes fruit, so pairing an assortment of melons with a slab of bluefin belly seemed an appropriate way to honor both ingredients. To add a little heft, heat, and complexity, each plate got a swipe of a mole-type sauce made from grilled tomatillos, poblano chilies, and pumpkin seeds, enriched with pork stock and lardo, and then blended smooth and strained. The sauce hid beneath a tidily geometric arrangement of fish and melons, waiting to surprise the diner with its assertive counterweight to the seemingly simple dish.

Melons can grow up here but require some care and protection to deliver ripe fruit in the short season. Their flavors, not quite tropical, but still exotically perfumed, suit a wide variety of applications both sweet and savory. Indian cream cobra melon, a pale, oblong variety originally from Africa, splits open when ripe; its mottled skin curls back like a cobra's hood. The yellow fruit's flowery quality played nicely with the more familiar flavors of red watermelon and orange cantaloupe, and all three provided a cool contrast to the warm fish and spicy sauce.

CELERIAC

1

A velvety celery root purée, fortified with some potato (about 25 percent) and mounted with copious butter, came to table in a copper cocotte. Atop the luxe tubers, a coarse condiment of charred corn and grilled kohlrabi—the former grilled whole, then stripped of kernels, the latter sliced into rounds and given pronounced grill marks before being diced—plus minced lemon drop chili for heat, all bound together with a deep venison broth flavored with a mixture of wild mushrooms.

2

Mexican sour gherkins tossed in a little chili vinegar with lovage, wild sage, and tarragon provided some greenery and a necessary hit of acidity to this transitional dish; the all-vegetable roster looked back to summer, but the broth spoke pure autumn and the texture purred comfort food.

VENISON

Venison, ground through the large die for more texture, cooked down into a hearty old-school *ragù* with venison stock, red wine, and wild thyme. In parts of Italy, especially around Bologna, one can tell if a family's recipe for *ragù* dates back to the era before Columbus's voyages; if it calls for tomatoes it's "new." This sauce, made of deer meat simmered in deer stock with a few aromatics, took its cue from the ancient tradition.

1

Venison, like tuna, enjoys the company of fruit. Blackcurrants, though domesticated, never lost their wild, foxy, herbal quality, making them an ideal match for deer (and duck). For this sauce, they cooked with maple syrup until they burst, then got puréed and passed through a chinois, with more whole currants added afterward for texture and pop before serving.

2

The pasta recipe was a simple variation of the standard house recipe, using 75 percent spelt flour and the remainder white. The kitchen cut the sheets into large squares, spooning *ragù* onto one piece and then adding another over to cover the meat.

3

To finish, rough chunks of black walnuts added their marvelous flavor and a strong textural contrast to all this tender fare. And borage flowers, among the only true blue foods, make a magical, starry garnish from early summer until the frost takes them.

ONIONS

No ingredient offers as many variations throughout the year as the allium family. From the wild garlic that pops up as soon as the sun hits the ground in March (and that sprouts again in the fall and doesn't die in the winter) to its plumper cousin the ramp, through scallions, garlic, bulb onions, and leeks, these sulfurous lilies put out all year long.

1

This dish celebrated a wide variety, prepared in different ways to showcase their various qualities. Leeks, roasted in embers in the wood oven, become sweet and tender, with an irresistible juiciness.

2

Halved white onions roasted in iron pans to soften a bit and pick up a little color. They got tossed with a little plum jam before plating for a slight sweet-tart accent.

3

Scallions, tossed in a little olive oil and salt, hit the grill and lingered there until they caught an assertive char; this method gives them an addictive quality second only to the leeks.

4

Beneath the vegetables, a fondue made from Comté rinds simmered in cream and then blended and strained. On top, strips of beef heart that smoked on the high grill until just cooked through, adding a rich meaty note to enhance the umami of the alliums and the cheese.

5

And the garnish, finely shredded raw scallion greens, added that delightful bite that makes them such a popular embellishment.

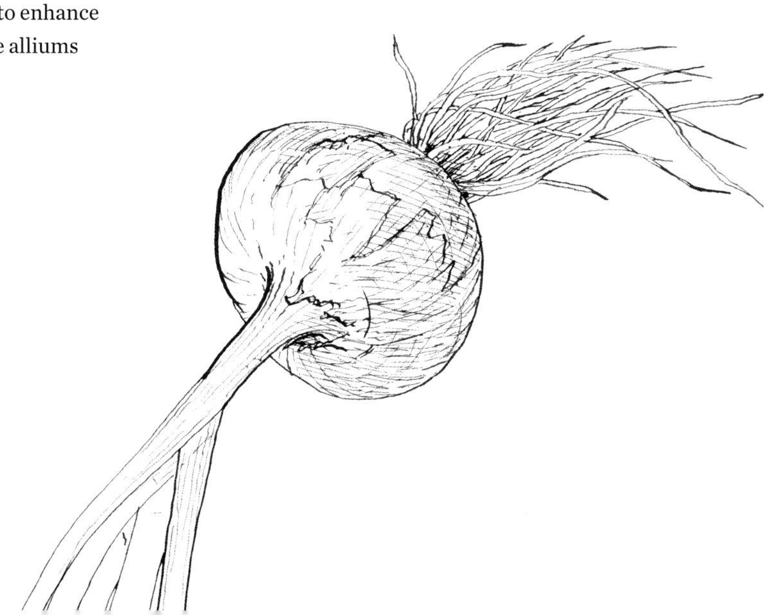

PEACH

With the countdown to the first frost ticking quickly, beautiful fresh peaches glowed like summer's receding taillights. Quartered, brushed with melted butter infused with black garlic and mixed with maple syrup, the slices went on the raclette in the dining room fireplace to catch a whiff of smoke and sizzle a bit to caramelize. Once hot, the peaches plated up with a schmear of Jori's peach butter and, yes, a triangle of grilled brioche because it's just that good.

BLACK GARLIC, caramelized at low heat over the course of months, originated in China. Zak likes to use black garlic in desserts, especially those involving dairy; it contributes a slightly dissonant and complex sweetness, not unlike molasses or tamarind, shaded with a tangy funk and an earthy umami. Think roasted garlic multiplied by ten. It has infused ice cream as well as a pastry cream that accompanied a porridge of whole grains simmered in maple sap.

1

Take whole garlic heads and pack them into a jar to fill it. Close the lid tightly and leave it in a dark room at around 100°F for a year. Good places for this at home might be the corner of your basement where the furnace lives, or on top of your hot water heater. If you have the technology to keep the garlic at 140°F for a month instead, by all means use it.

2

Open the jars after a month and let the cloves dry out a bit for another week or so until they're sticky, black, and about half their original size.

CHERVIL ICE CREAM

The final course involved careful counterpoint by a trio of related tastes: three different licorice-flavored herbs presented in three contrasting forms and textures. The main flavor in anise and fennel comes from anethole, the same molecule responsible for licorice's flavor, while chervil gets much of its character from the closely related compound estragole, also present in tarragon and basil (this accounts for its rounder, greener taste).

1

The cake used the same recipe as the anise hyssop cake on p. 196, but used toasted and ground anise seeds in place of the hyssop leaves. Use one third the amount of seeds since their flavors are so much more concentrated than leaves'.

2

Chervil, one of the four *fines herbes* in French cooking, has a subtle and elegant anise flavor, gentler than tarragon. This ice cream did a brilliant job of presenting that flavor in a correspondingly smooth and sensual form. Make this by infusing the cream with fresh chervil like the angelica gelato on p. 102.

3

The last component was a syrup made from Jori's Cynar, which includes a fair amount of fennel. Reduced gently with a bit of added sugar to an adhesive stickiness, it tied the plate together both literally and figuratively, and added the appealing bitterness of artichokes plus a subtle complexity from all the other botanicals she uses to make the liqueur.

The Elephant and the Snowdrift

ZAK

Mini cyclones of powdery snow whirled across the Taconic Parkway as I drove southbound in the aftermath of yet another weekly snowstorm during the now-legendary February of 2015. The sun was so bright I had both driver- and passenger-side visors down and my eyes cloaked in sunglasses. The driving followed a pattern. I'd hit a drift of snow and hydroplane onto a section of dark, wet pavement saturated with salt and water from a melted drift. The only way to manage this kind of driving is to keep the wheel steady and ride it straight through those moments when a drift throws the car, taunting you to jerk the wheel to recover from what is nothing but a momentary feeling that you've lost control.

The proper response to many situations in the snow can seem counterintuitive, just as the winter with which it comes is so often wrongly identified with isolation. For whatever reason, as I drove from Old Chatham to Hudson along the blustery and ill-kempt Taconic Parkway I was reminded of crossing the Cameron Highlands in the Malay Peninsula. Jori and I were winding our way up and down the heaves of black, baking tar flanked by banana trees and fractured guardrails; in a pinch it was the choice between guardrail or cracks and craters in unstable asphalt certain to swallow a Proton Saga's front end.

Driving through the bright and swirling snow recalled the caution with which I rounded the hairpin corners of those overgrown jungle roads, driving just slowly enough to avoid rear-ending an elephant in a chance encounter. On one such precarious descent, thanks to a communicative flash of the brights by an oncoming truck hauling a load of durian, we slowed, then stopped, our progress halted by an elephant crossing. He was in no hurry. Therefore, neither were we.

Just as during the extreme cold and snowy days of upstate New York, not much happens quickly in the tropics. And when an elephant's involved, we're all on his time. Jori approached the elephant with arm extended; her intention to touch it, her eagerness to find some way to communicate was clear. This was a wild elephant, a ton if an ounce. Reflexively, I uttered a word of caution. Then, heatedly, I warned. Without certainty or experience I spurted out some simple math concerning probability and size difference, as if that brought an authority to my concern. Heeding my admonitions she withdrew and we silently watched as the elephant watched us and moved on his way.

When I recently mentioned this memory to Jori she wrote to me, "It wanted me to touch it. It spoke to me." I believe her. I've always believed her. That's why we're here now, in the winter. The town, the county we call home, where we spend our money, grow our food, raise our animals, work with our friends and our farmers, where business is now slow but where, still, the work is happening, in this cold town this winter we are speaking to each other a little bit more than before. Fish & Game is unique in this county, this valley, this state. Hell, it's unique in the whole country. If we hadn't had the requisite experience, we might have approached our business with the reticence I expressed to Jori during her moment with the elephant. Instead, we are mapping a new paradigm. Building not just a restaurant, but a community. The Valley spoke to us, Columbia County in particular. And it wanted us to touch it, to feel it, to work with it to discover its flavors, to understand its rhythms, its terroir. No restaurant anywhere nearby works with the earth the way we do. Many tip the hat but few roll up their sleeves and truly dig in to divine the spirit and the flavor of our land.

When the ground is frozen and the digging slows, we have conversations. When the ground is soft and the migration from the city resumes once again, we're head down like draught horses, "pulling that eternal plough." But come winter, we can lift our heads for a moment and discover, contemplate and discuss the great work done by those who, through business, have become our friends. Our favorite venture through which we've discovered so many great artists and farmers is the Hudson River Exchange. HRE started with an explosion of conversation between bright, design-savvy and like-minded creative folks who are building not just marketplaces for artisans but a forum for Hudson Valley craft.

They are nurturing creativity, bringing together a strikingly talented mix of artisans. Because of them, I look around our restaurant and my home and see how their efforts have brought us so many varied goods and pieces that enhance our spaces and even improved the manner, through primitive yet superior tools, in which we eat. Their market, run in conjunction with the Basilica, is the highlight of the beginning of the cold season. During the darkest days of the harsh 2014–15 winter, Tony Stone of the Basilica poured an ice rink inside their giant space. He thought it was a cool idea and then, as clever and handy as he is and with a strong enough ego to back up his skills, he simply fucking poured an ice rink. This is speaking to the elephant.

The snow softens hard acoustics. Tires squeak along and people walk plush. There's no click, clomp, or clod. And Mona, Kate and Sarah, soft and easy, with competence and refined taste, quietly opened Talbott & Arding and deftly filled a need in Hudson that has our crew as happy and snacky as one could expect when the wind chill is -25°F. Melissa Auf der Maur, also of the Basilica, and I organized a few folks to gather and chat and skate on their industrial rink à la minute. I was overjoyed to be doing something in Hudson that was not of or about the restaurant. Kevin, Mike, and I made chowder. Jeff and Nina of Swoon made meatballs. Stella made lentil dip.

We socialized outside of Fish & Game on a day off. We lifted up our heads long enough to smile at others whom we admire, even hold in awe and, unexpectedly, we felt the warmth and appreciation they have for us. These people, who are elevating Hudson's cultural relevance, told us that they have never seen anyone so devoted to the work we do from scratch day in and day out, nor have they seen a restaurant with such a commitment to a place as Fish & Game. To find such colleagues among the doers, we are honored. We have recognized the winter as the time to approach the elephant and not veer off, lured by the siren call of a snowdrift or slow winter business, but to stay steady and believe Jori, believe in Hudson, believe in our community. The soil, the mission, the work, and the uncompromising commitment to quality all resonate and grow stronger, still, in the winter.

Winter

WINTER'S AUSTERITY PRESENTS A CHALLENGE TO THE LOCAVORE LIFE. It requires careful planning and frantic canning in equal measure if the preserved harvest in all its forms is to last until the first baby greens mark the arrival of spring. The crawlspace beneath the restaurant's kitchen, a cramped and uninviting space, becomes a gleaming trove of jewel-bright jars: vivid colors and flavors banked against the chilly privations of the season. Jori spends much of the fall pickling, canning, and otherwise preserving masses of fruit and produce, and the menu now features that bounty in all its forms: kimchis, vinegars, mostardas, pickled chilies, tomatoes, nubbly hands of ginger in syrup suspended like specimens in formaldehyde.

These products, processed by microbial metabolism or simply by boiling in sterilized jars, harken back to the necessary techniques used in wintry climes the world over for preventing starvation during the barren months. But eating these foods is not merely making do, settling for pallid simulacra of summer's glory. Many of these products, especially the fermented ones, gain all kinds of complexity by virtue of the process; the banking metaphor is especially apt because the act of preservation adds interest, literal and figurative, to the original fruit or vegetable. Jams and pickles benefit from extra sweetness or acidity (or both in mostardas), and a funky profundity enriches and enlivens vinegars and other ferments. Preservation represents the best possible argument for frugality and makes the minimalism that winter enforces a cause for celebration and innovation. Would you rather eat a cabbage or a jar of kimchi?

Fish & Game closes every March, giving the crew some much-needed time off and taking advantage of the slowest part of the year to recharge. Some take trips, some work on other projects, and some are never heard from again. All who return have plenty of energy, and the spring weather mirrors their sunny dispositions; by April the snow vanishes in the glare of the strengthening sun.

April also marked a significant shift that during the second winter, when Jori assumed full creative control of the bar program. Many of her liqueurs and potions had matured and were ready for deployment, so she and Madison got to work developing a variety of wholly original drinks. All deceptively simple, all with an enticingly medicinal aspect—reminding us of the apothecary origins of vermouth, and gin, and bitters, and cola for that matter—these drinks combined quenching refreshment with a bracingly healthful quality, the direct result of their fabrication from organically grown plants, hand-harvested and painstakingly fermented or extracted, using methods both ancient and modern for maximum flavor and refinement.

The Bar

1 OZ LADY JAYNE'S ALCHEMY CYNAR

4 OZ LE MAZEL CUVÉE CHARBONNIÈRES

Jori's Cynar, made from artichokes she grew in the garden (plus many hand-harvested botanicals both wild and domestic) aged for two-and-a-half years in a whiskey barrel. It's not as sweet as Cynar, and an anise flavor balances the artichoke character, pulling the experience somewhat toward Pastis territory.

The Southern Rhône's Domaine Le Mazel is a natural winemaker's natural winemaker. They add nothing at all to their wines at any stage of the process—no yeast, no sulfur, nothing—and they take nothing out via filtration. As a result, their whites often have a nutty, oxidative quality and some residual CO_2: both anathema to conventional winemakers but catnip to naturalists. Their Cuvée Charbonnières, a cloudy, faintly fizzy chardonnay, makes a perfect match for Jori's Cynar. The complex wine, with its supple acidic backbone, provides an elegant armature for the louche liqueur to drape itself seductively across. A little sparkling water enhances the aperitify vibe.

Combine both in a wine glass. Add ice and stir gently. Top with a splash of fizzy water and garnish with a flag of brandied cherries.

JUAN COLLINS

.75 OZ HERB VINEGAR SHRUB
(2:1 vinegar:sugar)*

2 OZ TEQUILA
CIMMARÓN BLANCO

GINGER SODA 1

Tequila and lime go together like peaches and cream, or Peaches and Herb, or herb and sex. Sadly, neither agave nor lime grow locally. A vinegar shrub, however, makes an excellent substitute for citrus, and Jori's herb vinegar picks up on the vegetal notes in the tequila to excellent effect.

Combine and shake with ice. Strain into a rocks glass. Add fresh ice, then top with ginger soda to fill the glass.

**all of Jori's shrub ratios are determined by taste, not some absolute formula. Since the pH, flavor, and intended use of each vinegar differs, each shrub needs to be mixed according to the requirements of those variables.*

Besides canning ginger in syrup, Jori also preserves it in sherry: just pack a jar with washed fresh ginger, then fill it with sherry and keep it in the fridge (it's not shelf stable at room temperature). The ginger retains its clean, sharp taste—almost indistinguishable from fresh—and the sherry acquires a bright gingery note. Jori's gifts include an extraordinary aptitude for creating preserves where the liquid holds as much culinary value as the solid.

This recipe is more of a snapshot; since the pantry contained ginger canned in syrup (1:3 sugar:water), ginger preserved in sherry, and frozen ginger, as the stores depleted the ratio of soda components shifted accordingly. The primary goal, besides delicious food and drink, is always to use everything efficiently so that nothing is wasted (except the customers at the bar who drink all these wonderful cocktails). As spring soldiered on, Jori and Madison tweaked the percentages to account for the fact that the ginger in syrup began to run out while plenty of the ginger in sherry remained.

12 OZ WATER

8 OZ THAWED FROZEN GINGER, CHOPPED

8 OZ JORI'S CANNED GINGER, CHOPPED

6 OZ CANNED GINGER SYRUP

½ TEASPOON SEA SALT

1

Purée all in a blender on maximum, then hang in several layers of cheesecloth or a jelly bag over a bowl for 24 hours. Pour 16 ounces at a time into a siphon and charge with two CO_2 canisters. Keep cold.

DR. MEPHESTO SWIZZLE

All that sherry-preserved ginger (and the gingery sherry itself) also needed something useful to do. Thus was born another drink, which derived principally from Jori's inspiration to infuse booze with turmeric, a relative of ginger purported to possess many medicinal applications in addition to its fetching orange color and appealing taste.

The name for this one comes from *South Park,* specifically "Cartman's Mom Is Still a Dirty Slut" from season two, wherein Doctor Mephesto reveals that Cartman's mom is a hermaphrodite. Turmeric flowers are hermaphroditic, so obviously any drink made with turmeric would logically refer to that canonical opus for its name.

10 DROPS 20 PERCENT SALINE SOLUTION

.5 OZ HUSK CHERRY-TOMATILLO JUICE
(from Little Miss Muffet, see p. 250)

.5 OZ TURMERIC LIQUEUR

.75 OZ BANKS WHITE RUM

1.5 OZ GINGER-INFUSED SHERRY (LUSTAU FINO)

Combine all in a highball glass, fill with crushed ice and swizzle. Garnish with a flower made from thin slices of sherry-preserved ginger.

TURMERIC LIQUEUR

1 QUART

1

Wash and chop fresh turmeric root. Juice in a tincture press, removing as much liquid as possible. Add a pinch of citric acid to maintain color and store the juice in the fridge as you work.

2

Add pressed roots to a quart jar and cover with grain alcohol for 48 hours. Press again and discard solids. Combine alcohol and fresh juice. In a saucepan, combine 1 cup water, 1 cup cane sugar, and 1 cup brown sugar. Boil until dissolved. Add syrup to liquid and shake to combine. Store in a jar out of sunlight.

THE BROWNSVILLE

The first time Jori had tequila mixed with coffee was in Brownsville, Texas, at the southernmost tip of the state. Her dad had a fishing camp in nearby Port Mansfield, so she and her sisters spent a lot of time down there. Shockingly, when she had her tequila and coffee experience, she was underage. Having also grown up drinking the Southern specialty of coffee with chicory root, Jori often likes to balance the rich blend with spices. At home she uses varying combinations of coriander, white peppercorn, fresh rosemary, bay, and cardamom, among others. Sometimes she adds her Lady Jayne's Alchemy bitters as well, lending their delicate aroma to the complex brew.

On first tasting Ransom's sweet vermouth, she immediately wanted to try it with coffee. Coffee is such a versatile flavor, playing equally well with sweet and savory, spices and milk—and of course it revives a flagging spirit—so making a hot coffee cocktail that shows off these affinities seemed like a worthy task. It didn't take long to settle on a sympathetic cohort of spices, apart from which the coffee is prepared according to the standard Chemex method.

The drink resembles mulled wine, with fragrant steam rising off the glass and the coffee's dark brown diluted by the clear tequila and burnished by the red wine to a glowing mahogany. But the fruity vermouth, bright spices, and vegetal tequila all play roles that support coffee's polyvalent complexity, keeping that bouquet center stage. At heart, it's still a cup of coffee. While warming, it's not scalding; the room-temperature spirits mitigate the heat. It's an ideal beverage for a dreary winter afternoon.

Because of the labor and long steep time involved in making the spiced coffee, Madison makes a big batch of it at the beginning of every shift, keeping it chilled in a jar until someone orders one. Then she uses an electric kettle to quickly heat up a drink's worth and assembles the cocktail.

3 BAY LEAVES

7G WHITE PEPPER

2G CARDAMOM PODS

5G CORIANDER SEEDS

77G FINELY GROUND COFFEE

1,145G WATER AT 203°F

1

Lightly crush the spices in a mortar and pour them into the bottom of a Chemex. Put the coffee in the filter and gradually pour the water over the top, stirring the grounds occasionally and adding more water as it subsides.

2

Once all the coffee has drained through, remove the filter and strain the coffee into your drink. If making ahead, pour the coffee (still with spices in it) into a jar. Store the jar in the fridge and reheat individual portions as needed.

.75 OZ RANSOM SWEET VERMOUTH

.75 OZ CIMMARÓN TEQUILA

3

Strain 2 oz of the spiced hot coffee on top. Serve in an absinthe glass on a saucer.

Caveat potor: if you drink too many of these, you'll be hammered but unable to pass out.

KINDERHOOK FARM

Valatie, NY

23 miles from Fish & Game

Though the ground is frozen and seeds are dormant, livestock production continues apace in the Hudson Valley. Kinderhook Farm, situated on about 1200 acres near the eponymous town, provides pastured, grass-fed beef and lamb (and some pork) to restaurants throughout the region while employing five people and keeping a sprawling parcel of gorgeous, undulating land uncontaminated by McMansions.

The farm operates under an Animal Welfare Approved certification, meaning it meets a stringent set of requirements for the animals' health and wellbeing. The sheep eat only pasture and hay from the property, while the cows require some extra hay and baleage bought from nearby farms. They get no grain, though; the Red Devon and Angus breeds they raise build plenty of muscle from grass.

Bought about ten years ago by Steve and Renee Clearman, the farm is run by Lee and Georgia Ranney and three other people. All the employees live on the farm. Like many meat farmers in the area, they spend a lot of time and effort growing the best grass they can; besides pasture mixes, they plant alfalfa, oats, and clover to ensure there's plenty of protein in both fields and hay. Moving the animals through the different pastures ensures good fertilization with manure, and for various far-flung unfenced hayfields they truck in manure composted behind the sheep barn.

The animals live outdoors all year long, though the sheep come into the barn at night for protection against predators. All of this adds up to happy animals, living the way they should. The lamb—from a growing flock of Dorper ewes—is deep red, with abundant fat, and the variety of plants that the animals graze lends the meat a rich, gamy flavor.

We cultivate life to feed on death
and, yet, somewhere along the way so
many of us have become squeamish about
the most natural act of man: survival.

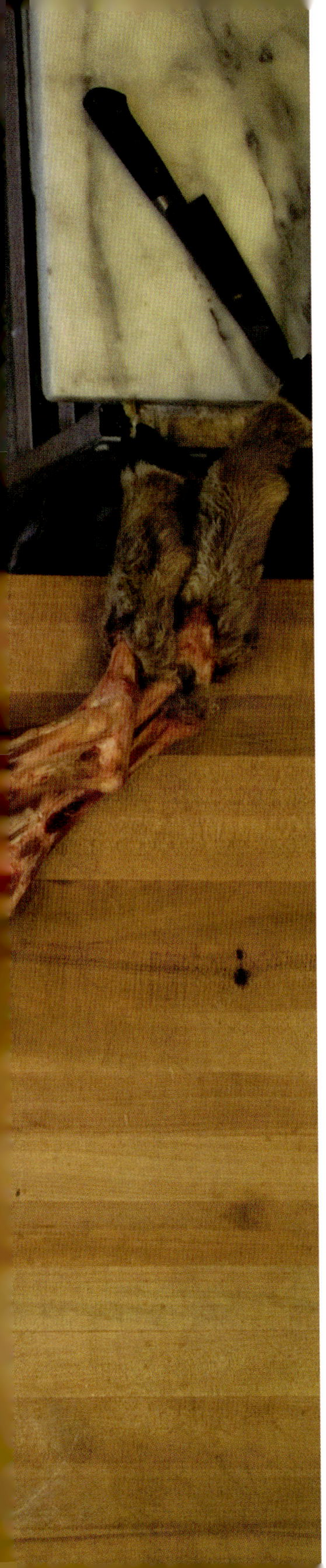

LAMB AND GOAT

No meat has a stronger affinity with herbs and spices, both fresh and dried, than lamb. Tender herbs like chives, chervil, tarragon, and cilantro (and the classic cliché, mint) play off the grassy flavors the animals acquire from grazing, while woody ones (like thyme, rosemary, sage, and oregano) enhance its wilder, gamier edge. Spice-wise, from tagine to gyro to kebab to curry to rendang, there is no point along the sprawling ancient silk road/spice route where lamb does not taste right at home. Lamb also thrives in the Hudson Valley.

Any serious meat farmer will admit that she's really a grass farmer; the animals grow themselves given quality pasture. Rotational grazing allows the manure-fertilized grass to recover between visits, providing peak biodiversity and nutrition. Many farmers follow their ruminants with chickens, who aerate the soil and spread manure far and wide as they peck and scratch for bugs. Goats are even easier than sheep, since they graze happily on all sorts of rocky, brambly land that other species won't touch; they adore the thorny, invasive rosa multiflora and even eat poison ivy. A couple years of heavy goat browsing can turn shitty scrubland into pasture suitable for pickier herbivores.

Culinarily, lamb and goat can be used more or less interchangeably, though goat grows less fat. It does not, contrary to popular belief, taste more gamy than lamb; if anything it has a milder flavor. Whatever the beast, whole carcasses hang in the walk-in for a month or so before butchering. Dry aging concentrates meat's flavor, darkens its color, and tenderizes it; it's a trifecta that pays off handsomely (though it decreases yield a bit through evaporation).

10

lambs per acre

20

weeks to maturity

70

pounds average hanging weight

LAMB PROSCIUTTO

Fresh lamb eats best at both ends of the cooking spectrum: dark pink inside or braised to a giving tenderness. All points between these two poles risk diminishing the glory of great lamb. (Serving lamb anywhere past medium rare should be a crime.) When the cooks braise it, it's never to a pulled pork level of shreddiness; the meat always retains a bit of chew. They accomplish this texture by cooking it, covered, at 165°F overnight (10–12 hours) with plenty of stock and whatever aromatics suit the flavor profile of its destination dish. The lower temperature gelatinizes collagen, softening the connective tissue between strands of muscle, but not as thoroughly as a hotter bath would. The result, though well lubricated by melted fat and slippery gelatin, still offers some textural character. Cooking it in the combi oven at 100 percent humidity prevents any exposed meat from drying out and becoming chewy.

Lambs and goats come apart into primals similar to other quadrupeds like pigs: shoulders, loins, legs, bellies. As with pork, loins sit on the high grill to catch some smoke and slowly come up to temperature. Shoulders tend to braise but will sometimes roast in front of the fireplace, as will back legs. Every cut other than the precious loin is fair game for grinding into a variety of sausages, though shanks braise beautifully. Tongues and brains, limited to just one per animal, often appear in little dishes the kitchen whips up for VIPs.

The great beauty of this preparation lies in the speed with which it reaches maturity; less fat and mass means that both the curing and hanging times are dramatically shorter than a ham requires. Just as with a pig leg, submerge the lamb leg in sea salt for one day per kilo, then wipe it off, and hang it. With no skin to impede evaporation, it should be ready in a month or two depending on temperature and humidity.

POSOLE

This posole started with Jori. One spring she talked to the good people at Common Hands Farm about growing some flint corn—the multicolored "Indian corn" often used in autumn decorations—because she wanted to work with some heirloom varieties. They grew a few rows, and after harvest, while it dried on the ping-pong table upstairs in Zak's parents' barn, the crew discussed what to do with it: polenta? Grits? Something else? Kalas (who also had the job of de-kerneling the dried cobs) suggested hominy.*

Hominy, known as nixtamal in Mexico, is corn treated with an alkaline solution to tenderize it and make its niacin bioavailable; it also gives it the particular flavor found in tortillas and tamales. Zak had made it once, in Mexico, with Diana Kennedy, the renowned Mexican cookbook author, and the idea stuck. He ordered some calcium hydroxide (slaked lime) on Amazon. The kernels soaked in a 1.5 percent limewater solution by volume, then got rinsed and simmered in water until tender but still offering some resistance to a nibble.

Concurrently, Sue at Blue Star Farm was ripping out all of her tomato plants in advance of an impending freeze. They still had a lot of firm green fruit on them, though, which after grinding in a food mill to make a sort of tomato verjus, lent an appropriately nightshadey acidity to the stew. The base is lamb stock reinforced with some of the pigskin stock that follows the disassembly of every pig; it tenderizes the skin, which can then be scraped, dried, and fried to make chicharrones, and results in a lusciously gelatinous stock that adds wonderful body to any soup or sauce.

1

The final dish comes together thus: sautéed shallot and garlic, then the stocks, then the tomato juice and some of Jori's salt- and oil-cured chilies simmer gently on the flat top with the corn, which still has some body to it. This allows the flavors to infuse without letting the grain get mushy like more domesticated strains are wont to do.

2

For pickup, diced braised lamb gets stirred in and fresh lamb sausage enjoys a quick grilling: a simple blend of lamb, pork fat, black pepper, coriander, fennel, cumin, and salt, they are best rare. Slice the sausage lengthwise to show off the sexy purple interior, and make sure every bowl gets a chili.

3

This dish, with minor variations, stayed on the menu for several weeks. Once it came off, Walter used the last of the hominy to make porridge bread, using a variation on his standard pain au levain recipe. A grilled slice of this, topped with a schmear of mustard polenta (reinforcing the corny goodness), formed the sturdy substrate for venison sausage (similar seasonings to the lamb, and also using pork fat) and pickled okra.

**Use a small knife or flathead screwdriver to remove one lengthwise row of kernels, then use both thumbs to pop the rest off by pushing them toward the opening you created.*

11,679

kernels de-cobbed

A PROCEDURE BEST DONE WITH A JOINT AND SOME JAZZ

GREEN PEPPER AND CORIANDER GOAT SAUSAGE

45 5-OZ SAUSAGES

5.5KG GOAT

1KG PORK FAT

10G CARAWAY

16G CORIANDER

16G BLACK CARDAMOM

10G GREEN PEPPERCORN

71G SALT

Though lamb fat ranks among the most flavorful lipids in the world, lambs tend not to grow very much of it relative to their meat. As a result, lamb sausages need some creamy pork fat ground in to achieve the proper proportion and texture. Stuff them into lamb casings for a traditional skinny vibe, or into pork casings for a little more leeway with the cooking time. If you're buying pastured meat and grinding it yourself, you can cook lamb sausages to the same pink that you would a loin chop.

JALAPEÑO LAMB SAUSAGE

42 5-OZ SAUSAGES

5KG LAMB
(shoulder/leg)

1KG PORK FAT

110G SALT

4 JALAPEÑOS

50 GARLIC CLOVES

1 NUTMEG

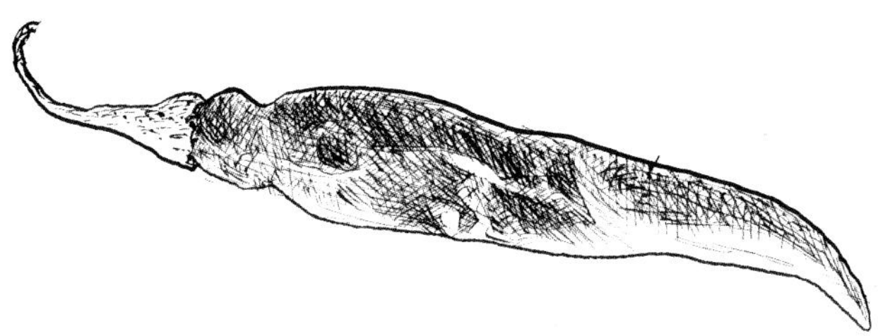

SPICED LAMB SAUSAGE

24 5-OZ SAUSAGES

5KG LAMB

2.5KG PORK FAT

1G JUNIPER

2G GREEN CARDAMOM

5G TASMANIAN PEPPER

2G FENNEL SEED

5G CORIANDER

2G WHITE PEPPERCORN

2G BLACK CARDAMOM

5G URFA PEPPER

1

For all three sausages, cut the meat and fat into chunks and chill thoroughly. Grind them through the large die into a bowl set in a larger bowl filled with ice water. For the jalapeño sausage, chop the garlic and jalapeños and grate the nutmeg, then add the spices to the salt and combine the mixture with the meat (For the other recipes, toast and grind the spices, mix them with the salt, then mix into the meat.). Grind the meat again through the small die, then wrap it and refrigerate it overnight. Stuff into lamb or pork casings.

STOCK

Copious stock is axiomatic in any kitchen that buys whole animals. As with so many other supposed by-products, the bones end up being as valuable as the main ingredient. Whether it makes the short trip to becoming soup, reduces to a glaze, or undergoes more elaborate transformations into sauces, stock is a culinary multitool, one of the fundamental and indispensable building blocks of a well-rounded kitchen. Fish & Game makes stock using bones only, without the addition of any aromatic vegetables or herbs, so that they can be flavored later according to their use on the menu. The result is a universally useful liquid, infinitely customizable, that no freezer should be without.

MAMMALS

PIGSKIN, which pork comes naturally wrapped in, makes a thick, gelatinous, and intensely porky stock. Each newly butchered animal's skin gets simmered for a few hours until it's thoroughly tender, then removed from the liquid. Scraped of all remaining fat and dehydrated overnight, the skin can then be deep-fried in grapeseed oil at 390°F to make chicharrones. The thick stock sees frequent action enriching other liquids—it imparts a lip-smacking stickiness to everything it touches—and occasionally gets reduced and frothed into a foamy embellishment (see p. 100).

PORK, LAMB, AND MUTTON BONES, after an initial spell on the grill, repair to the high shelf to roast and smoke for 4–6 hours. Keep in mind that they bathe in a light smoke up there, not at all like the inside of a smoker. Then the bones, snug in a pot of water, cook in the combi oven at 200°F at 100 percent moisture for 8–10 hours, meaning overnight. The wet atmosphere prevents evaporation, and gentle cooking makes for a clear result; boiling clouds stocks (although sometimes that doesn't matter). In the morning, the strained liquid reduces according to its intended use. Fish & Game uses little beef, but those bones get the same treatment.

WHEN A LEG OF PROSCIUTTO GETS CONSUMED, Kevin makes a lovely cured-tasting stock using the bone, fortified with onions, garlic, herbs, and whatever other pork bones might be on hand.

POULTRY

DUCKS tend to cook on the rotisserie, often after their legs are removed for confit or other purposes. Those carcasses, once relieved of their meat, get the same treatment as pork or lamb. (Geese are culinarily equivalent to ducks.) Bones from confit are not used to make stock.

CHICKEN STOCK usually gets made on the flat top because it's quick; a couple of hours suffice to extract pretty much all the carcasses have to offer.

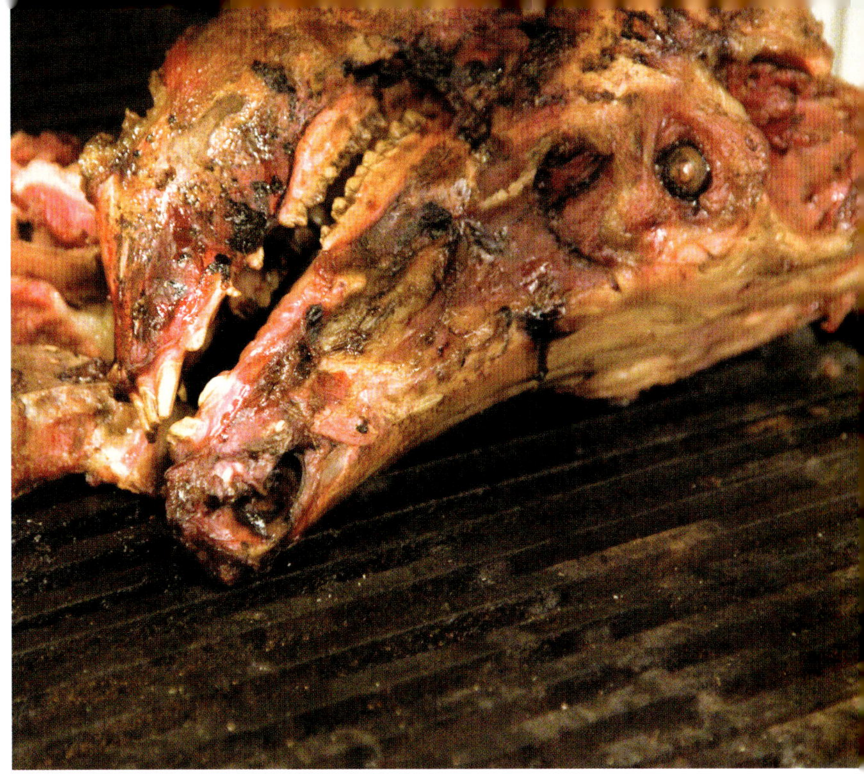

LOBSTER STOCK

SEAFOOD

BUYING WHOLE FISH MEANS A STEADY SUPPLY OF HEADS AND SKELETONS. These mostly end up as a traditional fumet, flavored with white wine, garlic, onion, and coriander, lightly simmered together for 45 minutes or so. Less traditionally, the kitchen also uses oilier fish like salmon and Arctic char the same way.

IF SHELLFISH STOCK IS REQUIRED, KEVIN WILL USUALLY STEAM MUSSELS just until they open, then strain off the liquid. The cooked mussels, which don't keep well, will often end up in family meal. (Mussels for menu courses get steamed à la minute, often over white wine or kimchi brine.) Lobsters, as with all other carcasses that move through the kitchen, get processed to extract every iota of flavor they have to give. (Crab stock is made according to the same method.)

1

After removing the tails and claws, put uncooked lobster heads and bodies in the bowl of a stand mixer fitted with the paddle and pummel them for a few minutes to expose lots of surface area. Roast them in a deep pan in a dry combi oven with full fan at 575°F for an hour or two. Deglaze the pan with cognac and burn it off.

2

Transfer shells to a deep pot, cover them with water, and simmer them gently (with a gently undulating surface) for 2½–3 hours, tasting regularly to make sure it doesn't get too chalky or bony tasting. Strain, chill, and store tightly covered in fridge or freezer.

LOBSTER OIL

1

Even after the long simmer, there is still a lot of fat-soluble flavor left on the shells that it would be a shame to waste. So once you've made stock, wring every glorious bit of lobster essence out of the shells by using them to infuse a neutral oil like grapeseed.

The shells to oil ratio is 1.25:1, so 625g of shells would need 500g of oil.

2

After draining the stock, dry the shells out on lined sheet pans in a 400°F oven for 10–15 minutes. Bash them some more in the mixer with the paddle, then bag the shells and oil at meatball pressure and cook sous vide at 88°C for 5 hours. Strain the oil through a double layer of cheesecloth and store in the refrigerator.

∞

number of things lobster oil makes better

ALL OF THE ABOVE

SOMETIMES THERE ARE SMALLER AMOUNTS OF STOCK, or a few bones lying around. Simmering bones in stock results in double stock, with twice the flavor and gelatin, and the happy ability to create delicious chimeras in the pot: a lamb with the head of a pig and the wings of a duck, for example. The dance of efficient consumption creates these miraculous liquids as a matter of course, and their ever-shifting nature adds a novel randomness to each iteration. Variety being the spice of life and all, the constantly shifting nature of fundamental ingredients like stock means that uniqueness is baked into every meal.

OTHER LIQUIDS can be key to perfecting the final potion. Kevin made a bouillabaisse once out of fish, shellfish, and smoked pork stocks, kimchi brine, white wine, tomato vinegar, and a full complement of aromatics. The profound and multidimensional result hit all the requisite notes of the classic, but with trademark soulful complexity. This is varsity, high-degree-of-difficulty soup ninja shit, but when you understand everything that went into everything and how they all play together then these advanced maneuvers can become commonplace.

VEGETABLES

ONIONS, which make a hell of a stock all by themselves, also comprise part of the standard aromatics added to bring a simple stock to a place of refined readiness. They and their alliumaceous cousins have been featured many times as the principal flavor in soups: grilled green onions for color and flavor, green garlic purée, wild garlic bulb stock with minced greens as a garnish, and even the onion soubise served alongside a spicy fish soup as a condiment to be stirred in by the diner (see p. 186).

MANY VEGETABLES produce trimmings during prep—greens, peels, stalks, roots, and the like—that are less sexy than whatever choice portion is destined for the plate. All these various parts can be simmered in stock to coax out their flavor and cant the flavor profile of the ultimate soup or sauce in a direction that reinforces the finished dish. Shiitake stems, for example, which can be unpalatably tough, nonetheless contain plenty of mushroomy umami; using them to impart fungal complexity to stock can underscore the flavor of the tender caps in the final product.

Besides deepening flavors, stocks work wonders as textural modifiers, adding body and flavor while they dilute. The difference between pumpkin soup and pumpkin purée, after all, comes down to a simple matter of ratio: is there more pumpkin or more stock?

ROMULUS CRAFT

Washington, VT

182 miles from Fish & Game

A significant part of Fish & Game's character comes from the skilled hands that fabricated important components of the dining experience: the wooden tables and bar, the steel napkin rings and rotisserie, and above all the variety of ceramics chosen to showcase each menu. A majority of the ceramics in regular rotation come from Romulus Craft, Ikuzi Teraki and Jeanne Bisson's studio in Washington, Vermont. Bisson hails from nearby Barre, Vermont, while Teraki, a Kyoto native, comes from a family of traditional kimono painters. They've been living and working side by side in the same spot for going on thirty years.

Bisson's talkative nature contrasts with Teraki's more taciturn demeanor. "Growing up here, I never thought 'It's so cold and only white people,'" she remembers. On moving to Vermont from California, though (they left Oakland to raise their daughter near family), "I realized how hard the winters are, and how there's very little diversity. But that's changing now." The choice of location proved wise nonetheless; the cost of living is low, and Vermont's extraordinary year-round beauty provides plenty of inspiration. "There's a lot of craft in Scandinavia because the winters are so dark and cold; there's nothing else to do,"

The clay body they use is porcelain, a formula that took years to get exactly right. It's made in Amherst, Massachusetts, using kaolin imported from England. The mix was developed for highly workable plasticity when wet and an extremely strong and translucent quality when fired. The finished ware becomes highly vitrified; the result is almost closer to glass than to ceramic. The clay is so fine, and the walls are so thin, that when tipping back a slender white mug to finish the coffee within, one sees a disc of light shining through the bottom, as well as bright ripples in the sides where Teraki's fingers pinched a bit tighter. His dexterity and prowess at throwing are astonishing; besides the extraordinary thinness and uniformity of the vessels, he also makes large, ornate chess sets, sold complete with boards made by a local woodworker.

While the shapes and sizes of their work vary tremendously, from monumental vases to tiny teacups, the color palette is limited to three oxides and a clear glaze, all mixed in house. The porcelain is bright white, and the oxides black, white, and red; by layering and mixing the oxides, they can achieve a wide spectrum of browns ranging from pale beige to rust to deep chocolate and everything in between. The clear glaze is glossy, and the oxides are matte, which allows for even

more visual and textural variations. They also use an airbrush to apply all the various mixtures they concoct, allowing for finishes that range from textured and speckled to glassy smooth. The seemingly infinite variations that can spring from a handful of variables represent an object lesson in minimalism.

Their spray booth, a jerry-rigged rural steampunk concatenation of hoses, ducts, and cables—including plastic yogurt containers as both an implement vessel and the nozzle for a dryer duct—while clearly functional, contrasts somewhat starkly with the pristine finished work. Though their kiln is electric—everything is fired to cone 6 (2180°F)—they have, over the years, developed a raku-style technique for producing a crackling effect. Applying a porcelain slip with slightly different properties over their regular body causes the top layer to crack as it shrinks during drying. Brushing oxide onto these areas and then sponging off the excess before firing results in a pattern of tiny black lines, needle-fine, against the bright white.

Teraki does all the throwing, and Bisson does the hand building; the wheel is his turf, the slab roller is hers. The roller creates large sheets of uniform thickness, from which she fabricates a variety of plates: ovals, rounds, squares, some

with smooth and graceful lips, others with sheer edges offering no safety to the food perched thereon. Fish & Game often serves ice cream on thick matte black square tiles with gently elevated corners—evocative of the flare on Japanese temple roofs—and a set of off-round plates with the same "stardust" finish (tan speckles blown onto the black on one side) probably see more use than any other plates in the restaurant.

Factoring in recycling (clay is infinitely reworkable until fired) they go through between a ton and a half to two tons of porcelain a year. Apart from occasional road trips to craft fairs, the couple keeps their carbon footprint small with minimal driving. They have no daily commute; they live upstairs in a modest apartment flooded with light from clerestory windows. On a recent visit, the space was perfumed with the smell of tomato sauce simmering low on the stove. They have nicer teacups than you do.

Their work resonates so well with the restaurant's food because it embodies the same confluence of consuming passion, technical excellence, and human warmth. Words like "master" and "virtuoso," like superlatives, get thrown around a lot in these days of attention-whoring hyperbole, but it's a rare person who can measure success by getting up every morning and doing exactly what she would do if it weren't her job to do it. Rarer still are people who work at such a consistently high level of refinement. They take it a bit easier on the weekends, but they're in the studio, quietly working, NPR playing low in the background, every day. Using a Sawzall metal-cutting blade to shape the handles of a group of large mugs into their characteristic tapered shape—thin on top, thick at the bottom, with a triangular cross-section—then smoothing them with a damp sponge, Teraki pauses to look up and smile. "We'll never retire."

HIROTAKE OOKA

Saint Péray, France

3,781 miles from Fish & Game

The petite village of Saint-Péray, just south of Cornas, sits tucked up against the steep cliffs that define the region's topography and wines alike: the easternmost edge of the Massif Central, the gigantic geological cornucopia that occupies much of central Southern France. Across the Rhône valley, parallel to the river, a glowering wall of jagged Alps looms blue in the distance, resembling nothing so much as Mordor seen from Minas Tirith (though without the sinister orange backlighting).

Tall, broad-shouldered, and speaking perfect French with a slight Japanese accent, Hirotake Ooka walks down the stone steps in front of his house, introduces himself, and bows solemnly. Then his tranquil face breaks into a big grin. "Should we go visit the vines?" Driving up a narrow, winding road to his vineyards, he fills in a bit of backstory. Ooka moved to France from Tokyo in 1997. Though he studied to be a chemist in Japan, he decided to leave school to become a winemaker, earning a diploma in Bordeaux as an agricultural technician.

He wanted a job with Thierry Allemand, the visionary most responsible for resuscitating Cornas's reputation, but found a position instead with Jean-Louis Grippat, whose business was bought by Rhône powerhouse Guigal in 2000. Ooka managed the Grippat and Vallouit vineyards in Hermitage and Saint-Joseph, all the while moonlighting with Allemand on weekends (Ooka originally chose the Rhône valley specifically because he loved Allemand's wines and subsequently modeled his own methods after his mentor's organic, low-intervention approach). In 2002 he left Guigal for Allemand and bought a vineyard as well as his home and winery, snug behind a high wall on a sharp curve near the center of town.

Bumping along a dirt road barely worthy of the word, brush scraping the underside of his van, he points out some of his parcels. He now owns eleven, totaling three hectares scattered throughout Cornas, like the one he parks above: steep, narrow, facing southeast. When he bought it, the hillside was all wooded; he cleared it himself because forested land costs far less than vineyards. He left a buffer of woods at the edges wherever possible to encourage biodiversity and reduce erosion. Crouching near the van, where cutting the road exposed a vertical section of earth, he indicates the four-inch layer of soil on top of crumbling granite, explaining that the vines have to find cracks and penetrate deep into the rock to get nutrients. As a result, they don't produce a lot of grapes, but the fruit is intensely concentrated with flavor: proof of the adage that poor soil makes great wine. "It's hard for the vines, but good for us."

It's hard for him, too, getting up at 5:00 in the morning to trudge up and down these steep vineyards, but his contentment with this life is palpable. And his wines reflect it. He and his wife, also Japanese (they met at French language school in Bordeaux), have three school-age children. She helps a little bit with the business, but apart from harvest time it's almost entirely him working in the vineyards and cellar. Ooka is a natural winemaker's natural winemaker; besides eschewing all sulfur and any interventions in the cellar, he tries to avoid any treatments—even biodynamic plant extracts—in the vineyards. He believes that vines thrive best under benign neglect, and that terroir expresses itself best with minimal human interference.

Cornas, perennially underrated, contains some excellent terroir but has suffered from hard conditions (those steep slopes of poor soil) and lazy producers (making dense, tannic, unfriendly wines). The label on Ooka's Cornas couldn't be further from that image: a child's drawing of grapes, leaves, rainbows, and insects. His domaine, La Grande Colline ("the big hill") is a translation of his family name, and most appropriate given the precipitous inclination of his vineyards, some of which easily approach a 30 percent grade. He works entirely by hand, pruning, training, and occasionally spraying; when he does apply nettle or horsetail tea, it is by means of a tank strapped to his back, hiking up and down the long vertical rows. "It's easier at the beginning of the season," he says, surveying the view. "I can hit a few rows at a time with the sprayer. Once the leaves fill out, I have to walk up every row."

His 2011 Cornas marked the beginning of his no-treatment approach, where he used no sulfur, no copper, not even any biodynamic plant-based sprays on the vines for the whole growing season. "It's just grapes. That's what I do." He identifies his most important role as choosing the right moment for harvest; he needs the sugar to be high enough to ferment well, but not so high that it becomes a problem. Speaking of the final alcohol percentage, he explains: "11 is good, up to 12, 12.5, but higher than that is bad. The yeast dies, the volatile acidity gets too high." Pick at the right time, though, he says, and "the wine makes itself."

His cave is carved into a cliff below an old chateau, about three minutes' drive from his house, sealed with a motorized roll-up door. Behind that modern contrivance sits a cave dug in the Middle Ages; the castle's ancient well connects to the back of the cellar and keeps going down. There's still water at the bottom, and more drips steadily down the walls of the vault. The cool, dank atmosphere within keeps the barrels tight and the fermentation slow. Most of the barrels are festooned with fluffy efflorescences of greenish mold.

His library of older vintages—a personal archive in which he eagerly rummages for bottles to taste—sits on metal shelves in back, right over the old well. Bottles and shelves alike are coated with an opaque film of damp dust. Swap the incandescent bulbs for torches and there's nothing going on here that did not happen five hundred years ago. A strange oily liquid has dripped from the ceiling onto the top of an upright barrel he uses for a tasting table, causing him to lean over and examine it up close. "I've never seen that before," he chuckles, and rinses a couple of glasses in the sink near the door.

While their profiles vary depending on the grape and the vineyard, his whites all share complex minerality, elegant acidity, and fragrant fruit; there's a precision to these wines, even the humble ones. Saint-Péray sits mostly on limestone, with a different character than Cornas. After pressing, his white juice may spend a day or two in a fiberglass vat to begin fermenting before it goes in barrel. Not surprisingly, the 2014 Chardonnay still has a bit of sugar; normally his whites ferment for a year since the cool cellar promotes long, slow fermentations. Very surprisingly, the 2009 Marsanne also still needs more time; it too is not completely dry yet. He shrugs. "I never force wine; I leave it until it's ready. I never heat it, stir it, nothing." Letting them sit in barrel for a couple of years, besides allowing them to thoroughly settle and clarify, also stabilizes the wines. "People say unsulfured wines don't keep, but that's not true." To prove it, he uncorks a 2006 Saint-Péray, beautifully mature, with lots of sesame seed on the nose—it would, most appropriately, kill with sushi.

Above all, Ooka's wines embody honesty and purity of expression. Beyond the immediately apparent pleasure and finesse in his mature reds, one finds a supple elegance wedded to a particularly Rhône-ish rusticity: the carnal, animal intensity of syrah tempered with a delicacy, refinement, and transparency. Cornas sits close to the southern end of the Northern Rhône, so it catches some Provençal heat; the orientation of its slopes ripens grapes quickly and gives vineyards some protection from the chilly Mistral in the winter. By defying the region's common tendency toward too-ripe fruit, though, his wines evoke some of the rarest flavors from farther north, where sunshine is more precious; the Côte-Rôtie, 40 miles away, or the legendary Hermitage hillside a few miles upstream.

His Saint-Joseph, all made from purchased fruit, features a large violet on the label, because that perfume marks a well-made example of the appellation. While his 2014 (only 11 percent alcohol) remains tightly closed, standing aloof, tart, and tannic, the 2013 is all smiles and caresses. The 2014 Cornas, while tannic, nonetheless conveys a ripeness, almost sweet, that meshes seamlessly with the supple structure. The 2014 spent barely a week in the vat before pressing and fermenting in barrel; this approach extracts a powerful combination of fruit and structure from Syrah, a grape that possesses both in equal measure.

While the vintages reflect the differing weather—and natural wines show more difference between vintages than chemical efforts, because there is no correction of "flaws"—Ooka ascribes their accessibility primarily to time in bottle. "Ideally, I let them sit in bottle for a minimum of six months before drinking. Ideally," he adds after a pause, laughing at the reality that business sometimes requires a faster pace. More enticing still, the 2012 drinks exceedingly well for such a young wine. Some famous Rhône reds go through a dumb period a few years after bottling, then open up with abandon after five or so more. Will this silky elixir, so fast out of the gate, hit a rough patch? "It's hard to say, but I think it will stay good."

MENU

WEEK OF JANUARY 30

SHAVED PORK LOIN

kimchi broth

PAGE 314

SHIITAKE

oyster, tomatillo, pork jus

PAGE 318

COD

sauce brunoise, butternut

PAGE 320

WHEY NOODLES

spicy offal sauce

PAGE 322

PORK SHOULDER

glazed green garlic, concord grape gel, spicy turnip

PAGE 326

CREAM

crème brulée, rye sugar

PAGE 328

CHOCOLATE GANACHE

rye crisps, rhubarb

PAGE 332

SHAVED PORK LOIN

This dish, with variations, appears on the menu with some regularity. Besides being extremely good to eat, it also represents a superbly efficient means of showcasing pork loin.

The chewy, funky pickles and deep broth offered a profound counterpoint to the velvety texture and flavor of pastured pig. Pinched with chopsticks and swabbed in soup, the meat acquired an uplifting acidity and additional smoky notes from the hot broth. Every element enhanced every other: pork in meat and broth, tangy fermentation in kimchi and daikon, classic pork-and-cabbage sympatico between meat, daikon, and kimchi juice. The heavy-bottomed bowls, hoisted to knock back the last drop of stock, underscored the heft of such a deceptively nimble starter.

1

Whole loins, still with bones attached, sit bathed in smoke on the high shelf over the grill for five or six hours until they're about 125°F in the middle, then cool off until they're ready to ride the deli slicer.

2

These tender folds of pink pork came adorned with wrinkled discs of Jori's daikon ice pickles and a sharp, pungent broth of smoked pork stock (made with those same bones) enlivened with kimchi brine.

ICE PICKLES

DAIKON

SOY SAUCE

WATER

1

Soy sauce is about 16 percent salt, so when diluting it the goal should be between three and five percent to ensure proper fermentation, which adds significant flavor and prevents mold from growing.

2

As long as the temperature outside freezes at night and doesn't rise above 60°F for any length of time, they can stay outside indefinitely. Jori pulls hers out in spring, when she sees bubbles beginning on the surface indicating accelerated fermentation. For service, the rounds are usually sliced into thin discs and quartered if their size requires it.

Over the first winter Jori made daikon “ice pickles” by filling a large Lexan tub with daikon and then covering the roots with diluted soy sauce. She left it outside, next to their house, until spring. The salt, combined with repeated freezing and thawing, pulls water out of the daikon and changes its texture, shrinking it and intensifying its flavor. The result was Goldilocks-esque: the top layer was bland, the bottom layer was too salty, and the middle layer was perfect. (This dish featured that magic middle layer.) The following winter, perfecting the method, she just made one layer so everything would remain the same salinity. She also reused the daikon-infused soy sauce from the previous year to double down on the pungent radish flavor.

SHIITAKE

Fish & Game is blessed with two great local mushroom farms: Zehr & Sons Farm in Ghent and Bulich Mushroom Farm across the river in Catskill. Both grow plump and tender shiitakes; their texture is not unlike an oyster.

1

This combination of oysters and mushrooms was served with a tomatillo fluid gel: Jori's grilled tomatillos and garlic, pureed and canned back in September, with .4% agar by weight incorporated by vigorous whisking, activated by boiling, gelled by chilling, and then fluidized by blending. This process makes for a sexy texture and enough body to stay where it's spooned on a plate without any running or sloshing around. Make this first.

2

Shuck the oysters but leave them in the lower shell. Place them on the grill for a few minutes to just cook through, then remove them from grill and shells (in that order). Keep them somewhere warm in their liquor.

3

Put the shiitakes in a pan with a bit of pork-skin stock enriched with butter and cook them until the liquid forms a glaze.

4

Nap the mushrooms in the shiny, sticky umami sauce until the pan is almost dry, but not quite. The gelatin from the skin stock and the fat from the butter should form an irresistibly glossy coating on the mushrooms.

5

Once they're done, wilt some baby spinach in a bit of butter. Spoon some gel on warmed plates, arrange two oysters on each plate and add a scattering of mushrooms.

COD

1

Large finfish like cod and hake often get filleted, portioned, salted, and then cooked in butter in the wood oven with a smashed clove of garlic and maybe a sprig of thyme.

2

Once they're fully sizzling, the key is to tilt the pan and baste them constantly with the butter until the skin is crisp and they're just cooked through.

3

This cod came to the table with butternut purée (roasted, blended, pushed through a tamis, seasoned) and a brunoise sauce of leek, onion, carrot, garlic, ham, and turnip (using the trimmings from making the tiles for the pork-shoulder dish).

4

This medley had a quick sauté in white wine, then got mounted with butter, pork jus, and a bit of maple.

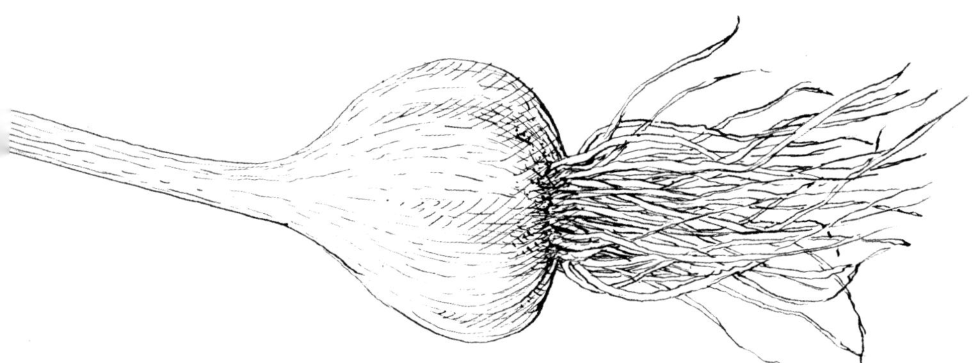

WHEY NOODLES

APPROXIMATELY 12 SERVINGS

1KG 00 FLOUR

4 EGGS

2 CUPS WHEY

This dish was inspired by dandan noodles, those mainstays of Sichuan street cuisine; Jori loves them and gets them every time she eats Sichuan. Any kitchen that regularly makes cheese or yogurt needs clever uses for whey. This is one of them.

1

Combine all in a mixer bowl with a dough hook and knead on medium speed until the surface bounces back almost completely when poked hard with a finger. (Turn the mixer off before you poke the dough.) Jori likes to knead it some more by hand, letting it get nice and stretchy, but you can forgo this step or just let it spin a bit longer in the mixer.

2

Wrap the dough tightly in plastic and let it rest for 30–60 minutes before running it through your pasta machine. You want to make sheets at the second-thinnest setting, then cut those with the spaghetti cutter. Separate individual strands and form nests with the noodles, dusting them heavily with flour so they don't stick together.

3

The sauce for these was an assortment of offal, which every conscientious kitchen will have on hand: the happy result of buying whole animals. In this case, there were pork livers, hearts, and kidneys, plus a bunch of duck gizzards. Because you eat nose to tail like you should, your organs will likely differ. No matter.

4

They all get sliced, salted, grilled rare, and then chopped and mixed with some ground pork and sautéed in chili oil with shallots, garlic, pigskin stock, and some vinegar until happily married but still saucy.

Briefly boil the noodles, drain them, divide them into warmed bowls and top with organ *ragù*.

Eat noisily, with much satisfied slurping.

PORK SHOULDER

ONE SHOULDER

1 GALLON WORT FROM CHATHAM SCOTCH ALE
(a heavily malted brown ale)

350G KOSHER SALT

200G BROWN SUGAR

42G PINK SALT

14G CORIANDER SEED, TOASTED

4 FRESH BAY LEAVES

1 ORANGE

2 HEADS OF GARLIC, SPLIT

2 CHILIES

1

Combine all ingredients in a pot and simmer for ten minutes so the liquid can infuse with the aromatics. Submerge the shoulder in the brine for 5–7 days and refrigerate. Rinse and pat it dry before roasting; this one turned on the spit for six hours.

2

This iteration of shouldery goodness combined the meat with grilled green garlic that was steamed and frozen back in June, frozen grape juice gelled with a little agar, and tiles of turnip cooked sous vide with butter and homemade sriracha—a teaspoon of the latter for every tablespoon of the former, and a bit of maple syrup—for an hour at 71°C.

3

The Concord grape juice gel (.4% agar to juice by weight, whisked in, boiled well, chilled, then blended) added a nice hit of sweetness and acidity.

This is not a falling-apart pulled pork style shoulder; it should retain the character and chew of the meat. Be sure to slice the pork on the thicker side so you can appreciate its texture.

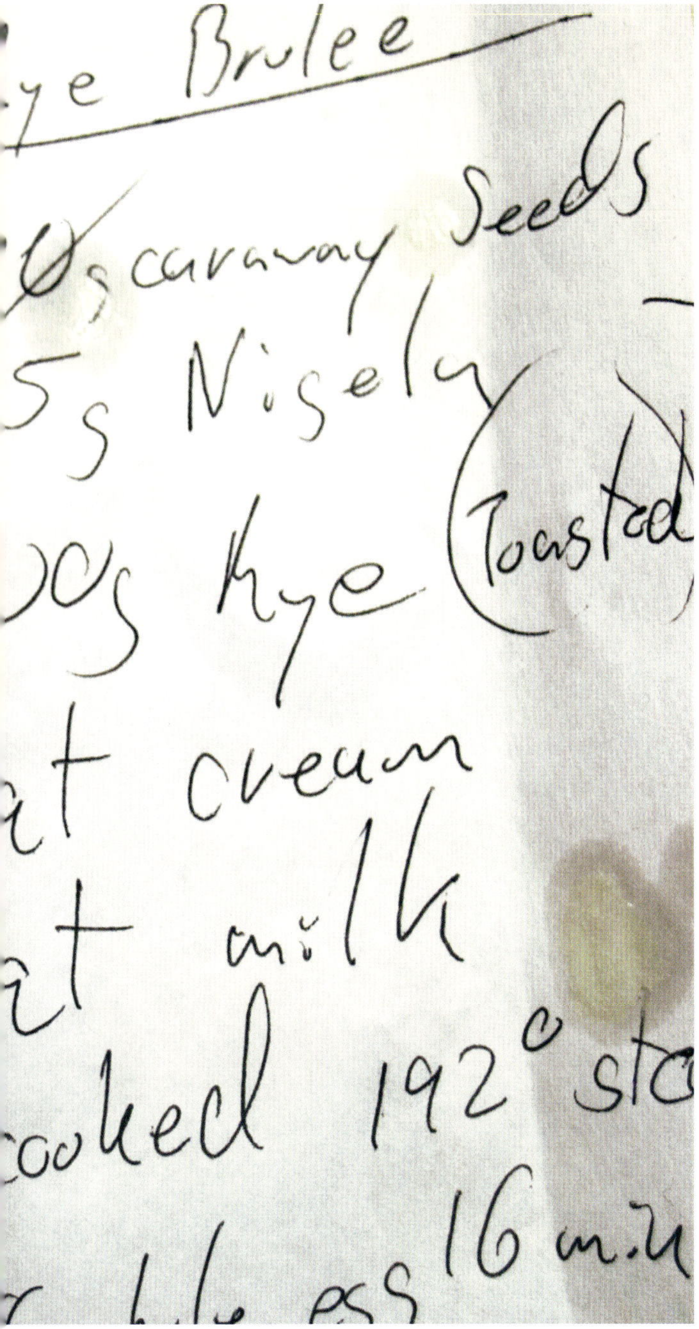

This dish originated on a ski trip to Vermont; the crew was shooting the shit and crème brûlée came up. Kevin suggested rye as a flavor, which resulted in this elegant pre-dessert.

CREAM

16 HALF-CUP SERVINGS

1 QUART CREAM

1 QUART MILK

8 EGGS

10 OZ DEMERARA SUGAR

FAT PINCH OF SALT

200G RYE BERRIES, TOASTED

30G CARAWAY SEEDS

5G NIGELLA SEEDS

1

Combine milk and cream, then add rye, seeds, and salt. Steep, covered, at a bare simmer for two hours, then strain.

2

Beat the eggs and sugar, temper with the hot cream, then strain the mixture into individual serving bowls.

3

Cover with plastic wrap and steam in a combi oven at 192°F for 16 minutes. Cool completely, sprinkle surfaces with sugar, and caramelize them with a torch right before serving.

CHOCOLATE GANACHE

ABOUT 20 SERVINGS

Zak, continuing to riff, talked to Walter about using rye with spelt and flax to make a crust for the main dessert on the same menu: a dark chocolate tart. The first version involved piping the ganache into walled crusts that Walter baked inside ring molds. The edges proved too irregular, so subsequent versions used rounds of dough stamped out with a 3-inch cutter so the ganache sat flush with the edges for a more elegant presentation.

GANACHE:

700G CREAM

810G CHOCOLATE
(70% Cacao)

250G BUTTER

80G GLUCOSE

2G SALT

1

Combine the cream, glucose, and salt. Bring them just to a boil and pour them over the chocolate and butter, using an immersion blender to thoroughly combine them. Keep the blender fully submerged to avoid mixing any air in.

2

Pour the ganache into 3-inch ring molds set on a wax paper–covered sheet pan and chill as soon as they're all filled. To unmold them, run a torch quickly around the outside of each mold and slide it straight up.

DRY MIX:

1 CUP DARK RYE FLOUR

½ CUP DARK SPELT FLOUR

½ CUP LIGHT SPELT FLOUR

1 TBSP SUGAR

1 TSP KOSHER SALT

3

Combine dry ingredients in a food processor; pulse a few times to incorporate.

WET MIX:

6 OZ (1½ STICKS) COLD UNSALTED BUTTER

1 TSP APPLE CIDER VINEGAR

½ CUP ICE WATER
(approximately)

4

Cut butter into small dice, add to dry mix, and pulse until coarse and sandy. Slowly add water just until it begins to come together.

5

Remove and flatten into a disk. Wrap tightly and let dough rest, refrigerated, for at least an hour. Then roll out into desired shape.

RHUBARB CONFIT:

RHUBARB

MAPLE SYRUP

1 PINCH OF SALT

6

Vacuum-bag ingredients and cook at 140°F for 40 minutes. Slice into small pieces before serving. Place a ganache on a round of crust, top with rhubarb confit and a pinch of Hawaiian black salt, and serve.

ZAK DOES NOT LOVE SWEETS. In fact, the entirety of the dessert chapter in his cookbook *Eat With Your Hands* consists of one sentence: "Eat fresh fruit!" He prefers to have the savory flavors of the meal crossfade with sweeter ones toward the end of the menu, but not disappear. More often than not, the pre-dessert will veer toward the sweet end of the spectrum and the finale will dwell in that half-sweet realm as well, never crossing fully over the line.

Ice creams are probably the most purely sweet desserts, but they will often be made with savory flavors like angelica or chicory. Vegetables appear frequently in desserts (carrot cake, zucchini bread, beet chips) and when chocolate makes its occasional appearances it stays pretty bitter. Kevin and Walter both adore sweets, so they're always trying to tilt the desserts in that direction. Zak tends to veto those moves, pulling them back toward flavors—earthy, bitter, sour—not traditionally associated with desserts, but that appropriately evoke Kevin's resentment.

Sugar is the most ubiquitous of culinary crutches. It's in mayonnaise, for crying out loud. If there's one thing that so-called Modernist Cuisine has taught us, it's that sweet and savory are artificial distinctions: burger with ketchup and a milkshake, anyone? Fish & Game's desserts (and they're usually not this austere) embody the notion that concluding courses should be seen as belonging to the meal, helping describe its trajectory, rather than standing apart from it.

HEY SWEETIE

PLUM TART

ABOUT 16 TARTS

This plum tart begins with a buckwheat crust of Walter's devising, which gets brushed with unsweetened dark chocolate and then filled with a mousse of egg whites and Jori's plum jam. The jam uses an old Russian technique that involves macerating the halved fruit with sugar overnight, then bringing the mixture to a boil and cooling it, over and over for several days, to evaporate the liquid and condense the jam without giving it the cooked flavor that afflicts most fruit preserves. Offering a tangy counterpoint to the tart, a quenelle of fresh ricotta, enlivened with mostarda syrup, a blend of various jars from last year: meyer lemon, tangerine, clementine, strained and reduced to a caramel. (Jori isn't making the citrus mostardas any more, since the fruit is rather non-local and she has enough on her plate as far as preserving is concerned.)

The dish contains creamy dairy, velvety mousse, crunchy crust, candied citrus, and chocolate, but all those traditional dessert flavors and textures have been subverted, gently and expertly, by reducing the amount of sugar they would normally be prepared with. While outwardly the dish looks every bit a sticky confection, the crust is savory, the chocolate is bitter, and the filling is barely sweet. The ricotta, enhanced with the mostarda syrup, is downright sour. Sounds dreamy, right? But the thing to keep in mind is how carefully modulated these flavors are, and how vibrant and focused the resulting harmonies—dissonant, sometimes, but compelling and beautiful, like Monk—become as they combine and overlap as they're eaten. And the grains, the cream, the eggs, and the fruit are the best the region has to offer. Every course should celebrate the product above all.

BUCKWHEAT CRUST:

1 CUP BUCKWHEAT FLOUR

¾ CUP AP FLOUR

½ TSP SALT

4 OZ BUTTER, VERY COLD

2 TSP CIDER VINEGAR

2–3 TBSP WATER, VERY COLD

1

Combine all dry ingredients and the butter, pulse in food processor until butter is about pea-sized. Add wet ingredients and pulse until sandy.

2

Let the dough rest, tightly wrapped, overnight; buckwheat has no gluten, but when fully hydrated it forms a gel that helps hold the dough together.

3

Roll out to about ⅛" thick, cut to desired shape, and push into greased tins with flared sides for easy removal. Blind bake for about 12 min at 350° with weights, then remove.

FILLING:

4 EGG WHITES, WHIPPED TO SOFT PEAKS WITH A TEASPOON OF CREAM OF TARTAR

2 LEAVES SILVER GELATIN, BLOOMED IN COLD WATER

2 CUPS JORI'S PLUM JAM, BLENDED SMOOTH

4

Heat one cup of the jam and dissolve the gelatin in it. Add the other cup of jam, then fold into the egg whites and refrigerate for a few hours.

5

Brush the cooled shells with melted unsweetened dark chocolate, then pipe in plum mousse and top with a few slivers of mostarda.

6

Serve a quenelle of ricotta whipped with mostarda syrup alongside and garnish with a sprig of chervil.

ICE CREAM

Ice creams feature frequently in the menu, either as a pre-dessert or the final course. They're an ideal vehicle for conveying an enormous range of flavors, from the traditional to the exotic. Zak is fond of using plants like chicory and angelica, which have earthy complexity and mesh beautifully with the sublime texture and sweetness of everyone's favorite dessert. In May, corn shoots thinned from the garden make a lovely pale-yellow confection. A few inches tall and saccharine sweet, those willowy sprouts pack a lot of flavor. Stone-fruit pits, cracked with a cleaver, infuse cream with the essence of peach or apricot enhanced by a subtly bitter aura.

Though a ginger sorbet once accompanied a roast pork course and they occasionally tilt toward savory, like a black garlic gelato, ice creams usually define the sweet extreme of the Fish & Game spectrum. Always served as one small spherical scoop, always with some crunchy accompaniment like streusel, nuts, or a cracker—the spirit of a cone in reductive, sophisticated drag—ice cream arrives on chilled plates so diners have enough time to eat it before it melts.

The ice cream base is a classic no-egg gelato mixture with a few modern enhancements. Old-fashioned recipes are grand, but ice cream is science and the additives (glucose, invert sugar, stabilizer) make an immense difference in the resulting texture. Sorbet—like cucumber, sour cherry, or ginger—is best made with fresh juice. Because it doesn't involve cooking, the idea is to keep the flavor as pure and unadulterated as possible. Which of these ends up on the menu depends on the featured flavor, and whether the scoop will be served alongside something else (like a grilled peach or a spruce tip cake). Sometimes the choice involves working forward from an ingredient (angelica makes wonderful ice cream) or backward from a dish (that grilled peach would kill with a scoop of fior di latte).

All these desserts get churned in the Pacojet, which is uniquely suited to producing superior frozen confections. One Pacojet canister contains thirty to forty servings, which is perfect for a restaurant with thirty-five seats. The canisters can be filled and frozen when convenient, and then spun as needed. Kevin churns them about four hours before serving, letting them temper in the freezer until service. Home ice cream makers work, but they don't deliver the same texture. Home-churned ice cream should also be eaten right away, after a brief temper in the freezer; it can turn to concrete if left overnight. Having said that, though, all of these flavors and permutations can make stellar desserts no matter what apparatus you own. After all, it's not how big, shiny, and expensive it is, it's how you use it.

FOR ICE CREAM AND GELATO,

Kevin infuses flavors (like angelica, chicory, and corn shoot) into cream with a two-step process: heating them together to 120°F for 4 hours and then moving the mixture to the fridge for another 16 hours. The solids are strained out before making the ice cream or gelato.

ICE CREAM BASE (FIOR DI LATTE)

30–40 SERVINGS

550G MILK
180G CREAM
42G NONFAT MILK POWDER
137G GLUCOSE POWDER
26G INVERTED SUGAR
50G SUGAR
4G STABILIZER
1G SALT

1

Combine the salt, sugar, and stabilizer. Heat the milk and cream, inverted sugar, and milk powder to 45°C and add the stabilizer combination, whisking to dissolve. Heat to 85°C, then chill.

2

Mature in the refrigerator for at least 4 hours, then scale into Pacojet containers and freeze. Churn without air and temper in the freezer until service.

CUCUMBER SORBET:

620G CUCUMBER JUICE
182G SUGAR
92G GLUCOSE POWDER
4G STABILIZER
52G LEMON JUICE

1

Heat the sugar, glucose, and stabilizer in a small amount of the juice just until they dissolve, then add the remainder of the juice and freeze.

Steve's Existential Crisis

STEVE

MOST NIGHTS TEND TO END UP LONG BLURS OF TIME WHERE THE SAME THINGS HAPPEN MIXED GENTLY WITH THE UNCOMMON.

Pool, dice games, four dozen roses, walks in silence, walks with words forgotten but the emotional output leaves its mark. Early mornings in diners ordering the strangest things off the menu just so another plate of breakfast doesn't show up.

An unsure and uneasy start. Knowing absolutely nothing of a craft leads you to trust people with any sort of knowledge in it. Whether it is in their hands, heart, or head.

Everyone toiled. Information exchanged. Food eaten to just catch up and try to understand what matters at the core of things.

I got into the habit of buying a new coat whenever someone close to me died. This ended with the only instance of me giving away a coat.

At some point I was told to read a story about what I would call ideals. Written by Osamu Dazai, "Hashire, Merosu!" The story itself goes back quite far in time. Dazai wrote his retelling in 1940. Friedrich Schiller did "Die Bürgschaft" in 1799. Gaius Julius Hyginus wrote "Damon & Pythias" back when the Greeks were "running" shit. This leads me to believe the story is much older than that due to their habit of going to Africa for knowledge research.

Kings need to be killed. At least Melos thinks so. Selinuntius not so much, but you know how that goes. Melos fucks up. Assassination fails. Resigned to death, Melos asks the king if he can be pardoned for a number of days to attend his sister's wedding. Afterward, he'll come for his death. King isn't about that. Selinuntius steps up. He's the placeholder. If Melos doesn't return in the allotted time he will go to death instead.

The king agrees. Melos is free. Selinuntius, locked up. Melos attends the wedding and walks back toward his death with no intention of betraying his friend. Insert life. All this bullshit delays Melos. He begins to run. Running at max is the only way he can get back in time to die.

Selinuntius is on his last minute of life when Melos runs into the city. There the two stand. Selinuntius demands Melos slap him because he began to doubt he was actually coming back. Melos demands the same slap from Selinuntius because he actually endangered his life.

And this is cooking. Trust. Devotion. Ideals.

Fuck off with love,
Steve

P.S.: It's all a comedy anyway.

Acknowledgments

PETER:

I would like to thank Zak, Jori, Kevin, Patrick, and the whole Fish & Game crew past and present for tolerating me over the course of three years and never stabbing me once even though I got to eat all the food and they didn't. It takes real chemistry to collaborate on a project like this, and we were blessed with copious quantities. (By chemistry, obviously, I mean wine.) Much gratitude also to Sarah Rainwater, for being such a badass designer and consummate professional, and to Casey Kittrell at University of Texas Press for his sage counsel and genuine enthusiasm for the book.

I owe an eternal debt to my ancestors who taught me to cook and eat: my grandparents Howard and Gertrude Beck—he fermented pickles and smoked chickens, she did everything else, they both gardened—and my mother, Claire Barrett, who had a huge vegetable garden and baked bread long before any of those things were even a little bit cool. Finally, I must thank my wife Christine and son Milo for putting up with me for the seeming eternity it took me to make this book. Without them, it would have gone much faster.

ZAK:

Fish & Game, this book, and various other experiments, endeavors, and culinary tangents would not be possible without my partner and confidant, Patrick Milling Smith. Thank you P! There is not a day that goes by when I am not bouncing ideas off of my other two partners, Kevin Pomplun and Jori Jayne: an intelligent, creative, compassionate, and highly dysfunctional family with which I could not be happier. A special thanks to crew past and present, new and old, and in particular my friends and longtime colleagues Mike Rice and Steve Hernandez, who have been just as important to the development of Fish & Game as anyone mentioned above.

Fish & Game would not be here, nor would the Hudson Valley be what it is, without all the talented, humble, craftsmen, farmers, and characters, in a word: artists with whom we have worked over the years. And let me not forget my folks, Jack & Linda, who have been so generous with their time and property, sacrificing privacy and suffering the sweet stench of decomposition as some of the world's finest sauces run through their necessary cycles in the far corners of the farm's barns. Thank you Peter Barrett for your talent, friendship, and perseverance, and thank you Sarah Rainwater for assembling all our ideas into something far more beautiful than I could have imagined. And thank you to Casey Kittrell and all the folks at University of Texas Press for believing in the book.

Finally, a special thanks to my son, Hudson, with whom I have missed countless weekends while bound to the pass at Fish & Game. He has handled my absence with grace and shown an understanding far beyond his years. He is also fortunate enough to have one hell of a bonus mom in Jori Jayne who has looked after him and given him more than I probably ever could. Jori Jayne, Hudson, and of course, Waylon… I am a lucky man!

JORI:

I'd like to thank Mother Moon + Father Sun.

"A thankful receiver bears a plentiful harvest"
—William Blake

KEVIN:

Well, they say it takes ten years to become an overnight success and to me that does not mean financial success but rather knowing that we all have each other's backs and trust. So it has only taken me twenty-five years to find partners like the ones I have found at Fish & Game. It is the whole team that defines F&G. So to the team that made this all possible, you know who you are, love you guys—no, not you, the other one—despite what I might say behind your backs… but generally it's to your face. THANK YOU!

what that dish needs is dobus sauce.

—KEVIN

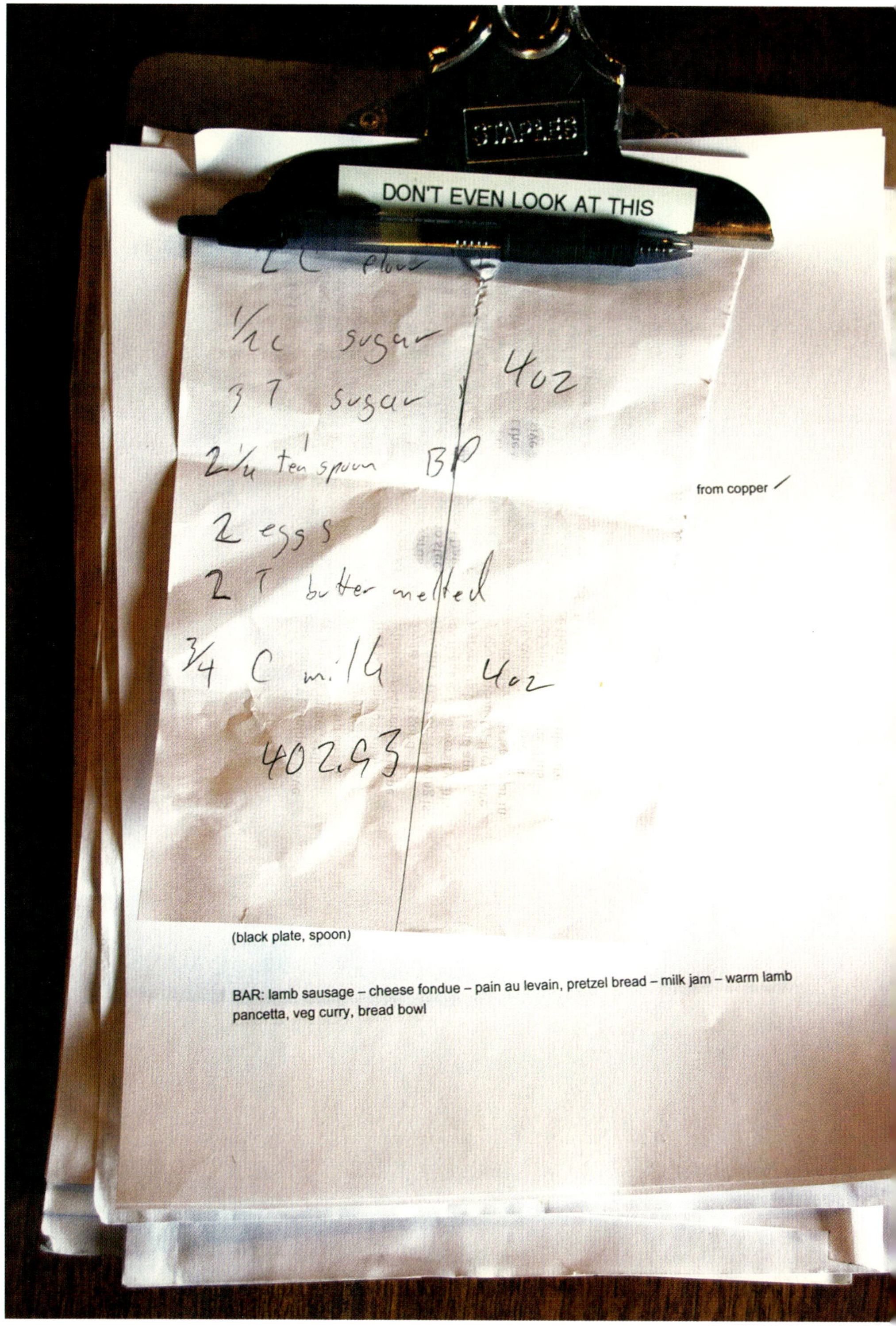

STAPLES
DON'T EVEN LOOK AT THIS
1/2 c sugar
3 T sugar
4oz
2 1/4 tea spoon BP
2 eggs
2 T butter melted
3/4 C milk
4oz
from copper
(black plate, spoon)
BAR: lamb sausage – cheese fondue – pain au levain, pretzel bread – milk jam – warm lamb pancetta, veg curry, bread bowl

Printed in China
First edition, 2017

∞ The paper used in this book meets the minimum requirements of ANSI/NISO Z39.48-1992 (R1997) (Permanence of Paper).

Library of Congress Cataloging-in-Publication Data

Names: Pelaccio, Zakary, author. Barrett, Peter (Food writer), author.
Title: Project 258 : making dinner at Fish and Game / Zakary Pelaccio and Peter Barrett ; photos and illustrations by Peter Barrett, with essays, comments, and recipes by Jori Jayne Emde, Steve Hernandez, and Kevin Pomplun ; book design by Sarah Rainwater
Description: First edition. Austin : University of Texas Press, 2017. Includes index.
Identifiers: LCCN 2016031578
ISBN 978-1-4773-1225-4 (cloth : alk. paper)
Subjects: LCSH: Fish & Game (Restaurant) Cooking. Seasonal cooking. Restaurants—New York (State)—Hudson.
Classification: LCC TX945.5.F57 P45 2017
DDC 641.5/64—dc23
LC record available at https://lccn.loc.gov/2016031578

doi:10.7560/312254

The Ox Cart Man

BY DONALD HALL

In October of the year,
he counts potatoes dug from the brown field,
counting the seed, counting
the cellar's portion out,
and the bags rest on the cart's floor.

He packs wool sheared in April, honey
in combs, linen, leather
tanned from deerhide,
and vinegar in a barrel
hooped by hand at the forge's fire.

He walks by his ox's head, ten days
To Portsmouth Market, and sells potatoes,
and the bag that carried potatoes,
flaxseed, birch brooms, maple sugar, goose
feathers, yarn.

When the cart is empty he sells the cart.
When the cart is sold he sells the ox,
harness and yoke, and walks
home, his pockets heavy
with the year's coin for salt taxes,

and at home by fire's light in November cold
stitches new harness
for next year's ox in the barn
and carves the yoke, and saws planks
building the cart again.